Meant to Be

A Memoir

Toby

Rabbi Marvin Hier

MEANT TO BE
A MEMOIR

The Toby Press

Meant to Be
A Memoir

The Toby Press LLC
POB 8531, New Milford, CT 06776–8531, USA
& POB 2455, London W1A 5WY, England
www.tobypress.com

Cover image: Bart Bartholomew

ISBN 978-1-59264-389-9

A CIP catalogue record for this title is available from the British Library

Printed and bound in the United States

For Malkie
my Eshes Chayil
who has accompanied me on my life's journey
and has made it possible

Contents

Acknowledgements ix

Where It All Began 1

Keeping Judaism Alive in a Distant Place 21

Teaching Our Children 51

Birth of the Simon Wiesenthal Center 61

Justice, Justice Shall You Pursue 81

Goodwill Ambassadors 133

Vatican Visits 177

When Grand Street Meets Hollywood 199

Expanding the Vision 225

Moguls and Stars Are People, Too 247

The Heart and Soul of It 271

Epilogue 285

Appendices 321

Index 335

Acknowledgements

The organization I was privileged to found would never have come into existence were it not for the extraordinary leadership of the men and women, those who've passed on and those who continue to serve with distinction, on the Simon Wiesenthal Center's Board of Trustees. A special debt of gratitude goes to my multi-talented colleagues at the Simon Wiesenthal Center, who have blessed and eased every day of the last thirty-eight years of my life. Many of them came to the Wiesenthal Center when it was just a dream. All of them have helped turn it into a respected, international organization. They have dedicated the best years of their lives to pitch their tents beside mine, and have become my dear friends. My deepest thanks to:

Rabbi Abraham Cooper, Associate Dean, a prolific writer and world-recognized authority on anti-Semitism.

Rabbi Meyer May, Executive Director, an extraordinary fund-raiser and strategic thinker.

Susan Burden, Chief Financial Officer and Chief Administrative Officer, who has played key roles in every Simon Wiesenthal Center exhibit and building project.

Liebe Geft, Director of the Museum of Tolerance, who has turned the Museum into one of the world's great institutions for teaching and promoting tolerance.

Rick Trank, Academy-Award winning Executive Producer of Moriah Films, who has helped develop Moriah into a preeminent film company.

Janice Prager, National Director of Development, who has turned fundraising into an art.

Avra Shapiro, Director of Public Relations, who, together with Assistant Director, Marcial Lavina, has disseminated the Center's message to the world media for decades.

Michele Alkin, Director of the Center's Global Communications and Internet Department, who, together with Associate Director of Communications, Felice Richter, broadcasts the Center's social action agenda to our constituents and social-media followers.

Rabbi Yitzchok Adlerstein, our capable Director of Interfaith Affairs, who has welcomed to his home many important religious leaders of all faiths.

Aaron Breitbart, Senior Researcher of the Simon Wiesenthal Center, who has a knack for finding the needle in the haystack.

Vivien Park, Controller, who, together with her staff, has dedicated herself to ensuring the highest standards of fiscal integrity.

Carrie Kneitel, our Art Director, for the wonderful design and graphics; Margo Gutstein for preserving our archival collection of more than fifty thousand books and artifacts; Mark Katrikh and Beverly LeMay, Directors of our Tools for Tolerance programs; Linda Blanshay, Director, Program Development; Leo Bravo, Director, Management Information Systems; and Donna Villalobos, Human Resources Manager.

I am eternally grateful to all of the Center's devoted staff, many of whom have been with us for decades, along with the hundreds of Holocaust survivors and Simon Wiesenthal Center volunteers, under the direction of Elana Samuels, who have given so generously of their time, and have had such a profound impact on the Center and visitors to the Museum of Tolerance. None of this would be possible without the technical expertise of Jim Hinton and Ron Morita.

Special thanks to our security people, including Patrick Burke and his team at Universal Protection Service for keeping us safe.

And to our capable staff on the front lines in the United States and abroad: Martin Mendelsohn, former head of the US Justice Department's Office of Special Investigations for his wise counsel; Dr. Shimon Samuels, Director of International Relations; Avi Benlolo, President of Friends of the Simon Wiesenthal Center in Canada; Dr. Efraim Zuroff, Chief Nazi Hunter and Director of Eastern European Affairs; Mark Weitzman, who covers the United Nations and Congress; Audrey Fox, an "operator" in every sense of the word, who can find anyone, anywhere; and Alison Pure-Slovin, Director of our Chicago office, and Rick Eaton, Senior Researcher for Hate and Terrorism on the Internet.

Special thanks to Matthew Miller, Publisher of The Toby Press, for his immediate interest in this book and his encouragement in writing it. I could not have found a better publisher.

Thank you to my Editor, Sheryl Abbey, for her insights, patience, and constant reminders that my Lower East Side dialect, while essential to the character of the book, needed to be wedded to proper English. To Gila Fine, Editor in Chief of Koren Publishers, for her great attention to detail and organizing this book.

Thank you to my wonderful assistant, Dana Mones, who spent months working and re-working drafts of the book while politely lecturing me on the virtues of patience, and to Ashley Forbes, for her dedication when Dana was on leave.

None of my life's journey would have been possible without the selfless dedication of my family. I will never forget the love, devotion, and sacrifice of my parents, Jack and Rose Hier, and my in-laws, Harry and Hanna Levine, of blessed memory, who made Malkie and me who we are. I am forever grateful to Adele and Sol Mermelstein and their wonderful children, Razie and Sendy Berger, Estee and Menachem Lipman, Shavie and Elchanon Isner, Elisa and Chaim Mermelstein; Lorraine and Irving Lazarowitz and their lovely children, Ronald, Marla, and Jimmy. Thank you to my wonderful sisters, Esther Hier, and Myra and her husband Dr. David Klein, and their wonderful children, Naomi and Scott Klein,

Jessica and Dr. Jason Klein, and Shayna and Dr. Daniel Klein, all of whom, since Malkie and I left New York more than fifty years ago, have graciously opened their homes to us and showered us with love and care, in the tradition of our forefather, Abraham.

Chapter One

Where It All Began

I t has been more than fifty years since I left New York City's Lower East Side. But that immigrant neighborhood of crowded tenements, synagogues, kosher delis, and Yiddish theaters has never left me. The people and places I first encountered on its bustling streets did not just form a backdrop to my childhood; they shaped my view of the world and my place in it. Every decision I've made, every project I've undertaken, can be traced back to those endearing characters on Cannon, Columbia, Grand, Delancey, Essex, and Henry Streets.

There was our family dentist, Dr. Celnicker, who cut costs by making temporary fillings from yesterday's newspapers. "Moishele," he said to me one day as I looked past my scuffed saddle shoes and out the window to Clinton Street from his reclining dental chair. "Do you want me to use the sports section, or would you prefer the movie section?"

"I wouldn't mind Joe DiMaggio's box score!" I answered.

Across the street, the Syd and Howe Candy Store sold chocolate syrup that made the best egg creams in the neighborhood. Every Friday, cars lined up on Houston Street, trunks opened wide, waiting to be filled with two-gallon glass bottles. One afternoon as I was sipping an egg cream at the soda fountain, a Chassid barged in waving a bottle overhead. "It's just milk and chocolate—it's kosher, right?"

"Absolutely," replied Joe the Fountain Man. "Just don't drink it with a *fleishig* (meat) kugel."

Harry the Pickle Man was a fixture of the neighborhood. My buddies Willie Lehrer, Sheldon Miner, and Seymour Brier and I would sometimes meet at his stall between Sherriff and Columbia Streets, and tussle for the best positions around Harry's stout wooden barrel. Convinced that the bottom of the barrel yielded the most flavorful pickles, every woman had the same request for Harry, better known by his Yiddish name, Hershele:

"Please Hershele, *zei a zoy gut* (be so kind) and give me *nor fin hintin* (only from the bottom)."

As I watched Hershele submerge each glass jar—and the sleeves of his heavy wool coat—into the dilled brine, I decided it must be the wool that gave his pickles their unique flavor.

Some of the great Jewish sages of our generation lived on the Lower East Side. Strolling down East Broadway, you might overhear your neighbor offering, "*A gutten tag, Rebbe*" (Have a good day, Rabbi) to Rabbi Moshe Feinstein, the world-renowned Lithuanian rabbi and scholar. Or you might see a young mother waiting outside the famous Boyaner Rebbe's shul to beseech him to say a special prayer for her sick child.

Politicians regularly made appearances in the neighborhood to garner the Jewish vote. I shook hands with Senator Herbert Lehman and Mayor Robert Wagner on Rivington Street. The first time I saw an American president was on Delancey Street, along with some 20,000 others who shouted, "Give him hell, Harry!"

President Truman looked back and shouted, "I just tell the truth, and to them it feels like hell!"

My parents were typical Lower East Side Jewish immigrants. My father, Yankel, had set out for America in search of work to help support his mother and sisters, who remained in the small village of Jalivga, Czechoslovakia. His father, Moishe, for whom I am named, had died several years earlier, and Yankel had taken on the responsibility of providing for the family. In January 1921, he boarded the *ss Poland* and arrived at Ellis Island. (The name *ss Poland* would come to haunt him later, when Hitler's ss murdered many members of our family in Poland.)

Like many other immigrants eager to make their way in America, Yankel officially changed his name. But brusque, American English could not convey my father's warm, gentle manner to the people who knew him best, and "Jack" forever remained "Yankel."

My father set an example of religious devotion tempered by humility. Each morning, en route by subway to his job as a lamp polisher at locations throughout the city, he read the Yiddish newspaper, *Der Tag Morning Journal,* and recited *tehillim*. He refused to work on Shabbos, though the consequence was periodic unemployment. Unable to financially contribute to our shul, he fulfilled the obligation of giving tzedaka by preparing kiddush and organizing the sale of High Holiday seats. One of his favorite quotes was from the collection of Jewish ethics and advice, *Pirkei Avos*, "It is not for you to complete the task, but neither are you free to desist from it."

My mother, Raisel Frost, arrived in America with her mother, Freidel, and her younger brother, Moishe, in the mid-1930s. Her father, Daniel, a follower of the Belzer Rebbe, had difficulty obtaining a visa. Several years later, he and my mother's older brother, Chuna, joined the family on Cannon Street, and Daniel went to work for Streit's Matzo Company.

My mother, a petite five-foot-two brunette with piercing eyes, was as vivacious as my father was composed. She was the life of every party, with a ready and distinctive laugh. When she gossiped with her friends in the women's balcony in shul, the cantor had no chance of being heard.

My mother was a stereotypical Jewish mother, self-sacrificing and completely devoted to her children. Every day she walked more than a mile, many times in the icy New York City winter, to bring me a fresh bagel in time for recess at the Rabbi Shlomo Kluger Yeshiva on Houston Street, where I attended elementary school, and to deliver hot cups of soup to my sisters at their public schools. After letting a salesman talk her into buying a new pair of shoes for herself when she bought me a pair for my bar mitzvah, she soon returned them, claiming they were too expensive, and that "for the few hours that the bar mitzvah takes, nobody will look to see if the mother of the bar mitzvah boy is wearing new shoes."

Over the years, delightful stories about my mother accumulated. When she once came to Los Angeles to visit me, a man who admired her spunk asked her age. She looked him straight in the eye, and in her unmistakable Yiddish accent, retorted, "Mister, even if I would know how old I am, I wouldn't tell you!"

Once, when we returned home from a trip and were helping my mother unpack, I discovered a small blue teapot in her luggage. "Ma, where did you get this?" I asked in surprise.

"Moishe," she replied, "Remember when I wasn't feeling well, and you told me to order some tea? So they sent up the tea with some honey and a little pot. I wanted to pay the man who brought it, so I asked him how much it cost. So he says twenty-one dollars. *'Far a gloos vasser you vant twenty-one dollars?'* (You want twenty-one dollars for a glass of water?), I asked. But that's what he wanted, so I paid him. After he left, I said to myself, 'It couldn't be twenty-one dollars for just plain water, so it must be that it includes the teapot.' So I packed it in my suitcase."

My parents met at one of the many social events regularly held for new arrivals on the Lower East Side. I imagine they found in each other traits they each lacked: my mother's vitality countered my father's calm; his dependability balanced her spontaneity. They married in 1938, and moved to a small apartment at 71 Cannon Street, where I was born on March 16, 1939. My sister, Esther, was born in 1943 and Myra followed in 1949.

While our living conditions were poor, our lives were rich. Like most Lower East Siders cramped into tiny apartments, we turned the streets around us into our living room. We visited with family, met with friends, and connected with the world-at-large by strolling down Rivington or Grand Streets, or popping into Simcha Glick's Candy Store or Sam's Deli.

Much of our lives revolved around the Litovisker Shul, which, like dozens of other Lower East Side synagogues, provided a sense of community for hundreds of Eastern European immigrants. The shul community felt like an extended family—so much so, that men who shared the same Yiddish first names were re-named according to their physical features, like *Hoycher Yakov* (Tall Yakov), and *Kleiner Yakov* (Short Yakov), *Darrer Nachum* (Skinny Nachum), and *Grobber Nachum* (Fat Nachum) and they didn't seem to mind.

The Hagler and Mikola families vied for dominance in shul politics. My father's cousins, Yichel, Hersh Leib, and Mendel Hagler, were traditionalists. Each week, they sat in the same seats, and asked the same people to lead services. Mendel, Chazkel, and Hershel Mikola embraced innovation, claiming that traditional religious customs needed to be adapted to the New World. One Shabbos morning, when Yichel Hagler sent up Reb Noach, his regular choice, to lead services, Hershel Mikola reached his limit. "Yichel!" he bellowed, "Are you deaf? God Himself is pleading for us to get someone new to speak to Him!"

The Haglers were staunch supporters of the Democratic Party, and Yichel served in the powerful position of captain of the Lower East Side precinct. One Shabbos, just before Election Day, Yichel, a stocky man in his late sixties, strode to the bimah (Torah reading table) to make his usual pre-election pitch: "*Ich vil dermanen yeden einem...*" (I want to remind everyone) "*Gedenkst alle zollen vooten far di Demecratin row B un nor row B*" (to vote only for the Democratic ticket: row B and only row B).

An angry Mendel Mikola responded, "Why haven't you called Katz, the plumber, to fix the shul's leaky toilets? Is it because he's a Republican?"

Yichel's brother, Hersh Leib, fired back, "*Republicans zitsten nor ouf de hoycher fensters*" (Republicans only sit in high towers).

Chazkel Mikola put in his two cents: "Listen, you've got no business telling everyone in the shul to pull down the lever for row B. What if Hitler ran on row B?"

Realizing where this was headed, Rav Weinberger, the shul's rabbi and a distinguished scholar, staved off the fight by issuing a rabbinic ruling. Slowly caressing the wiry white beard that concealed the edges of his face, he declared, "It is immoral to mention Hitler's name in connection with the Democratic Party, and it is obligatory for each Jew to scrutinize the candidates before voting, just as it is required to have proper intent when performing mitzvos." He emphatically concluded, "The toilets should be above politics, and fixed immediately." With that, everyone charged downstairs to kiddush, where they were fortified by the herring and kugel, and continued to argue about Hitler, Katz the Plumber, and the merits of voting row B.

The Litovisker Shul had its somber moments, too. Four times a year, the recitation of *yizkor*, the prayer for the dead, subdued its otherwise lively atmosphere. One Yom Kippur, when I was ten or eleven, waiting outside the shul during *yizkor*, as was the custom for those whose parents were still alive, I noticed that the memorial service was taking a long time. When I re-entered the shul at the prayer's conclusion, I asked my father, "Dad, why does *yizkor* take so long?"

For the first time, my father acknowledged a grim reality: "Moishe, many of our friends are saying *yizkor* for their parents and for others who were killed by the Nazis."

"Does it take this long in Zaide's (grandpa's) shul, too?" I asked, hoping it didn't, and we could go there instead.

"I'm afraid it's the same in every shul, Moishele," my father sadly replied.

Another passing reference to the Holocaust came from Rabbi Rosenblum, one of my teachers at Yeshiva Rabbi Shlomo Kluger, the week that Israel was created. Rabbi Rosenblum entered our classroom, as he did each morning, with a stick in one hand, and a Yiddish newspaper in the other. Before beginning our lesson in *Chumash* (Five Books of the Torah), he embarked on his daily ritual of briefly perusing the day's headlines. This morning, he spent extra time scanning the paper before raising his eyes and asking, "*Nu it veist vos hot parsirt heint?*" (Do you know what happened?) "*Mir haben a Yiddishe medina!*" (We now have a Jewish state!) While wiping away tears with a handkerchief, he then mumbled, "*Nein yhar tzu shpett*" (Nine years too late).

Rabbi Rosenblum did not explain his reaction to the day's astonishing news. He didn't have to. His tears spoke louder than any speech on the subject. I inferred, as I had from my father's *yizkor* remarks, that the Holocaust was a pivotal event to which an unspoken rule applied. Much like Jewish tradition approaches the study of the seminal work of Jewish mysticism, the *Zohar*, one should not discuss it too much, nor delve into it too deeply.

A few years later, I learned that even if I didn't understand the Holocaust, I could glean purpose from it. I was studying for my bar mitzvah with Rav Yankele Flantzgraben, the Senior Rebbe of my elementary school, a revered Talmudic scholar, and special teacher, who made each of his students feel as if he were his only concern. One evening, while listening to me recite my Haftorah, Rav Flantzgraben interrupted me, "Moishele," he said, "Every bar mitzvah boy has to learn something from the *churban* (destruction) that befell *K'lal Yisroel* (the whole of Israel) during the Holocaust. He can't just get up and recite his Haftorah as if the world is the same as before, as if nothing happened to our people. Every bar mitzvah boy has an opportunity to make up for what the Nazis took from us. As the Torah teaches, 'and Moshe took with him the bones of Yosef,' so must every young man commit himself to take those 'bones' with him throughout his life, and replenish what was lost."

Soon after my bar mitzvah, my parents enrolled me in the Rabbi Jacob Joseph Yeshiva (named for New York's first and only Chief Rabbi), where I attended high school. Rav Yitzchok Tendler introduced me and a thousand other boys to the riches of Talmud study. The Talmud, we were taught, brings relevance and vitality to the Torah. The exploration of this central text, we learned, would make us part of the living history of the Jewish people—an unbroken chain of tradition, philosophy, and practice transmitted from one generation to the next.

Throughout my studies at the yeshiva, I learned many life lessons. One year, just before the festival of Shavuos, which marks the giving of the Torah, Rav Tendler shared a beautiful explanation of why a Jewish king is obligated to write two Torah scrolls. "One that he keeps in his palace, and another that he takes with him on his travels." Rav Tendler explained, "A king, to whom subjects bow in deference, may come to believe that he is the center of the universe. Therefore, he is obligated to write an additional Torah scroll which he keeps at home in order to remind himself that he, like every other human being, has a Creator before whom he must stand in judgment."

After school, I shed my *yeshiva bocher* (young student) persona, and played punch ball, basketball, and stickball with neighborhood friends, some religious, some not. I couldn't wait to get home after a full day of studies to hang a hoop on the wall of our narrow third-floor landing and play one-on-one with my pals, Arnold Eisenberg and Leonard Sponder. In the evenings, we transformed our hallway into Madison Square Garden. Ignoring the velvet yarmulka on my head, I morphed into the Knick's premier guard, Dick McGuire, while Arnold made the moves of the Celtic's Bob Cousy, and Leonard pretended to be "Sweetwater" Clifton. On Sundays, we perched on the edges of seats in the Yankee Stadium bleachers, rooting for our hero, Joltin' Joe DiMaggio.

The two worlds I inhabited rarely converged. At times, I was the exemplary child of Jewish immigrants, dutifully attending synagogue in suit and tie, enthusiastically debating Talmudic nuances. At others, I was a typical, sports-loving American kid. I never invited my non-religious friends to join me in shul for the Simchas Torah or Purim holidays or to my home to study. I never introduced my yeshiva classmates to my neighborhood friends for fear that each side would be put off by the other.

My behavior was a reflection of the prevailing attitude in the Orthodox community of those days. Fearful of secular society and its potential to lure us away from Jewish tradition, my parents, like other religious Jewish immigrants on the Lower East Side, created an insular environment that excluded non-Jews and non-Orthodox Jews alike. As my social consciousness developed in my teenage years, I became bothered that the older generation was ignoring the fundamental Jewish teaching that "all Jews should be guarantors for one another."

My opinion grew stronger one Shabbos, when an earnest man with two young sons came to the Litovisker Shul for the first time to say *kaddish* (memorial prayer) for his wife, who had recently passed away. Hesitantly, he approached the *shammes* (sexton) to ask for a prayerbook with English transliterations. Unable to find one, the *shammes* recommended he go to another shul on East Broadway, about a mile away. As I overheard the brief interaction, and watched the dejected threesome leave the shul as the regulars carried on with the service, I sensed that they were headed home, alienated—perhaps forever—from the Jewish community.

I also could not understand why the Holocaust, one of the greatest tragedies in all of Jewish history, was relegated to the sidelines of Jewish communal life. I became preoccupied with the question of how the Holocaust had been allowed to happen. I found Rav Flantzgraben's answer, *"Dos iz gevein a himmel zach"* (This is a matter for the heavens), insufficient.

My teenage worldview was being formed as much by movies as by Talmudic tales. Each Sunday at the Delancey, Apollo, or Palestine Theaters, I cheered the sheriffs as they rounded up posses of do-gooders to confront the outlaws, and counted on the cavalry to come to the rescue in every Indian raid. I believed that for every Jesse James there was a Wyatt Earp, a Roy Rogers, and a Gene Autry. "Where were the good guys when it came to saving the Jews?" I thought.

I wondered about the Jews themselves. Where were the Mordechais, Esthers, and Bar Kochbas among them to warn of the impending catastrophe? How could they have ignored the words spoken by Ze'ev Jabotinsky in Warsaw in September 1938?

> For three years I have been imploring you, Jews of Poland, the crown of world Jewry, appealing to you, warning you unceasingly that the catastrophe is near. My hair has turned white and I have grown old over these years, for my heart is bleeding that you, dear brothers and sisters, do not see the volcano which will soon begin to spew forth its fires of destruction. I see a horrible vision. Time is growing short for you to be spared. I know that you cannot see it, for you are troubled and confused by everyday concerns…listen to my words at this, twelfth hour. For God's sake, let everyone save himself, so long as there is time to do so, for time is running short.

Many years later, in 1995, my eyes would fill with tears when Israel's most decorated soldier, Ehud Barak, would say while visiting the Auschwitz concentration camp, "We arrived here fifty years too late." And I would react similarly when, in September 2003, Israeli pilot-officer Amir Eshel, the son of Holocaust survivors, broadcast a message as he led a formation of three F-15 Eagles on a fly-over of Auschwitz, "We pilots of the Air Force, flying in the skies above the camp of horrors, arose from the ashes of the millions of victims and shoulder their silent cries, salute their courage, and promise to be the shield of the Jewish people and its nation Israel."

As the years passed, the Lower East Side changed. Blocks of squalid three- and four-story tenements were cleared to make way for low-income, high-rise development projects. Most Jewish families whose apartments were torn down moved to Brooklyn. The same was true for shuls and schools that had been a part of the Lower East Side's vibrant Jewish life for more than fifty years.

My parents moved into a large public housing project on FDR Drive, a peripheral area of the neighborhood, where the majority of residents were not Jewish. Later, they relocated to the Amalgamated Co-Op Building on Grand Street to be back in the heart of what was left of the most famous Jewish community in America.

Life changed for me, too. After graduating from high school in 1956, I decided to enter the Rabbi Jacob Joseph Yeshiva's *beis medrash* program. There, I would spend the next six years poring over ancient texts and debating religious law and practice in order to become a rabbi. While my friends headed off to college or went into business, I could not imagine another path for myself.

At the time, however, there was no telling what the future would hold. As I walked under the blue-grey steel beams of the Williamsburg Bridge on my way to the yeshiva each morning, I contemplated my future. I wondered how I would earn a living and support a family. Knowing my parents were unable to help me financially, I considered whether there was enough stability in the rabbinate.

As I prayed each day in front of the ark's carved oak doors in the yeshiva's *beis medrash* (study hall), I assured myself that my dilemma paled in significance compared to the challenges my parents and grandparents had faced and overcome. I knew it was wise to be practical, but I sensed that unlike previous generations, I had the opportunity to pursue the studies that challenged and nourished me. I immersed myself in the sea of the Talmud, under the guidance of some of its most learned scholars, who themselves had studied with the great Talmudic sages of pre-World War II Europe.

What a privilege it was to study in the same *beis medrash* as Reb Yakov Safsel, known as the Visker Iluy (Genius from Visker), one of the most accomplished scholars ever to have attended the world-renowned Slabodka Yeshiva in Poland. Whenever the yeshiva's main study hall was crowded, I walked across the street to the small Agudas Anshei Maimed shul, where Reb Yakov sat and learned. Then in his late seventies, Reb Yakov was a diminutive man, hunched and thin. But his mind was expansive. My yeshiva friends and I would often test Reb Yakov's memory by pretending to have forgotten a Talmudic source. Each time, completely unprepared, he precisely quoted the passage we were referencing, as if he had studied it the day before.

I developed a special relationship with Reb Yakov. On cold winter days, he liked to sip hot tea through sugar cubes he delicately positioned on his tongue. One day, to curtail the amount of sugar Reb Yakov was ingesting, Reb Chatzkel moved the sugar cube box out of his reach. Sensing Reb Yakov's frustration, I reached up to the shelf when Reb Chatzkel left the room, rescued the box, and returned it to the amused and grateful Reb Yakov. His wink in my direction signaled that he had bestowed special status upon me.

Taking advantage of this, I decided to test the widely held belief that Reb Yakov concentrated his studies on the early Talmudic commentaries, and ignored the later ones. I selected a question posed by one of the great late commentators, and presented it, as if my own, to Reb Yakov. He quickly digested the question, and began pacing the *beis medrash*, deep in concentration. After several minutes, he walked toward me and declared, "Write your address on a piece of paper.

When I have time, I will send you an answer." For the next ten years, Reb Yakov sent me dozens of letters in response to my question.

Other rabbis regaled us with inspirational stories they had learned from their rabbis. Between puffs of his cherished Havana cigars, Rav Tendler recounted moments with Reb Boruch Ber, the Talmudic prodigy and head of the Kaminetz Yeshiva in Poland. Rav Tendler explained how Reb Boruch Ber never read a newspaper until Hitler came to power. Asked why he suddenly became interested in the news, Reb Boruch Ber replied, "When Jews are suffering, if I don't know their problems, how can I advise them and share their pain?"

Rav Shumel Dovid Warshavchik recalled the last time his Rebbe, Reb Elchonon Wasserman, head of the Novardok Yeshiva, one of the world's largest yeshivas, was in the United States. With tears in his eyes, he recounted how Reb Elchonon's loyalty to his students cost him his life:

> The Rebbe was here in New York in March of 1939, raising money for his yeshiva, when the war broke out. Many pleaded with him to stay in America and to send for his two children. But Reb Elchonon dismissed them, "I have four hundred children in my yeshiva. How can I leave them behind? I am a soldier, and a good soldier must go to the front." Reb Elchonon returned to his yeshiva, and was murdered by the Nazis two years later.

It was in the yeshiva, where I heard the inspiring words of the distinguished Rav Yosef Shlomo Kahaneman, the former Rabbi of Ponevezh, who immigrated to Palestine after the Nazis destroyed his yeshivas and murdered his family members. He addressed us during one of his many visits to America to secure financial support for his new yeshiva in Israel. He began his remarks, "Please listen to the words of an old man, who has come here all the way from Yerushalayim, who stands before you today in this holy place to speak with you, for what I am sure is the last time in his life." In awed silence, we listened as the Rabbi of Ponevezh implored us to do something meaningful with our lives, something that would bring honor and credit to the entire Jewish people.

In the *beis medrash*, Rav Mendel Kravitz, the head of our yeshiva, and the man from whom I received rabbinic ordination, often shared the teachings of his Rebbe, Rav Aharon Kotler, widely regarded as the *gadol hador* (greatest sage of our time). Rav Kravitz quoted Rav Aharon, who explained why the Talmud says that God judges every mortal human being three times: on Rosh Hashanah, upon his death, and just before the final resurrection of the dead. He taught that Rav Aharon understood the first two times to be logical, but pondered the need for God's additional judgment before the resurrection. He explained that there are people whose accomplishments extend well beyond their lifespans. God suspends His final judgment to take into account the cumulative impact of each and every life in order to remind us that each person has an obligation to do good work in his generation and to plant seeds to affect future generations. God, in turn, credits such people with the residuals of their accomplishments.

I was privileged to meet Rav Aharon Kotler on two occasions during my yeshiva days. Twice, Rav Kravitz asked my *chevrusa* (study partner) David Greenwald and me to drive Rav Aharon from his Borough Park home to the yeshiva, where he was scheduled to deliver his annual lecture. We approached his apartment with trepidation (I had proudly displayed Reb Aharon's Great Sages card under the glass top of my bedroom desk throughout my childhood). But when the rabbi's wife, Rebbitzen Chana Perel Kotler, showed us into their modest apartment, with furnishings both ordinary and familiar, we felt immediately at ease. We offered to help the rabbi put on his raincoat, but the dignified Rav Aharon declined: *"Ich ken iz ton a layn"* (I am capable of doing it myself). People nodded toward Rav Aharon and reached out to shake his hand as we made our way to the parked car. Such a respected figure could not lead the simple private life he might have wanted.

My time in the yeshiva had its light moments. Rav Tendler once went on a hilarious rant against the increasingly popular bar mitzvah teaching aid, the tape recorder. "Boys," he said, "You know why I am against this? I will tell you. Recently, I went to a fancy bar mitzvah of a rich man's son. So they call the boy up to the Torah, he goes up, kisses it with his tallis, and recites the blessing, '*Barchu es Hashem hamvorach.*' As is the custom, the congregation then responds, '*Baruch Hashem hamvorach l'olam va'ed.*' Suddenly, the bar mitzvah boy shouts back at the congregation, 'Shut up! I know the blessings!' You see what happens when a tape recorder becomes a teacher," concluded Rav Tendler.

One spring day, when we needed a break from our studies, a few friends and I decided to head south for an afternoon at the Asbury Park Amusement Center. When I managed to pop three balloons in a darts contest, I was presented with a five-foot-tall stuffed polar bear. Eager to show off the oversized prize to my sisters, I boarded a bus (paying an additional fare for the bear) then a train to Delancey Street rather than East Broadway in order to avoid the yeshiva, whose rabbis would surely frown upon my having played hooky to indulge in secular pleasures. The train pulled into the Delancey Street station, the doors opened, and I cautiously stepped onto the platform, my vision impaired by the life-size bear in front of me. As I craned my neck around the bear's rounded ear, who should be directly facing me, but my Rebbe, Rav Warshavchik. He took one look at the bear, then at me behind it, and said with an affectionate grin, "So Moishe. This must be your *chavrusa*, Reb Dov Ber. One thing I can promise you, he is going to get *smicha* (rabbinic ordination) a lot sooner than you will!"

The Purim holiday is traditionally a time for pranks, and I was the chief prankster. At the yeshiva's Purim party in 1960, an emcee announced to the hundreds of rabbis and students gathered, "We will begin the evening by listening to a tape recording of a recent lecture given by Rav Kotler. Following this, a student will impersonate Rav Kotler." The emcee played the tape, and the rabbis nodded their heads in fervent agreement with Rav Kotler's finest points, which he delivered at a rapid-fire pace, in a Yiddish dialect that was difficult to follow, even for those for whom Yiddish was a first language. When the lecture ended, the emcee announced, "I'm sorry to inform you that the young man who was supposed to come up on stage next cannot be with us. But he did not want to disappoint you, so he kindly sent us the tape you just heard." Realizing that the rabbis had been fooled, the entire student body burst into laughter.

I was soon identified as the practical joker, who not only had imitated Rav Kotler's distinctive speaking style, but had quoted freely from invented sources that bore no relationship whatsoever to the lecture topic. Rav Tendler was so impressed with my impersonation that he asked to borrow the tape to play for his *mechutin* (father of his daughter-in-law), the world-renowned Rav Moshe Feinstein. Rav Tendler later told me that Rav Moshe listened attentively to the tape, then, with a big smile across his face, quoted the verse from Genesis in which Jacob disguises himself as his brother Esau, "The voice is the voice of Jacob, but the hands are the hands of Esau."

Like most of my friends studying in the *beis medrash*, I felt an obligation to ease my parents' financial burden. Every year, I teamed up with friends to sell *aravos*, one of the four plant species used during the Sukkos autumn harvest festival. We left our homes at 4:00 am to catch a train to Yonkers, where the Saw Mill River empties into the Hudson, and spent the morning cutting and gathering red willow stems along the riverbank. We brought the willows in huge plastic bags to the retail market on Canal Street, where we sold them for ten cents a branch, earning a respectable five hundred to six hundred dollars each.

After three years of our annual *aravos* project, I hit upon an idea to improve our earnings. Since our asking price was dependent each year on how insect-bitten the leaves were, I suggested we take a few branches to the Bronx Botanical Garden to see if the experts could help us figure out what to do about the bugs.

Off we went to the botanical garden, where a botanist identified our willow as *salix purpurea*, and, intrigued by our description of the Jewish tradition of shaking it each day of Sukkos, suggested we have a professional nursery grow them. He made a few phone calls, then provided us with contact information for a nursery in Princeton, NJ.

The next day, Fishel "Pepsi" Hochbaum, Max Kaminetzki, and I negotiated a deal with the Princeton nursery to grow fifteen thousand *aravos* for the following year. Over the next few years, we steadily increased the order, until we reached two hundred thousand branches annually. We paid the nursery four cents per stem, and sold them for ten. While our profit margin was reduced from our first years, our volume was dramatically increased, bringing our net individual incomes to a stunning four thousand dollars—and we no longer needed to wake at 4:00 am to catch the train to Yonkers.

Our entrepreneurship enabled us to forge special relationships with the *gabbais* (rabbis' assistants) who ordered *aravos* for the major Chassidic sects in New York. Reb Yossel Ashkanazi, the *gabbai* of the Satmar Rebbe, was so impressed with the quality of our *aravos* that he ordered twenty five thousand units and invited us to the Rebbe's home so the Rebbe could give us a blessing.

Almost overnight, a few yeshiva boys from the Lower East Side had become *aravos* moguls. But our dominance of the market did not last long. Two years later, I received a terse call from my partners informing me that I would no longer be receiving my usual share of the profits. Apparently, we had been out-foxed by our long-time competitors, the Buxbaum brothers, who spotted our trailer's NJ license plates, and honed in on our supplier, to whom they offered more money and signed an exclusive five-year contract. While the incident brought to an end any aspirations I might have had to become a businessman, I nonetheless took pride in knowing that along with my yeshiva buddies and the botanist from the Bronx Botanical Garden, I had changed the way *aravos* are grown and sold in America.

No resume of a young man from the Lower East Side would be complete without a stint in the Catskills. My gig was as busboy, then waiter, at the West End Country Club in Loch Sheldrake. The West End was an ideal escape from New York City's steamy summers for hundreds of middle-class Orthodox Jewish families. The resort had all they needed: a shul, a pool, and Jerry Lewis, just up the road at the posh Brown's Hotel.

Food was the main attraction in the Borscht Belt, where guests lined up outside the hotel's vast dining halls a half-hour before they opened, three times a day. One afternoon, waiting near the kitchen to pick up an entrée for a guest, I noticed the hotel's co-owner, Izzy Leibowitz, mixing his famous spring salad, elbow-deep in cottage cheese. Ever frugal, Izzy slid the leftover cottage cheese down his hairy forearms into a plastic vat. When I returned to the dining room, a hefty woman with a thick Brooklyn accent assailed me: "What did I tell you when we checked in? We have been coming here for ten years, and whenever they serve spring salad we expect seconds, because it's a Leibowitz special."

I quickly apologized, delivered another portion, and concurred, "You are absolutely right, Ma'am. The West End spring salad certainly is an Izzy Leibowitz special."

While life as a waiter meant long work hours, little sleep, and even less pay, adequate compensation came in the form of socializing. At the West End, I met an assortment of people I never would have encountered at the Rabbi Jacob Joseph Yeshiva. On Saturday and Sunday nights, I listened to guest entertainers singing popular American and Israeli songs. And at the West End, I met my life's partner.

During our daily, two-hour break between lunch and dinner, I often played ping pong with Adele Mermelstein, who came to the hotel each summer from Borough Park with her husband, Sol, who had survived Auschwitz, and their two children. During one of our matches in the summer of 1961, when she was clobbering me with her superior serve, Adele matter-of-factly said, "I'd like you to meet my younger sister. She's a counselor here. She's very smart and good looking." She did not need to add another word. I knew that everyone admired the Mermelsteins and I knew that I was a sheltered young man who lacked the confidence to initiate a conversation with a young woman.

The next day, Adele introduced me to Marlene, known affectionately as Malkie, and her parents, Hanna and Harry Levine. As advertised, she was intelligent and attractive. We had many complementary traits: she liked to laugh, and I liked to tell stories; she loved cookies and I was in a unique position to supply them. We saw each other many times that summer, and when the season sadly drew to a close, she extended the pleasure it had brought by accepting my offer of a date when we returned to the city.

17

Once back at the yeshiva, however, I realized I was in a predicament. In those days, no young woman would consider seriously dating a young man who had no idea how he was going to support a family. I continued on in my studies, indefinitely postponing a date with Malkie, although we spoke often on the phone.

Then, one December day, Rabbi Bernard Goldenberg, the senior rabbi of Congregation Schara Tzedeck in Vancouver, Canada visited my yeshiva to seek recommendations for filling the position of Assistant Rabbi. I typically spent my days studying with other rabbinical students in the Agudas Anshe Maimed Shul. But that day, when we discovered that the shul's heater was broken, we relocated to the main yeshiva building. Much to my surprise, and perhaps only because I was seated nearby, Rav Warshavchik called me over to introduce me to Rabbi Goldenberg. We spent the afternoon discussing the Vancouver position, and by the end of the day, Rabbi Goldenberg made me an offer. The Yiddish words my beloved grandmother, Freidel, regularly repeated to me rang in my ears: "*Alles in leben iz barshert*" (Everything in life is meant to be).

Excited and emboldened by my new job offer, I made arrangements to take Malkie on our first formal date. Our dinner at Manhattan's famous Lou G. Siegel's restaurant was memorable, both because Malkie was impressed that Rabbi Goldenberg had offered me the position from a large pool of qualified candidates, and because I didn't bring enough money to pay the bill. I had done the math while savoring the delicious flanken, and realized I was about to come up short. Embarrassed and desperate, I scanned the restaurant for someone from whom I might borrow money, stalled by telling Malkie every story I knew, and prayed for a miracle. When the waiter presented me with the bill, Malkie unexpectedly came to the rescue. "Will twenty dollars do it?" she asked. My granddaughter, Rachel, would later tell me that that moment marked the beginning of my fundraising career.

A few months later, I was ordained as a rabbi, and asked Malkie to marry me. I used the money I had saved from the *aravos* business to buy her an engagement ring. We were married on September 8, 1962 at the Riverside Plaza Hotel in Manhattan. We celebrated with our parents, Malkie's grandmother, Kayla, and my grandmother,

Freidel, all of whom had sacrificed so much for us. I danced with Rav Yankele Flantzgraben, Rav Yitzchok Tendler, Rav Shmuel Dovid Warshavchik, Rav Mendel Kravitz and the other rabbis with whom I had studied, and my friends, Dovid Greenwald, Heshie Weinreb, Shobsie Knobel, Leibeish Topp, Yakov Goldberg, Alan Press, Sheppie Borgen, Shimshon Bienenfeld, Fishel Hochbaum, Dr. Jerry Hochbaum, Max Kaminetzki, and Harvey Hoenig with whom I spent my unforgettable formative years.

But the day was bittersweet. Malkie and I knew that in just one week, following the traditional *sheva brachos* celebrations, we would be leaving the Lower East Side and Borough Park, the only worlds each of us had ever known. As we said our final goodbyes to family and friends after the wedding, my father shared one last story from the Litovisker Shul that lightened the mood.

"Moishe," he said, "Everyone in the shul is worried about you. I asked them what they are worried about, and they told me I must be crazy to let my son go off to a Communist country to be a rabbi. Rabbi Horowitz himself said to me, *"Er nemt a shtellar by Castro. Dorten hast min yidden!"* (He's taking a position with Castro. They hate Jews there!) "Dad," I replied, "You have nothing to worry about. I'm not going to Vancuba, I'm going to Vancouver!"

Chapter Two

Keeping Judaism Alive in a Distant Place

The scene at the airport the day Malkie and I left for Vancouver was reminiscent of the sorrowful farewells of Jews leaving Eastern Europe for America in the 1920s and 1930s. Our relatives and friends, who had come to say goodbye and wish us well, did nothing but cry. Other passengers looking on might have thought the plane was headed for a distant planet.

Once aboard, Arthur Fouks, a lawyer and leading member of Vancouver's Jewish community who had observed the scene, introduced himself and admitted, "Rabbi, your family gave me the impression they were losing their children to another religion! I know you are coming to our shul, so let me be the first to welcome you, and to congratulate you for making the right decision. I can assure you, you're coming to a great community, but more importantly you're coming to a community that really needs you."

As we drove into Vancouver for the first time, Malkie and I were captivated by the city's natural beauty. The blue waters of the Pacific

Ocean hugged the city's edge. The rugged peaks of the North Shore Mountains formed a breathtaking backdrop. We were mesmerized by the snow-capped Canadian Cascades and Vancouver Island.

New York City was no match for this striking Canadian seaport. We had often boasted to guests visiting New York that Central and Prospect Parks were the most beautiful parks in America, but the lush gardens of Vancouver's Stanley and Queen Elizabeth Parks put New York's urban amenities to shame. We had never seen streets so clean. We wondered if the well-tended garbage cans were ever used.

It did not take Malkie and me long to notice the differences between New York and Vancouver etiquette. As we innocently crossed a traffic-free downtown street, oblivious to a red pedestrian light, we felt the sharp scrutiny of a passerby. I was sure my yarmulka was what had drawn attention, but a young woman patiently waiting at the traffic island for a pedestrian light to turn green set me straight. "You know," she said amusedly, "the traffic lights are not here for decoration. And I'm sure wherever you are going will still be there thirty seconds from now."

However enthralled we were with Vancouver's natural splendor and unhurried atmosphere, we were disillusioned by its small Jewish community. More Jews were packed between Cannon and Grand Streets in the Lower East Side than lived in the entire province of British Columbia. The city had just two major synagogues: the Conservative Congregation Beth Israel, and the Orthodox Congregation Schara Tzedeck. There were no religious day schools, except a fledgling Talmud Torah.

At least Schara Tzedeck had an impressive facility. The synagogue's main sanctuary seated twelve hundred and included three women's balconies. The facility also housed an auditorium, classrooms, a *beis medrash* and a *mikvah* (ritual bath). When we arrived, the community had just broken ground on a new wing north of the synagogue property, which made us hopeful that Schara Tzedeck had a vision of developing into a large, vibrant community.

The central and most respected figure in Vancouver's Jewish community was the man who had hired me, Rabbi Bernard Goldenberg. Rabbi Goldenberg was serious and scholarly. He was a consummate pulpit rabbi and a skilled orator, who was sought after in both the Jewish and non-Jewish communities.

Rabbi Goldenberg astutely predicted that Malkie and I would be disappointed by our first encounters with the Vancouver Jewish community. He knew the disheartening statistics: barely two dozen families in the entire city observed Shabbos; fewer than seventy-five people came to Schara Tzedeck's Shabbos services unless there was a bar mitzvah or an *aufruf* (groom called to the Torah before his wedding); there were no religious couples our age, and no kosher restaurant.

When Rabbi Goldenberg and his wife, Shirley, graciously invited us to join them at their Wolfe Avenue home for our first Shabbos dinner, they brought us straight into their living room for a little chat. "We know what you're going through," Rabbi Goldenberg assured us. "It's going to take a few months for you to adjust. Shirley and I want you to know that we felt the same way you're feeling now when we first came to Vancouver eleven years ago. We kept asking ourselves what we were doing here. Believe me, we expected to send our children to yeshivas. But then we realized, if we wanted to reach the majority of our brothers and sisters—who don't live on the Lower East Side—then, as leaders of the community, we needed to make sacrifices."

Rabbi Goldenberg reminded us that in New York he had been one of the leaders of Torah Umesorah, a prominent Jewish educational organization, and a colleague of Rabbi Joseph Kaminetsky, the organization's pioneering founder. "I could have remained in a senior position there for many years," Rabbi Goldenberg said, as he repositioned the yarmulka on his head. "But I promise you one thing: what you can achieve here, you can't achieve anywhere else. Here, you can help shape a community's future, and accomplish great things for the Jewish people. If you give it a chance, you will never regret having come to Vancouver."

Six months later, Rabbi Goldenberg called me into his office to share a guarded secret. "Moishe," he said, "I'm teaching you the ropes, because in another year or so, I will be leaving Vancouver, and you'll be the person to succeed me."

I was excited and overwhelmed by the news. It was thrilling to imagine that I would become the rabbi of the city's oldest and largest Orthodox synagogue, but staggering to think that I, a twenty-five-year-old *yeshiva bocher*, would be responsible for serving the spiritual needs of an entire community, including addressing all twelve hundred of them on the High Holidays.

Rabbi Goldenberg helped ease my transition to being a pulpit rabbi by inviting me to stand in for him at a variety of events over the coming months. My first public appearance was on *Religion on the Line*, an interfaith program that aired each Sunday on the Canadian radio station, CJOR. Rabbi Goldenberg assured me, "Moishe, you are perfectly capable of answering the questions they will ask you, which will only be about Jewish tradition and practice." Reluctantly, I agreed to my first radio interview, which nearly became my last. The radio panel included a Catholic priest, a Protestant minister, and a Hare Krishna follower. After my colleagues expressed their views on the topic at hand, the moderator turned to me and asked if I agreed with their comments. "I agree with some of the previous remarks," I replied. "But I must say that I disagree with the comments made by the last speaker, Mr. Harry Krishna." There was a long pause, then the panelists burst into laughter. The switchboard lit up with calls.

Next, Rabbi Goldenberg invited me to deliver my first Shabbos sermon. I prepared a speech aimed at motivating members to become more actively involved in synagogue life, which I entitled "Even Synagogues Need Marines." As I approached the pulpit, I felt a wave of insecurity come over me.

Fortunately, the congregation was receptive, and a congenial crowd gathered at kiddush to offer congratulations. Only Meyer Feldstein, who had grown up in the synagogue and was the director of its funeral chapel, noticed a quirk of mine that would be the cause of many future embarrassing moments in the rabbinate and beyond: my tendency toward mispronunciation. "Rabbi, I want to tell you something," Meyer began. "My father loved rabbis. But he had a tradition that whenever a rabbi got up to speak, he would fall asleep. Don't get me wrong. He didn't mean anything disrespectful. It's just that the sermon was a perfect time for him to relax, and relaxing usually turned into snoozing. I inherited that tradition from my father. So when you got up to speak, I dozed off. But when you got to the part about how every synagogue needs a Marines *corpse*, I immediately snapped to. I thought you needed my help with a funeral!"

Fully prepared or not, I took up my new position as rabbi of Congregation Schara Tzedeck in July 1964. By then, we had two children, Ari, who was born in October 1963 and Avi, who was born in June 1965. I was less than half the age of most regular attendees, who had arrived in Vancouver as Eastern European immigrants before or immediately after World War ii. I knew I had to retain the loyalty of the older generation if Schara Tzedeck was to survive, but I needed to attract members of the younger generation – most of whom attended services just a few times a year – if the shul was going to grow.

I decided my first task would be to persuade key shul members to invest in the synagogue's youth programs. I approached Jack Diamond, a Galician immigrant who had become a successful businessman. Jack was proud to belong to an Orthodox synagogue despite his non-Orthodox practice, and was well respected within the community. When some had questioned the wisdom of appointing a young rabbi to serve congregants twice or three times his age, Jack had supported me in his trademark, no-nonsense style. "Now look here," he said. "I rebuilt this synagogue in 1947 and I have twenty-three seats that I continue to pay dues on. Some of them are for people who have passed away, like my parents. If we don't bring in a rabbi our children can relate to, in twenty-five years, all our names will be on the seats of a shul that died because we didn't do the right thing."

Jack agreed with my assessment that programs for young people were essential. He made sure the synagogue's president, David Chertkow, was on board. A short time later, we secured the funds, and announced that we were beginning a program of Shabbos services, lunch, and afternoon activities for teens. I considered whether it was appropriate to offer such a program, given the reality that most parents would be violating Orthodox Jewish practice by driving their children to the shul on Shabbos from homes miles away. But I decided that providing a traditional Shabbos experience was crucial, and could not be replicated on a different day of the week. I also knew that if we failed to inspire young adults in their formative years, we would lose our chance of ever reaching them.

The initial turnout was impressive. Nearly thirty kids, many from families that came to synagogue only on the High Holidays, showed up that first Shabbos. Most spent the entire day with us, and remained for *havdalah* (ceremony marking the end of the Sabbath day) and an evening party, which included a Three Stooges movie and popcorn. They continued to come each week, and we soon needed to hire an assistant to help Malkie and me run the program. Our success reinforced my belief that the shul's future was not dependent on my sermons or the cantor's singing, but on our effectiveness in reaching out to young people.

After several months, a core group of teens coalesced. In December 1965, the group attended its first national conference, a week-long Yeshiva University-sponsored Torah Leadership Seminar in Los Angeles. Twenty-five Vancouver teens made the two-day trip by train and Malkie and I chaperoned.

The train chugged along craggy coastlines and stark wilderness as the sun set. We burrowed into our cabins for the night. Hours later, awakened by the click clacking of the train, I discovered that Malkie and I were alone. I frantically woke her, and together, we searched the length of the train, terrified that our teens had deserted us in Seattle. Only after we made our way to the refreshment car at the train's end, did we find our rowdy group, devouring snacks from the vending machines.

The next day, a chance meeting on the train would spark a transformation in Jewish education in Vancouver. A group of Bay Area teens headed to the same youth conference boarded our train in Oakland, accompanied by a charismatic young man named Rabbi Pinchos Bak. Pinky, as he was known, had a trim beard, piercing brown eyes, and kinetic energy. From the moment he stepped onto the train until the conclusion of the conference a week later, he did not stop shmoozing, singing, or dancing with every kid he could buttonhole.

Pinky and I spent a lot of time together that week in Los Angeles. He told me that he had graduated from Yeshiva University, and was working at an afternoon Talmud Torah at the Oakland Synagogue, where Rabbi Saul Berman was the spiritual leader. He was uncertain about his professional path, but knew that if he were to choose a career in Jewish education, he would prefer to teach in a full-time day school or yeshiva, than in a part-time synagogue Hebrew school.

As the week unfolded, I realized that I needed to bring Pinky to Vancouver. Malkie and I envisioned Pinky as principal of the city's only Jewish day school, the Vancouver Talmud Torah. The school had a student body of one hundred and fifty, and a faculty that consisted mainly of Israeli teachers who taught modern Hebrew and Israeli history but little Judaism. In our opinion, the Talmud Torah needed to be infused with the spirit of Torah, and Pinky Bak, with his love of Judaism and contagious enthusiasm, was the person to do it.

My challenge upon returning to Vancouver was to convince the Talmud Torah's trustees, most of whom were Conservative, to interview this Orthodox young man. I made my pitch to key trustees, emphasizing how it was in the interest of the entire Vancouver Jewish community to raise proud Jews passionate about their heritage. I reminded them that leaders of the Conservative Movement, including Rabbis Abraham Joshua Heschel, Louis Finkelstein, and Mordechai Kaplan, had studied with Orthodox rabbis. To its credit, the board agreed to interview Pinky.

A few months after our fateful train meeting, Pinky arrived in Vancouver for the interview. He outlined his educational philosophy, which showed his concern not only for curricula and academics, but motivation and inspiration. The board immediately responded to Pinky's approach and charisma, and offered him a contract. In the summer of 1966, Pinky and his wife Karen moved to Vancouver, and he became the principal of the Vancouver Talmud Torah.

Pinky invigorated the Talmud Torah, and galvanized Jewish educators to create something new in Vancouver. Within a short period of time, his dynamism inspired a group of rabbis and teachers from New York's Yeshiva University and Baltimore's Ner Israel Yeshiva to join the school's growing faculty. Joel Cutler and Rabbis Yale Butler, Elchonan Oberstein, Shlomo Schwartz, Raphael Minkowitz, and Eddie Epstein came aboard. So did Rabbi Abraham Cooper, whom I had met at the Los Angeles conference, and Aaron Breitbart, who was referred to me by a relative. Rabbi Cooper would later become the Associate Dean of the Simon Wiesenthal Center, and Aaron Breitbart its Senior Researcher.

This devoted team expanded the curricula and created a vibrancy that could be felt beyond the school walls. Stimulated by the new energy, we opened a National Conference of Synagogue Youth (NCSY) chapter at Schara Tzedeck. We organized fun activities and provided great food, while teaching *niggunim* (repetitive melodies) and insights from the weekly Torah portion to teens from all segments of the Jewish community.

Our wives were essential partners in our efforts. Malkie and the others hosted dozens of teens on Shabbos and holidays, and ran activities at *Shabbatonim* (weekend retreats). They helped create a warm atmosphere that was undeniably part of our success.

At the many teen activities we organized, I often taught lessons from Rabbi Joseph B. Soloveitchik, the great twentieth-century Talmudist known simply as "The Rav." I stressed the themes in the Rav's teachings that I thought would resonate, such as the Rav's interpretation of the biblical verse, "And he [Abraham] sat at the entrance of the tent in the heat of the day." I explained how the Rav understood that Abraham purposely positioned himself at the entrance to his tent in the midday sun, despite the fact that it would have been more comfortable inside, because the Covenant of Abraham demands that every Jew stand guard, engage with the world, and contribute to it, despite the challenges even in the "heat of the day."

In the 1970s, more than forty of our Vancouver teenagers—almost all of them from non-observant homes—went to the US and Israel to study in yeshivas. Many others embraced Jewish tradition by wearing yarmulkas and keeping kosher. I was proud of the spiritual development of our young people, though I understood it was sometimes the cause of friction with parents who feared they were losing their sons and daughters.

Such was the feeling at the Calgary Jewish Community Center, where I was invited to speak in 1968. Marc Belzberg, the son of Samuel and Frances Belzberg, prominent members of Vancouver's

Jewish community, had warned me that I might face animosity in Calgary, particularly from his family members who were concerned about their increasingly observant nephew in Vancouver. I kept this in mind as I prepared my remarks.

More than two hundred people assembled at the community center on an icy winter's night. Many women wore fur coats. I delivered my speech, and indeed, was assailed with questions that revealed trepidation about religious observance.

"Rabbi, how can you teach students that it's okay to wear *tzitzis* (prayer shawl fringes) outside their clothes when we live in a predominantly non-Jewish society?" asked one skeptic.

"Aren't you taking us back to the Middle Ages?" asked another.

"Isn't it disgraceful to set ourselves apart from the communities we live in?" raised a third.

"In the Jewish tradition, we often answer a question by raising another question," I began. "The question I'd like to raise is, 'Why are so many of you wearing fur coats?' I know it's cold here in Calgary. But if the purpose of wearing fur is to stay warm, then why not put it on the inside of your coats? Since your furs are all on the outside, there must be another reason you are wearing them. My guess is that you want to show everyone how proud you are of your husbands, who bought you those coats. How ironic that when it comes to fur coats, we are comfortable sharing our pride, but when it comes to our heritage, we frown upon it.

"You all know Monty Hall, the Canadian host of the television program, *Let's Make A Deal*." I continued, "So like Monty Hall, ladies and gentlemen, I say to you, 'Let's make a deal.' I will go back to Vancouver and tell all the young men in my shul wearing *tzitzis* to tuck them inside their pants, if all of you wearing fur coats will now turn them inside out. Is there anyone here who would like to make that deal?"

There were no takers. After a long silence, we went onto the next question.

Meanwhile, Vancouver's Jewish teen scene was abuzz with activities. Our NCSY teens established friendships throughout Canada and the US. Lee Samson, a West Coast NCSY director, who would later become a Wiesenthal Center trustee and major benefactor, inspired our teens during his frequent visits to Vancouver.

Many of our students participated in Yeshiva University's summer programs, which included visiting Warsaw and Cracow, Vienna, or Budapest before traveling to Israel. Dr. Abraham Stern, Director of Yeshiva University's Youth Bureau; Rabbi Pinchas Stolper, Founder and National Director of NCSY; and other innovators in Orthodox education, took note of our achievements.

Our momentum continued to build until 1974, when we faced a difficult setback. Pinky Bak, the young man who had inspired so many, announced that he was leaving Vancouver to start Yeshiva Mesivta Ohr Torah with Rabbi Shlomo Riskin in Riverdale, New York. We could not argue with Pinky's assessment that he had accomplished his mission in Vancouver. Pinky had turned the Talmud Torah into a first-class Hebrew day school that provided hundreds of students with a traditional, yet relevant and exciting, Jewish education. Sadly, we reconciled ourselves to the truth that his talents were now needed elsewhere.

Three years later, the bond we continued to feel with Pinky despite his physical distance, was tragically severed. While dancing with students, including my son, Ari, at a Purim celebration at his New York yeshiva, Pinky collapsed and died of a heart attack. He was thirty-two. Malkie and I were paralyzed by the news. Vancouver's NCSY teens, Talmud Torah students, and parents grieved as if they had lost a family member.

Even after leaving this world, Pinky continued to motivate us as teachers, parents, friends, and Jews. We strove to emulate him, always remembering his poetic words:

It is a dream of generations
To raise our children in the tradition of our fathers
To inspire them with the ways of the past
To challenge them with the hopes of the future.

It is a dream to see them live in freedom and dignity
To see them walk in a posture so definite, so self-reliant

That watching them will inspire others
To come along.

Many of the young men and women touched by Pinky and the rest of Vancouver's exceptional cadre of Jewish educators went on to become leaders of Jewish communities around the world. Some moved to Israel. Others established remarkable organizations, like Marc Belzberg and his wife Chantal who founded One Family, which supports and rehabilitates Israeli victims of terror, and Rabbi Kalman Samuels and his wife Malkie who created Shalva to support special-needs children and their families. Whatever they achieved later in life, large or small, Schara Tzedeck's young adults took with them the confidence of knowing they had grown up in a place that cared passionately about their Jewish future.

The full impact of our efforts to inspire Vancouver's Jewish young adults was driven home to me in the fall of 2010, when Malkie and I celebrated Sukkos with our children and grandchildren in Jerusalem. As we strolled in the Shaarei Chesed neighborhood where they lived, a young woman called out to me.

"Rabbi Hier! It's Laura, Laura Dunner from Vancouver. Do you recognize me?"

As I crossed the street and took a closer look, I couldn't believe what I saw. Laura, one of the first teens who had come to the youth services at Schara Tzedeck, was now Laura Wasserman, a middle-aged woman wearing modest clothing and a head covering.

"What are you doing here, Laura?" I asked in astonishment. "I thought you were living in New York."

"We do live in New York, but we also own an apartment here in Jerusalem. Our children all go to yeshivas and study in *kollels*, and we wanted them to have a home here."

"Where is it?" I asked.

"Right here, just a few houses up from your children.... And you'll never guess whose home we had the privilege of buying: Rav Shlomo Zalman Auerbach. Before Rav Auerbach's children agreed to sell the house to us, they looked over our family history. Luckily, they decided ours would be a good Jewish home. They even let us keep his bookshelves so that our family will always have a connection to Rav Shlomo."

I was stunned. Laura's exploration of Judaism, which began thirty years earlier in Vancouver, had led her to live in the former home of one of Israel's most respected rabbis, whose funeral was attended by more than three hundred thousand people. After chatting for a few more minutes and saying our goodbyes, Malkie and I continued on our way, savoring a gratifying moment in which we felt part of a Divine plan that had mysteriously brought one young woman into our orbit, then guided her to become owner of a home in which one of Jerusalem's greatest sages had lived.

Settling our family in Vancouver, regularly hosting Shabbos guests, and helping to revitalize the Talmud Torah and Schara Tzedeck teen programs was not enough for Malkie. So she decided to go back to school. In 1971, she earned a bachelor's degree with honors from Simon Fraser University, and, in 1973, a master's degree in urban planning and statistical analysis from the University of British Columbia. Art Phillips, the mayor of Vancouver, appointed her to the City Planning Commission, which made the Jewish community proud, but forced her to use the excuse that she didn't talk during Shabbos services to avoid the issue of discussing real estate projects that many Schara Tzedeck members had pending before the commission.

Meanwhile, I set out to reinforce Schara Tzedeck's successful youth programs with parallel initiatives for the older generation. To best reach out to members in their forties and fifties, I focused on cultural programs that would connect them to the larger Jewish world. We established Giants of the Twentieth Century, a program that brought prominent Jewish thinkers, businessmen, politicians, musicians, and writers to Vancouver to broaden members' perspectives on Judaism and rekindle their appreciation for Schara Tzedeck.

A newly formed men's club took charge of the program. Gordon Diamond, Murray Goldman, Al Kolberg, Morley Shafron, Azer Horowitz, Bill Orenstein, and Max Fugman raised the necessary funds. Gordon's wife, Leslie, with whom I worked closely, chaired many of the public events. Joe Segal, who helped revitalize the shul, and served with distinction as its president for many years, provided critical support with his wife Rose, as did Morris and Dena Wosk and Leon and Evelyn Kahn.

Within a short time, we launched the program, which was a virtual "Who's Who" of the Jewish world. Israeli statesmen Menachem Begin, Moshe Dayan, and Abba Eban came to speak, as did Rabbis Dr. Samuel Belkin, Sir Israel Brodie, Ahron Soloveichik, Aaron Lichtenstein, and Dr. Norman Lamm, Cantor Jan Peerce, and writer Chaim Potok.

Rabbi Shlomo Carlebach, "The Singing Rabbi," was one of our Giants. Reb Shlomo feverishly danced around the bimah with dozens of NCSY teens and our *gabbais*, Isaac Tyer and Hyman Dashevsky, each in their seventies, who, overcome with emotion, wiped away tears with handkerchiefs. At a rare, quiet moment between songs, Hyman turned to me and said, "Rabbi, *zeit mein chasina in the alta heim hob ich nischt azoy getansed*" (I haven't danced like this since my wedding in the old country).

Reb Shlomo repeated the scene the following day at the University of British Columbia, where I also served as Hillel Director. This time, thousands of non-Jewish students in the main campus auditorium linked arms and swayed along with Reb Shlomo's stirring versions of the Chassidic songs, *Od Yishama* (There Will Yet be Heard) and *Am Yisroel Chai* (The Jewish People Lives). Jewish students, who previously might have found such traditional music old fashioned or irrelevant, looked on, bewildered but proud.

We brought Rabbi Dr. Samuel Belkin, then president of Yeshiva University, to the Vancouver Talmud Torah, where he made a powerful impression on teenagers and parents alike. Rabbi Belkin explained the Talmudic teaching that if a student's father and teacher simultaneously lose something, the student is obligated to search for his teacher's lost item first.

"Do you know why this lesson never offended Jewish parents?" Rabbi Belkin asked, then answered, "Because it was never applicable, because parents never abdicated their role as teachers. On the contrary,

Jewish parents have always considered it their primary responsibility to be their children's role models."

There were funny and embarrassing moments with our guests, too. Kelly Cohen, an active shul member who had more enthusiasm than Jewish education, insisted on being part of a committee that was to greet and present a gift to Rabbi Shlomo Goren, the Ashkenazi Chief Rabbi of Israel, upon his arrival at the airport. As Rabbi Goren disembarked the plane and approached our entourage, I noticed Kelly placing three, large round boxes on the tarmac. When Rabbi Goren approached, I improvised, "Uh...Rabbi Goren, this is Kelly Cohen, who would like to make a special presentation to you."

"Chief Rabbi," Kelly stated, "Now that you have left the army and become Chief Rabbi, you deserve to wear the best hat in the world. So here is the finest English homburg."

"Mr. Kelly," Rabbi Goren responded in his heavy Israeli accent, "You want to give to me a hat? How do you know my size?"

"I don't. That's why I bought three hats for you to choose from. You can take them home and decide which fits best."

"And what will I do with the rest?" he replied, baffled.

"Well, you can give one to the prime minister," answered Kelly.

"Mr. Kelly, the prime minister is Golda Meir. I don't think she will want to wear a homburg."

Rabbi Goren wore one of Kelly's hats throughout his stay in Vancouver, and years later quipped, "Rabbi Hier, remember that gentlemen that gave to me a hat when I visited you in America? He should come to Israel. I could use another one."

Thousands of Vancouverites flocked to hear Israel's leading political figures speak at Schara Tzedeck. Menachem Begin, a hero to many, urged them to be proud Jews, and to realize that they were living in one of the greatest moments in Jewish history. Moshe Dayan regaled them with heroic stories of the Israel Defense Forces. Abba Eban reminded them of the double standard continuously applied to Israel at the United Nations.

I was especially proud of the way the Vancouver Jewish community received two distinguished heads of yeshivas, Rav Ahron

Soloveichik and Rav Aaron Lichtenstein, the brother and son-in-law, respectively, of Rabbi Joseph B. Soloveitchik. I feared that only the few members who observed Shabbos and a handful of NCSY teens would show up to hear these leading Jewish scholars. In the end, Schara Tzedeck members turned out in force, their interest piqued, perhaps, by my frequent references to the Rav. A large contingent also came from Congregation Beth Israel.

Both Rav Soloveichik and Rav Lichtenstein wowed their audiences. When they entered the auditorium, people stood out of respect; when they spoke, the audience was spellbound. Both rabbis showed an impressive familiarity with secular literature and philosophy, and a deep understanding of contemporary political issues that surprised many people in the audience. Their astute and articulate presentations relieved the anxiety that some parents felt about their children becoming more observant, and enabled many of them to support their children's decisions to attend yeshivas or Yeshiva University years later.

One of the most moving experiences of Schara Tzedek's Giants of the Twentieth Century series was the weekend we spent with Cantor Moshe Koussevitsky. A lyric tenor who had served as a cantor in Vilna and Warsaw before escaping the Nazis, Koussevitsky was the greatest cantor of our time. People came from all over the Northwest to hear him, including other cantors who formed a special choir to accompany him during Shabbos services and a Sunday concert.

Cantor Koussevitsky led us in a magnificent Shabbos *davening*. But it was in a more intimate setting that I was most touched by his presence. Koussevitsky had a custom of chanting *havdalah*, the ceremony marking the end of the Sabbath, for his mother at the end of every Shabbos, no matter where he was. Saturday night, at the home of Professor Moe Steinberg, thirty of us gathered around the great cantor as he spoke to his mother by telephone in Yiddish.

"*Mama, dos rett Moishe ich gey yetzt machen havdalah*" (Mother, this is Moishe. I am going to make *havdalah*).

"*Far mir iz keimul nisht oys* Shabbos *biz ich herr dein shtimmer un havdalah*" (For me, Shabbos is never over until I hear your voice and your *havdalah*), she replied lovingly.

Their conversation reminded me of the biblical scene in which Rachel waits by the side of the road for word from her children. With this thought in my mind, I listened to Koussevitzky sing the most beautiful rendition of *havdalah* I had ever heard.

The next day, Cantor Koussevitsky deeply stirred the audience at a concert in the shul's Wosk Auditorium. During his beautiful interpretation of *Vileyerushalayim Ircha* (And to Jerusalem Your City), an older man in the audience began to sob. Following the concert, he explained to Koussevitsky:

> I am a survivor of the Holocaust. I drove here from Seattle to hear you. When you sang the song about Yerushalayim, I couldn't stop myself. I was in your shul, the Tlomackie Shul, in Warsaw in 1938 when you sang this very song. A few years later, I lost my whole family—my parents, my grandparents.... Tonight, when you sang the song again, and I heard the words "And to Jerusalem Your city, rebuild it soon in our days..." and I saw, standing behind you, the Israeli flag, I thought God is sending me a message...He is telling me that what happened in Poland will never happen again.

In the early 1970s, several leading Orthodox rabbis began to question the role of non-Orthodox Jews in Orthodox synagogues. Concerned that non-Orthodox members would undermine their roles as their congregation's sole authorities on Jewish law, they put forth a proposal at an Orthodox Union National Convention in New York to bar them from holding key positions in Orthodox synagogues. Most of the proponents had pulpits in New York, and little experience with Jewish life in smaller communities.

Based on my experience in Vancouver, I adamantly opposed the proposition. At the convention, I proudly recounted that no one had ever attempted to overrule my positions on religious issues since I had become rabbi of Schara Tzedeck. In addition, I shared that it was the non-Orthodox members of Schara Tzedeck who had donated the most time and money to our educational programs in order to ensure that their children and grandchildren would have strong Jewish identities. Without the involvement of such leaders, I argued, many Orthodox shuls in cities with small Jewish communities would simply fold.

In Vancouver, non-Orthodox Jews contributed essential funds to all the Orthodox organizations and institutions, including NCSY, Chabad, the Vancouver Talmud Torah, and the Community Kollel. They also made important contributions to Yeshiva University and the Orthodox Union. Thanks to Syd and Joanne Belzberg, David and Lil Shafron, and Fred and Arnold Silber, Vancouver's Orthodox Jewish community expanded and thrived.

Much to my relief, the proposal was voted down.

Being the rabbi of the largest Orthodox synagogue in the city made me a de facto spokesman for Jewish affairs. Within the first few months of my rabbinate, I received an unusual call from an official in the Mayor's Office who asked how many people could sleep in our synagogue in the event of an emergency, such as a Soviet nuclear attack. Hoping he had a sense humor, I replied, "I have no idea, but during my sermon on the Jewish High Holidays, my congregation sleeps twelve hundred!"

I used my increasing visibility within the larger Vancouver community to be politically active. Horrified by the April 1968 assassination of Martin Luther King, Jr., I organized a fundraising drive for King's widow, Coretta Scott King, with my colleagues Wilfred Solomon, rabbi of the Conservative Congregation Beth Israel, and Harold Rubin, rabbi of the Reform Temple Sholom. Within a few days, we raised several thousand Canadian dollars. When Mrs. King's book, *My Life with Martin Luther King, Jr.*, was published shortly after, she sent me a copy, which she inscribed: "To Rabbi Marvin Hier. With deepest gratitude for your support and contribution toward the continuation of my husband's work."

Rabbi Solomon, Rabbi Rubin, and I collaborated again in October 1971 on the most pressing global Jewish issue of the day, the struggle to liberate Soviet Jewry. We agreed to stage a press attention-getting scene at the Vancouver Hotel, where Soviet Prime Minister Alexei Kosygin was staying during a visit to our city. Knowing when he was scheduled to leave, we decided to stake out the area near the hotel elevators and chant "Free Soviet Jews Now."

But when we met at the hotel coffee shop to go over the details of our plan, a bizarre incident prevented us from confronting the Soviet premier. A young man, noticeably agitated, entered the coffee shop, grabbed a coffee pot, and threw its hot contents at us. Customers shouted, the police were called in, and the man was restrained. Amidst the commotion, Kosygin left the hotel.

That evening, I recounted the episode to Malkie and a rabbi who was staying at our home while visiting Vancouver to solicit funds for his New York yeshiva. "Your efforts failed," the rabbi stated smugly, "because it is God who decides these matters, not mortal Jews. It is up to God to create miracles, not us, as we say every day in our prayers, *"Ki hu levado baal milchamos"* (He [God] alone fights our battles).

I looked the rabbi straight in the eye and countered, "You know, it's very strange. One of the first things you asked me when you arrived at my home was if I could give you the Schara Tzedeck membership list so you could approach potential donors. As you are well aware, in the very same prayer in which we say 'God alone fights our battles,' we also say '*Ki hu levado zoreya tzidakos'* (He [God] alone plants the seeds of charity). It seems when it comes to raising money for your yeshiva, you are willing to sow the seeds that God has planted, but when it comes to attempting to rescue millions of suffering Soviet Jews, you want God to do all the work."

Because Schara Tzedeck was the oldest and most established synagogue in Vancouver, I was occasionally invited to meet visiting political leaders. In 1971, Malkie and I received an invitation to a formal dinner hosted by Queen Elizabeth, Prince Philip, and Princess Anne at Victoria's Government House, the official residence of the Lieutenant Governor of British Columbia, to mark the centennial of British Columbia becoming a Canadian province. We were invited as Vancouver's senior clergy, along with sixty other guests.

Our immediate concern was the non-kosher food. I called Government House and, explaining our dietary restrictions, asked if we could be served fresh fruit on new dishes. The event staff graciously assured me they would accommodate our needs, and apologized that Her Majesty's seal could not be imprinted on the new dishes in time.

We arrived at the Tudor mansion, Malkie in white gloves, as required by the invitation, and me in my standard dark suit and black velvet yarmulka. We entered a wood-paneled room with brick fireplaces where a cocktail hour was underway. While we sipped colas and chatted, I spotted the Chief Justice of British Columbia, at whose parents' funerals I had officiated. I pointed him out to Malkie, and we headed in his direction. Much to our surprise, when the Chief Justice saw us coming, he quickly turned away, apparently giving the impression that he did not want to be seen in our company. As Malkie and I exchanged expressions of disbelief, we were invited into a grand, chandeliered banquet hall. We were seated beside the French Ambassador to Canada, at an antique dining table that seemed to stretch without end and upon which silver candelabras, elegant flower arrangements, china and crystal had been impeccably set. As promised, new dishes were awaiting us. While other guests were served an elaborate first course, a skilled waiter diligently delivered our sliced apples.

Unexpectedly, the lights began to flicker. I leaned over to the Ambassador and joked, "I didn't realize we are so poor in British Columbia that we can't pay our electric bills."

Surprised, and a bit embarrassed on my behalf, he explained, "Rabbi, I see you haven't been to one of these affairs before. The flickering lights signal that Her Majesty wants us to change our seats in order to meet other guests around the table."

"What are we going to do about our kosher dishes?" I thought to myself. Following the Ambassador's lead, Malkie and I simultaneously rose from the table. With a few discrete hand signals, we indicated to one another that we would take our kosher dinner plates with us. The Chief Justice noted our exchange, and cast a disdainful look our way.

At the conclusion of the dinner, we listened to congratulatory remarks, and toasted the royal family. Next, we followed the

Lieutenant Governor's instructions to form two lines through which the Queen, Prince Philip, and Princess Anne would pass, like the Israelites through the divided Red Sea. While making his way through the passage, Prince Philip spotted my yarmulka, stopped momentarily, and initiated a conversation. "Sir, I take it you are a rabbi. Would you, by chance, know the Chief Rabbi of Great Britain, the Reverend Israel Brodie?"

"Your Royal Highness, sure I do," I said, "The Chief Rabbi was recently a guest of ours. We know him and his wife very well."

"Excellent. He's a very bright man indeed."

The Queen, just behind him, joined in with questions of her own. "How many Jews are there in British Columbia?" she wanted to know.

"Approximately twelve thousand," I immediately responded, delighted by my good fortune at having been singled out for a royal conversation.

"Does each community choose its own rabbi, or does a seminary send them along?"

"Every congregation chooses its own rabbi, Your Majesty."

Just then, I felt an assertive tap on my shoulder. I quickly turned around to face none other than the Chief Justice, who, moments earlier, had been mortified by my presence. He extended his hand and announced for all to hear, "Rabbi, so good to see you."

I forced myself to return the handshake. Back at Schara Tzedeck the following week, I delivered a sermon on Jewish pride, in which I said that it shouldn't take the Queen of England to render one Jew kosher to another.

The novelty of my first royal encounter had faded and my confidence grew when I was invited to deliver the invocation at an international conference of Christians and Jews at which Prince Philip was guest of honor several years later. Malkie and I were seated with an English, kilt-wearing officer of the royal yacht, *Brittania*, who foolishly blurted out: "Canada is just too ethnic for me. It has too many competing interests that weaken the country's national identity." Looking my way, he grinned and added, "Take, for example, the good rabbi here, who just gave us a wonderful invocation. We are all eating Her Majesty's food, but he insists on eating his own."

Malkie and I were shocked. I couldn't hold myself back.

"Sir," I said, "with the greatest of respect, if you are not embarrassed to wear a skirt and expose your knees, I don't think I should be ashamed to eat kosher food."

During my tenure as rabbi of Congregation Schara Tzedeck, major political events brought the community together, changed the trajectory of Jewish history, and helped shape my worldview. Congregants flocked to Schara Tzedeck on June 10, 1967, the final day of the Six Day War. Surely, they would have been better informed by staying home to watch the television news. But on that Shabbos, the sixth day of Israel's harrowing fight for survival, members of our community wanted and needed to be with one another.

The same was true during the Yom Kippur War in October 1973, when hundreds of people who had not planned to be in synagogue came to Schara Tzedeck to stand in solidarity with the people of Israel. The mood was somber. Some asked Mike Kuzik, our non-Jewish synagogue caretaker, to turn on the office radio; others made regular visits to their cars to get the latest bulletins. Everyone prayed.

In my fifteen years at Schara Tzedeck, I was never so moved as that year, during *Neilah*, the final prayer service of Yom Kippur. The building seemed to shake as 1,200 voices chanted the concluding line of the service in unison, "*Hashem, Hu haElokim*" (Only He is God) again and again, climaxing in the final, seventh repetition. Cantor Moishe Preis then led us in "*Hatikvah*," the Israeli national anthem: "As long as the Jewish spirit yearns toward Zion, our two-thousand-year hope will not be lost..."

I looked around the men's section into the faces of our Holocaust survivors: Leon Kahn, Irio Gray, Izzy Tischler, David Weinberger, Dave Shafron, and Leo Lowy, many of them standing beside their sons. Remarkably, each looked confident that this newest attempt to destroy the Jewish state would fail. Their expressions conveyed the power of prayer to transform fear into trust.

Such moments of Jewish solidarity reminded me of Rabbi Soloveitchik's interpretation of the two Jewish covenants, the one God entered into with the entire Jewish people when He gave them the Torah at Mount Sinai, and the one He sealed with Abraham in the Land of Canaan. The Rav taught that the Sinai covenant comes with a clear obligation to keep God's commandments. Some Jews adhere to this obligation, while others do not. But the fulfillment of Abraham's covenant, he taught, is more mysterious. Every Jew, the Rav argued, fulfills Abraham's covenant when he reads a biased article against Israel or learns of the latest terrorist attack and feels an immediate sense of outrage or dread. The Rav understood that in that moment of empathy, no Jew, no matter how assimilated, can free himself from Jewish fate, because, like Abraham, he is part of a covenant that obliges him to confront a hostile world and attempt to change it by turning fate into destiny.

There are many reasons why we Jews have survived nearly three thousand five hundred years of persecution and turmoil. I am convinced that one of them is our ability to laugh, even during the most trying circumstances. When I left the Lower East Side, I was certain that the personalities that had filled my youth with laughter were unique to New York City. But after moving to Vancouver, I realized that every Jewish community has its special characters.

Kelly Cohen of homburg hat fame was one such individual. Kelly was Canadian-born, the son of an owner of a successful clothing store chain, who lived on an expansive property, where he raised horses. Kelly was single and in his fifties when he began to delve into Judaism for the first time.

At services one morning at Schara Tzedeck, while he was sitting *shiva* for his father, Kelly naively asked, "So Rabbi, am I allowed to have sex during *shiva*?" While everyone laughed, I deflected the question by directing Kelly to the elderly Reb Velvel Schuster, who had known Kelly's family for many years. Knowing Reb Velvel was a little hard of hearing, Kelly repeated the question: "So, Reb Schuster, am I allowed to have sex during *shiva*?"

Reb Velvel scolded Kelly, "*Di naar!*" (You fool!) "*Vos far a zex?*" (What kind of six?) "*Far a taten darf min zitsen zibben nisht zex!*" (For a father you have to sit seven days not six days!).

Reb Velvel, an elegant man with a trimmed goatee, was a wonderful character in his own right. While he served for many years as Vancouver's *shochet* (one who slaughters animals according to kosher law), he nonetheless wore an impeccable dark suit daily. Reb Velvel and Reverend Bernard Liebowitz, the synagogue's sexton, worked very closely with me during my fifteen years as rabbi of Schara Tzedeck. I, along with the rest of the Jewish community, admired and respected him.

Late one drizzly Friday night on a walk home from a friend's house, Reb Velvel wove in and out of streets, temporarily hiding under store awnings to protect a special black hat he wore only on Shabbos and holidays. Two members of the Royal Canadian Mounted Police who were surveying the area from inside their police car thought Reb Velvel's behavior strange and wondered if he was casing stores for a future robbery. The policemen flashed their headlights on poor Reb Velvel, and ordered him to put his hands up. They asked for his driver's license, which he could not produce, because, as an Orthodox Jew, he didn't carry a wallet on Shabbos. Next, they asked what he did for a living. Unable to come up with a better English translation of the Yiddish *shochet*, Reb Velvel mumbled that he was a slaughterer. With that, the police detained him. Soon after, the misunderstanding was cleared up, but the story lived on in Vancouver lore. Often, when Reb Velvel was called upon to perform his secondary job as the community *mohel*, nervous fathers would quip, "Remember, Reb Velvel, today you're the circumcisor not the slaughterer."

Then there was the inimitable Abrasha Wosk, a character so authentically Jewish, he might have walked right out of a Sholem Aleichem story. While most shul members shied away from serving on committees, Abrasha couldn't get enough of them. He was, at various times, not only a member, but the chairman of the Seating Committee for the High Holidays, the Cantor's Committee, the *chevra kadisha* (burial society), and the board of the Home for the Aged. He often carried a leather briefcase with nothing in it but a gavel.

One day early on in my tenure at Schara Tzedeck, just before the High Holidays, I happened to overhear a conversation between Abrasha and a young couple from out of town.

"Would you be the Abrasha who we were told is in charge of seats for the High Holidays?"

"Yes," replied Abrasha in his gruff Eastern European accent. "Vat can I do for you?"

"Well," the woman explained, "We are from Montreal and unfortunately will be stuck in Vancouver for the High Holidays."

Knowing Abrasha's love for his adopted home city, I knew trouble lay ahead.

The man continued. "We are very familiar with the process of assigning synagogue seats. But before we go any further, you need to know who we are. Our family is best friends with the Bronfmans, the owners of Seagram's. Our families belong to the same synagogue in Montreal, where we are used to sitting in the front, by the eastern wall, for one hundred dollars a seat."

"Now lemme see if I understand you," Abrasha replied. "Your parents are big shots in Montreal and dey are de best friends mit de Bronfman family. You vant to sit near de eastern wall and pay for each seat one hundred dollars." Abrasha elaborated, "Look I don't vant no trouble vit such an important family like yours. I don't vant that you only should see de seats from a chart. So please, be so kind, and come downstairs vit me to see de real seats."

A few minutes later, as I peered out my office window, I saw the couple running down the steps of the synagogue, and heard Abrasha puffing his way up the stairs to my office. In a voice filled with pride he said, "Rabbi you know dem two shnooks from Montreal dat were just here? I taught dem a lesson they vill remember for the rest of their lives. You know vat I did vit them? I vent downstairs vit dem and took dem right to the bathrooms. I opened de door to de toilets and I told dem, 'You vant two *mizrach* (east) seats? Here are your damn seats! Now gimme the two hundred dollars and you can go home and tell your big shot parents dat here in Vancouver, if you vant to sit in *mizrach* for two hundred dollars you can sit in de toilets!'"

As chairman of the *chevra kadisha*, Abrasha worked closely with Jack Diamond, who headed the synagogue's cemetery board. When a wealthy Edmonton shopping center developer passed away, a member of his family asked Jack the cost of holding the funeral at Schara Tzedeck, where they were not members. Knowing the family's financial capability and believing that each family should support the shul according to its means, Jack quoted them fifteen thousand dollars for the plot, stone, and perpetual service. They agreed to the price, and the funeral was held. When the family had not paid the fee a week later, Abrasha pleaded with Jack to let him serve as collection agent. Jack acquiesced, and Abrasha took over the case.

Abrasha rang up the family, "Hello. Dis is Abrasha speaking, de chairmen of Congregation Schara Tzedeck's *chevra kadishem*, de people who prepare de body. I understend you got de bill that Mr. Jack Diamond sent to you. Iz dat right?"

"That's right. But we have no intention of paying you fifteen thousand dollars. It's an outrageous sum. As a matter of fact, the way I feel about it, I'm not paying a thing."

"Let me make sure eef I understand you. You say dat de price is too high, and you're going to pay nothien—absolutely nothien?"

"You've got that right!"

Lowering his voice for dramatic effect, Abrasha continued, "Vell, in dat case, let me tell you vat I'm going to do. As soon as I hang up dis phone, I am calling up my boys in de *chevra kadishem*, and I'm telling dem, 'Go right down to de cemetery and dig up de body.'" Then, building to a crescendo, Abrasha concluded, "In two hours they vill deliver your brother right to your office. Then you can bury him yourself for nothien as far as I am concerned!" The next day, the family delivered the check.

One evening, Abrasha convened the Cantor's Committee to interview a potential new cantor. Abrasha failed to tell us in advance that we would be conducting the interview by telephone. Despite our concern that we would not be able to adequately judge the candidate's voice, each of us picked up a phone in a different synagogue office, and Abrasha took charge.

"*Chazan!*" he announced brusquely, to the innocent candidate in Toronto. "You have on de phone Abrasha, chairman frum de Cantor's Committee frum Schara Tzedeck in Vancouver. Vee heard some very good things about you, but I'll be honest. The reason we vant to talk to you on de phone is dat some *chazunem* vant to take second honeymoons, free trips, so dey say they are looking for jobs and go for interviews. In Vancouver, we're too smart for dat. Dats why I have my whole committee on the phone. So now please be so kind and deliver for us a *Kol Nidrei*."

The candidate cleared his throat, and sang a lengthy, rather mediocre rendition of the Yom Kippur prayer. Before anyone could say a word, Abrasha delivered his verdict:

"Cantor I vant to tank you very much for singing dat *Kol Nidrei*, but I'm afraid dat as far as me and my Cantor's Committee is concerned, '*Iz shoen nebach nooch Neilah*' (For you it may be *Kol Nidrei*, but for us it's already after *Neilah*). The final service is over!"

My sons were also a regular source of amusement, though an occasional cause of embarrassment. One Rosh Hashanah, just before I was to deliver my sermon to what was typically one of the largest crowds of the year, our *gabbai*, Yitzhak Tyer, tiptoed to the pulpit to inform me of a worrisome development. "Rabbi," he whispered, "We have a problem. There is a long line waiting downstairs for the bathrooms."

"What happened? We have plenty of bathrooms."

"Well, it seems your boys climbed under the stalls and locked them from the inside. Then they took shoes from the cloakroom and put them in the stalls to make it look like people were still in the toilets. But you know our Canadians. They are so polite, they are waiting and waiting and nothing is happening."

"Reb Yitzhak, this isn't a problem, it's a catastrophe!"

Ari and Avi had an easy time avoiding Malkie and me in the after-shul crowd, and managed a temporary stay of punishment by sheepishly showing up at home amidst a dozen guests for the holiday meal. That evening, after everyone left, Malkie and I finally gave then a stern talking-to. But when the boys went to bed, we laughed with one another at how our devilish duo had proven the adage that the rabbi's children are usually the worst behaved children in the congregation.

In 1976, on the occasion of our thirteenth year in Vancouver, Congregation Schara Tzedeck honored Malkie and me at a community-wide dinner. Rabbi Berel Wein, Executive Vice-President of the Orthodox Union, praised our service to the community. Former Prime Minister of Canada John Diefenbaker sent us a lovely personal note, in which he wrote, "Thank you for your lives of devotion and dedication, which will long be remembered." The synagogue generously presented us with a special gift: a three-month sabbatical in Israel.

We knew then, as did some of our closest friends, that the time had come for us to make a difficult decision. We could no longer ignore the fact that we wanted Ari and Avi to have yeshiva educations that simply were not available in Vancouver. The sabbatical in Israel would give us time to think things through.

We had a magical three months in Jerusalem. The boys attended yeshiva. Malkie and I kvelled over Israel's accomplishments in its first twenty-eight years. We discussed the issue of moving from Vancouver at length, but as our last week approached, we remained undecided.

Malkie suggested I take the boys to visit Rabbi Yisrael Altar, the Gerrer Rebbe, one of the great sages of our generation, who had rebuilt Ger into the largest Chassidic dynasty in Israel after it had been nearly obliterated by the Nazis. Malkie wanted our boys to receive a blessing from the Gerrer Rebbe before we left Israel, and she wanted me to seek his advice on whether or not we should stay in Vancouver.

Ari, Avi, and I stood on line with hundreds of black-hatted men outside the Jerusalem stone building in the Chassidic Ge'ula neighborhood, where the Rebbe had a *beis medrash*. As was the custom, I wrote my question on a small piece of paper. I explained that I was a rabbi of a large congregation in Vancouver, Canada, and that we'd had some success sending young people to yeshivas and increasing their religious observance. But, I noted, I had a personal dilemma: there were no yeshivas for my sons in Vancouver. I asked the Rebbe, Should I remain there or move to a larger city like Los Angeles to start a yeshiva?

Taking note of our non-Chassidic suits and ties, one of the Rebbe's assistants accompanied us to the front of the line. Twenty minutes later, we were in the long rectangular *beis medrash*, where the Rebbe leaned against a wooden lectern.

I gingerly approached the Rebbe with Ari and Avi at my side, the three of us drawn in by his bright eyes and meticulously groomed white beard. The Rebbe gave the boys the blessing that they should follow in the ways of their forefathers. Through silver-rimmed glasses perched on the end of his nose, he read my note, then looked me over astutely, and decisively responded: "*Gayit zor fort. Ihr vet haben grois hatzlacha*" (Go immediately. You will have great success).

Back at our apartment, I repeated the Rebbe's words to Malkie, who was as astonished by them as I was.

That night, we flew back to Vancouver so I that could officiate at the wedding of one of our students, Paul Claman. At a *sheva brachos* meal a few days later, Sam Belzberg pulled me aside. "Rabbi," he began. "My wife, Fran, was at Paul's wedding Tuesday night, and says that you were not your usual self. Is something going on?"

Sam and Fran had only recently become members of Schara Tzedeck, and were not enthusiastically involved because they were concerned about their son Marc's increasing level of religious observance. If my change in demeanor was noticeable to them, perhaps it was obvious to everyone.

I told Sam honestly, "Fran is very perceptive. Malkie and I are probably leaving Vancouver for Los Angeles, where we want to start a yeshiva."

Sam probed further, asking whether I had any connections to the Los Angeles business community and if such a move was worth the risk. When I told him I had no particular donors in mind, he was skeptical whether it could succeed.

"Mull it over for a month or so, Rabbi," Sam advised. "If you still feel strongly about it, then come see me, and we'll talk some more."

A month later, I shared with Sam my full plan to create a yeshiva for post-high school students, especially those who did not come from Orthodox backgrounds. Samuel Belzberg, a man I would never have imagined would support a yeshiva, immediately understood the need. He told me he was willing to help, and to enlist the support of his brothers, Bill and Hyman. Together, they would pledge five hundred thousand dollars—a fortune in 1977—to purchase a building that would become home to Yeshiva University of Los Angeles (YULA), and, eventually, the Simon Wiesenthal Center.

Sam also accepted my suggestion to take a leadership role in the new institution. He became the Founding Chairman of the Board of Trustees of Yeshiva University of Los Angeles, and later, the Simon Wiesenthal Center, positions in which he served with great distinction for nearly twenty-five years. Sam introduced me to many of his friends and business associates in New York and Toronto and promoted the new yeshiva, and later the Center, in his travels around the world. Sam's brother, Bill, spread the word in Los Angeles, particularly among active members of the Jewish Federation and the Hillcrest Country Club. Those introductions paved the way for years of organizational support, without which both YULA and the Simon Wiesenthal Center would never have succeeded.

Another act of remarkable generosity made it possible for Malkie and me to embark on the next phase of our lives. A year before we took our sabbatical in Israel, Jack Diamond had recommended that builder George Biely visit our home on West 26th Street to identify the source of our basement flooding.

"Rabbi," George said on his way out, "There is nothing to say except you live in a crappy house."

On a rainy night a few months later, I answered a knock at the door. It was Jack. "Rabbi," he said, "Have you got a few minutes to take a stroll around the block?"

Despite the drizzle, we walked to nearby Cambie Street, where Jack pointed out a white, two-story house with a "For Sale" sign staked in the front lawn. I hesitantly followed him, as he rang the doorbell and a young man invited us in. We entered the living room, and Jack insisted, "Rabbi, sit down. I don't want you to faint when I tell you this."

Intrigued but worried by the introduction, I sat down on what appeared to be a brand new couch. Jack went on, matter-of-factly.

"A few of us got together and bought and furnished this house for you. There are just two details you need to know. The first is that as long as you live in Vancouver, you can't take a mortgage against the house. The second is that this is your property, not the synagogue's. You've been here for thirteen years without a retirement package. This home is your retirement package. Whenever you leave Vancouver, it's yours to sell."

Jack handed me a list of names of the families that had purchased the house. He passed over the keys, suggested I call Malkie to tell her and the kids to come see their new home, and walked out the door.

Malkie was elated as she meandered through the spacious, four-bedroom home with a large back porch and unobstructed mountain views. This was the very house she had always admired. Never had she dreamed it would be ours. Never could we have anticipated such generosity.

We lived in the house on 26th Avenue for only a few years. But the sale of the house, together with Sam Belzberg's support for our new yeshiva, enabled us to move to Los Angeles. Our years in Vancouver were formative and deeply meaningful. Now, with the words of the Gerrer Rebbe ringing in our heads, and gratitude to our friends filling our hearts, we took the next step in our journey.

Chapter Three

Teaching Our Children

Founding an educational institution in a city in which I had no roots and few connections posed a serious challenge. Trying to create a yeshiva whose student body would represent the full gamut of American Judaism, from unaffiliated, to Reform, Conservative, and Orthodox Jews, made the challenge all the more daunting. Yet that was exactly what I set out to do—establish a post-high school yeshiva for students from all Jewish backgrounds.

The fifteen years I had spent working with teenagers as the rabbi of Congregation Schara Tzedeck and Hillel Director at the University of British Columbia had convinced me that there were young people everywhere eager to reconnect with the faith they had abandoned or never really known. I saw how they were drawn to the social interaction and sense of community that NCSY and Yeshiva University's Torah Leadership Seminars offered, and how stimulated they were by traditional Jewish studies taught in ways that were accessible and alive at Ohr Samayach, a Jerusalem yeshiva where I volunteered during our sabbatical. I was committed to building an institution modeled after these successful programs.

I believed that Los Angeles was the ideal location for such a yeshiva. The city had one of the largest Jewish populations in the country. Although the overwhelming majority of Jewish Angelinos were too infatuated with southern California weather to attend synagogue on Shabbos, a small but vibrant Orthodox community supported the Hillel, Yavneh, Toras Emes, and Emek Jewish elementary schools. These schools were poised for future growth, while Jewish high schools and post-high school institutions were disproportionately underdeveloped. I was confident that there was a constituency of college-age students looking to deepen their Jewish identities that could be attracted to our yeshiva.

Before we could launch the yeshiva, however, we needed to accomplish two vital tasks—acquire a building to assure potential students and parents that we were a stable institution with a viable future, and develop a *hashkafa* (philosophy) to define and promote the kind of education we were offering.

Harvey Tannenbaum, a Los Angeles native and son-in-law of Sam and Fran Belzberg of Vancouver, was looking into the real estate situation for us. Harvey had met his wife, Cheri, at an NCSY event in our shul, and I had officiated at their wedding. In early December 1976, he called me with the exciting news that he had found a possible site for our yeshiva: "Rabbi Hier, the building is just what you are looking for. I think you should fly down right away to see it."

By the end of the month, I was in LA, and Harvey was driving me to a Pico Boulevard property in West LA, minutes from Century City. The two-story, E-shaped building sat on a two-acre property surrounded by tall trees, adjacent to a large parking lot. Before I had stepped foot in the building, I knew this was it.

I immediately phoned Sam Belzberg with the news. Sam thought West LA was a great location for our yeshiva, but questioned whether we needed such a large property. I assured him that schools, like shuls, often grow quickly, and moving every few years can be expensive and difficult. Sam said he would discuss the issue further with his brother, Bill, who lived in Beverly Hills.

Within a few weeks, Bill Belzberg had negotiated the asking price down from one million two hundred thousand dollars to nine hundred and thirty thousand dollars, and had opened an escrow account with the five hundred thousand dollars his family had pledged toward the project. A few months later, Bill delivered the news, with a biting sense of humor, that the escrow had successfully closed: "Now Rabbi, don't forget to let me know when the yeshiva boys start moving into the neighborhood, so I can move out! On the other hand, maybe this yeshiva deal is good news. When the Hillcrest Country Club a few blocks away hears about it, maybe they'll finally lower their membership dues and I can get a discount."

Now that we were on our way, the enormity of the undertaking began to hit me. Unlike Schara Tzedeck, where I had the support of the shul's members and board, the new building and all that would take place in it would be my sole responsibility. Was the West LA location a good one, given that the majority of shuls and kosher restaurants were situated in the Fairfax neighborhood? Would I be able to deliver on the promises I had made to the Belzberg family and other Vancouver friends who had generously donated more than $100,000 to the project? Would we attract enough young people to make the yeshiva viable? Even though we had acquired a building, I worried that establishing a Los Angeles yeshiva might remain an unfulfilled dream.

At the same time, I realized that all the signs were pointing in one direction. The Gerrer Rebbe's blessing, the Belzberg's funding, and the wonderful property that had so quickly come our way were signaling me to move forward. I focused on the tasks at hand and trusted my grandmother's motto, "Everything in life is meant to be."

On an early spring morning in 1977, I peered through the front door of our newly acquired, vacant building, eagerly looking for the janitor to let me in. A tall, slender African-American man with deep worry lines on his forehead came to the door.

"I'm Rabbi Marvin Hier, the new owner of the building," I announced enthusiastically.

"Jack Rufus," the janitor replied. "I expected you'd be coming sooner or later. I was just going through the building one last time. This was kinda my second home, you know," he said with resignation.

"Aren't you going to stay on with the Reese Davis people who we bought the building from?"

"Nope. They merged with Vista Del Mar and told me they don't need me anymore.... Maybe you could use a good janitor and handyman with all these kids you are bringing in?"

"Well, I don't exactly have any students, and we haven't hired any teachers yet," I reluctantly acknowledged.

Jack scratched his head in disbelief. "You mean to tell me, you don't have any students or teachers but you bought this building? Rabbi, I don't mean any disrespect, but that doesn't make much sense to me. That's like going horseback riding without a horse."

In order to explain myself and bolster my faith in the project, which he had momentarily sapped, I told Jack a classic Chassidic story. "Two young men were grumbling that they had no children, even though they'd each been married for years. They went to a great rabbi and asked him to bless them so that their wives would give birth. The rabbi gave his blessings and a year later, one of the wives gave birth. When the second man heard the news, he returned to the rabbi. The rabbi said to him, 'I know that you want me to tell you why my blessing worked for your friend but not for you. I will tell you.... When your friend received my blessing, he immediately took his wife to buy a baby carriage. He showed that he had faith in the blessing, and so the blessing was able to come true.'

"Jack, I have faith in my dream. But instead of a baby carriage, I bought a building. If you have a little faith in me, and help us out for a while, I think there will be a place for you when the students get here."

A wide smile spread across Jack's face. "You really mean that?" he asked, shaking his head. "Here I thought I was going to hand over the keys to some new owner, but instead I wind up with a job at a school with no kids!"

Jack led me through a maze of small, empty rooms that had been appropriate for the building's prior use as a children's therapy clinic, but was hardly suitable for a yeshiva. Assuming we were going to demolish the building and construct a new one, Jack innocently pointed out that the building had no lights; the previous owners, operating on the same assumption as Jack, had removed the sockets. My first requests of Jack were for him to buy six folding chairs and install a phone with a long extension cord so that I wouldn't have to run the hundred-yard dash every time it rang.

One of the first calls I received was from Dr. Norman Lamm, a distinguished pulpit rabbi, philosopher, and teacher, and the newly elected president of Yeshiva University. Dr. Lamm had heard about our plans from his brother, Rabbi Maurice Lamm, spiritual leader of Congregation Beth Jacob of Beverly Hills. Dr. Lamm invited me to New York to discuss the yeshiva with him in greater detail.

I immediately realized what a breakthrough this could be. Partnering with Yeshiva University, the oldest Jewish educational institution in America, would give our project immediate credibility and accelerate student recruitment. I seized the opportunity, and made my travel plans.

Dr. Lamm greeted me in his warm, book-lined office on the university's Washington Heights campus, and introduced me to Rabbi Jacob Rabinowitz, Dean of the university's Erna Michael College of Hebraic Studies, and Dr. Sheldon Sokol, its Vice President for Business Affairs. As we settled into deep armchairs, Dr. Lamm explained his interest in our project:

"The university has wanted to establish a presence on the West Coast for some time. That's why my predecessor, Dr. Samuel Belkin, founded the West Coast Teacher's College there, with the hope that it would eventually grow into a full-fledged yeshiva. Unfortunately, this never came to be."

Dr. Lamm then moved to specifics: "I asked you to come here today, Rabbi Hier, because I share your view that the West Coast is underdeveloped. Yeshiva University would like to participate in your project in a meaningful way. We can't assume any financial obligation. But Rabbi Hier, I know what you have accomplished in Vancouver, and I am sufficiently confident in your abilities to get this done that I am willing, if we come to an agreement, to lend you Yeshiva University's distinguished name and to offer you its educational expertise."

I was stunned. I had not attended Yeshiva University, and had not signed up a single student to my new yeshiva, yet the university's president was willing to entrust me with the Yeshiva University name. I told Dr. Lamm how grateful I was for the opportunity to have our yeshiva affiliated with his fine institution, and how we were prepared to assume full financial responsibility for the yeshiva's operation. Within a few weeks, we reached an agreement, and the Yeshiva University of Los Angeles was born.

Along with the Yeshiva University name came its educational philosophy: *Torah u'madda* (Torah and secular knowledge). This approach resonated with me, despite the fact that it was not the one in which I was educated. My experience in Vancouver had convinced me that a balance of traditional religious studies and secular academic studies was exactly what was needed in a new West Coast yeshiva.

With a building and a *hashkafa* (philosophy), we could now begin the practical work of institution building. Rabbi Lamm soon appointed Rabbi Rabinowitz as Yeshiva University's liaison to YULA and Dr. Socal as its Financial Advisor. Rabbi Rabinowitz immediately began helping us develop a plan to assemble a faculty and recruit students so we could open the yeshiva in the fall of 1977.

Key positions needed to be filled. We hired Rabbi Moshe Meiselman, a nephew of Rabbi Joseph B. Soloveitchik, who himself was a great Talmudic scholar and held a doctorate from MIT, as YULA's Director of Academic Programs. Rabbi Abraham Cooper, who, with his wife Roz, had first come to Vancouver, at my urging, became School Administrator and Director of Admissions. We invited ten outstanding Yeshiva University graduates to establish a *kollel*, which would enable them to continue their religious studies at a high level, and would provide our students with capable and energetic young teachers and mentors. Among them was a young couple, Rabbi Meyer and Shulamith May. In a short time, Rabbi May would become the organization's Executive Director.

At the same time, we formed a Board of Trustees. Sam Belzberg served as Chairman of the Board, and Roland Arnall, a prominent Los Angeles real estate developer, as Co-Chair. Roland, in turn, approached Esther Cohen, a daughter of Holocaust survivors who had an uncanny ability to reach out to people across the religious spectrum. The creation of a board that included many prominent individuals helped promote the message that our yeshiva would serve the needs of the wider Los Angeles Jewish community.

Over the next few months, from a temporary office Roland generously provided, I oversaw the conversion of the former clinic into a proper school campus. We renovated the building to include a dozen classrooms, a large *beis medrash*, and a dormitory wing to house fifty students.

As the campus neared completion, Malkie and I prepared to leave Vancouver. Our departure was bittersweet: we had watched children grow into adults, shared in families' joys and sorrows, been embraced and nurtured by the community. But our leaving also marked a beginning. As we moved into our new home in the Beverlywood section of West LA a few blocks from the new yeshiva, and enrolled Ari and Avi in the local day school, we reminded ourselves why the Torah lists the names of the many places the Israelites stopped on their way to the Promised Land: because human beings are reflections of their earthly journeys; each stop along the paths of their lives defines them, shapes them, and enables them to continue on their way.

In September 1977, Yeshiva University of Los Angeles proudly opened its doors to nearly sixty students from diverse backgrounds, aged eighteen to sixty-five. Most were Americans who had grown up in the Reform and Conservative movements. A few came from Canada and Israel.

It was deeply gratifying to reconnect to my roots in the yeshiva world. YULA's desk chairs were a step above the worn, wooden benches of my yeshiva days, and the bindings of our books were not yet frayed like those from which I had studied. But the substance of those volumes, which had been authored over twenty centuries, remained an unchanged testament to the timelessness of our traditions.

As I peeked into our newly refurbished *beis medrash* and classrooms, made possible by generous gifts from the Belzberg family and later from Betty and Zvi Ryzman, Jacob and Pnina Graff, and David and Judy Hager, and saw our first crop of eager students seated at its tables, I was overwhelmed by the thought that our little yeshiva would contribute in its own way to the unbroken chain of Torah study that had sustained Jews over the centuries. YULA was joining the ranks of Torah academies around the world, from the great Eastern European Volozhin, Slabodka, and Chachmei Lublin Yeshivas to the hundreds of yeshivas in America, England, Israel and elsewhere that were continuing the legacy the Nazis had attempted to eradicate.

YULA's first years were exciting and rewarding. Students quickly acquired the skills of analyzing Jewish texts, and immersed themselves in prayer and Talmud study. YULA offered an intimate atmosphere and easy access to rabbis, which students loved, and from which their studies benefitted. I kvelled whenever I saw YULA students running up Pico Boulevard with their yellow and black yarmulkas flapping in the wind; we had chosen yellow to give positive new meaning to the color that had signified degradation and shame in the Nazi era. When I davened with students in the *beis medrash* or spoke at yeshiva events, I felt enormous pride in our achievements.

As a result of our early successes, and just two years after we had launched our yeshiva, leading members of the Los Angeles Orthodox Jewish community came to us with an urgent appeal. They wanted us to open a high school, and their argument was persuasive: "YULA is a success," they told us, "but the community's most vital need is a high school. We had hoped that Rambam, the school that we have been involved with, would fill the void, but it's not working. We need YULA to run a high school under its auspices."

As much as I wanted to reach the thousands of college-age students around the country, whom I knew were suited to our yeshiva, I couldn't challenge the assertion that priority should be given to creating a quality high school for the local Jewish community. The Board of Trustees agreed, and we shifted our emphasis. In 1979, the Yeshiva University of Los Angeles High School opened on the original YULA property, which we retrofitted, renovated, and later rebuilt and inaugurated as the new Jack and Gitta Nagel Family YULA Boys Campus. In 1981, we purchased a property on Robertson Boulevard in West LA that was later rebuilt to become the Gindi Family YULA Girls Campus.

YULA's outstanding faculty and staff, who spent the next months and years building a school of excellence, made my role as Founder and Dean a pleasure. My friend and colleague, Rabbi Meyer May, raised millions of dollars as YULA's Executive Director. Rabbis Moshe Meiselman and Shalom Tendler, its Heads of Yeshiva, set a high bar and provided skillful guidance. YULA's Principals, Rabbi Herbert Hexter, Dr. Bruce Powell, Rabbi Dovid Landesman, and Rabbi Heshy Glass, developed exceptional curricula. Rabbi Nachum Sauer, a renowned scholar, was the Senior Rebbe. For many years, he provided spiritual inspiration as rabbi of the YULA Minyan. Together with parents, devoted teachers, and administrators, this remarkable team developed a school that fostered religious growth, love of learning, and personal and communal responsibility.

One memorable incident encapsulates the school's emphasis on both faith and action. Early one morning in January 1994, the late Dov Abramson was repairing books in his second-floor office when the walls began to shake: the Northridge earthquake had hit the San Fernando Valley. Dov rushed to the school's *beis medrash* to check on the condition of the thousands of sacred books it housed, and spent the next several hours re-shelving those that were strewn across the floor. When he completed the job, he overheard two men on their way to the yeshiva's daily morning *minyan* marveling at how every book was in its proper place: "Can you believe it? Not one book fell down! It's a miracle from God."

Dov chimed in, "God does perform miracles. But sometimes even He needs a little help."

In 2005, I stepped down as Dean of the Yeshiva University of Los Angeles after having served proudly in that position for twenty-eight years. A new Board of Trustees made up of dedicated parents and led by the capable David Nagel would now take YULA to the next stage in its development. They would follow in the footsteps of philanthropists Sam Belzberg and Roland Arnall, who had staked their reputations on my dream, and, later, the Jack Nagel family and hundreds of others, who stepped up to continue to make that dream a reality.

Since its founding in 1977, more than two thousand young men and women have graduated from YULA. They have gone on to attend leading yeshivas and every Ivy League university. They have won basketball championships and model UN programs. They have become pulpit rabbis and heads of yeshiva, doctors, scientists, authors, and entrepreneurs. YULA's graduates are leaders of Jewish communities everywhere.

Although Malkie and I are associate members of Rabbi Elazar Muskin's Young Israel of Century City, I still *daven* on Shabbos and Jewish festivals at YULA because, there, surrounded by thousands of sacred books, I am reminded of my roots as a young student in the yeshivas on the Lower East Side.

As I look back at YULA's founding, I am reminded of the interesting relationship between the patriarch Jacob and his son, Judah in the Torah. Jacob never praises Judah, despite the fact that he brilliantly negotiates with the Egyptian Pharaoh's highest-ranking official, whom we later discover to be Jacob's long-lost, favorite son, Joseph. Instead, Jacob sends Judah on a new assignment, as the Torah tells us, "and he sent Judah ahead of him…". The Talmud interprets this to mean that Jacob sends Judah to the Land of Goshen to build a school—a yeshiva—for the seventy members of his family who would soon move there. The Talmud's message is clear: business dealings and political negotiations are important; but education is the only guarantee for the long-term future of the Jewish people.

Chapter Four

Birth of the Simon Wiesenthal Center

I n the summer of 1977, shortly after arriving in LA from Vancouver, Malkie and I took Ari and Avi to visit the Los Angeles La Brea Tar Pits, one of the world's most famous fossil sites. The tar pits were formed when subterranean bitumen bubbled up to the earth's surface, creating large areas of natural asphalt. They contain animal skeletons that have been preserved over tens of thousands of years.

During our tour of the site, a young girl innocently asked the tour guide: "Will dinosaurs come back to earth one day?" The amiable guide smiled and reassured her that the earth's changing climate conditions prevented dinosaurs from returning.

As I considered this fact, I thought about human creatures, whose time on earth is dependent as much on political conditions as environmental ones. No one can reassure us that the political climate has changed so dramatically since the time of Adolf Hitler, for example, that another tyrant like him will never again come to power.

This thought prompted a string of questions to unravel in my head. How many of the visitors who came to the La Brea Tar Pits to learn about prehistoric animal fossils knew anything about the cataclysmic events that had engulfed our world in the 1930s and 40s? Why didn't America have a major Holocaust education center like Israel's Yad Vashem to teach the story of the murder of six million Jews—one-third of the world's Jewish population? Why hadn't the American Jewish community—the world's largest—built a major Holocaust museum?

The more I looked for plausible explanations, the more concerned I became about the lack of an American institution dedicated to Holocaust remembrance and education, and what that absence said about the state of the American Jewish community. Perhaps American Jews were still traumatized by the Holocaust. Maybe they had a false sense of security that caused them to forget the unexpected turns history can take. Whatever the reason, the absence of such an institution suddenly felt stark.

A month later, on a walk back from a Shabbos *minyan* that had recently been organized at the Ramada Inn Hotel in West Los Angeles where a number of friends, including, Harvey Tannenbaum, Dr. Larry Platt and Dr. Mark Goldenberg, would pray, I mulled over the idea of creating a Holocaust remembrance and education center at YULA. By the time I arrived home, I was eager to discuss it with Malkie, who, over the years, had served as my most valued sounding board. I expected her to respond with, "Moishe, it's off the wall. You just started a yeshiva. Before we even know if it's going to succeed, you want to start a museum? What does the Holocaust have to do with a yeshiva anyway?" Instead, Malkie listened intently then encouraged me. "It's a great idea!" she said. "It will have an impact on the whole community. I think you should do it."

The idea dominated our conversation around the Shabbos table, and, by the time we finished the cholent, it had evolved into an action plan. The following week, I discussed it with Sam Belzberg and the other members of the YULA Board of Trustees, and with Dr. Lamm and his team at Yeshiva University, who were enthusiastic and supportive. They recognized that the time had come for American Jews to face the challenge of teaching the lessons of the Holocaust.

In 1977, Holocaust memories were being roused around the world. Holocaust survivors living in the Chicago suburb of Skokie were shaken when the United States Supreme Court defended the right of the neo-Nazi National Socialist Party of America to march through their streets. Italian Holocaust survivors were humiliated when Herbert Kappler, the former head of the Gestapo in Rome, who had organized the deportation of thousands of Italian Jews to Auschwitz and had ordered more than three hundred civilians shot in the infamous Ardeatine Caves incident, was smuggled out of an Italian prison, and brought to freedom in Germany.

Anti-Semitism was also beginning to take the form of anti-Zionism. In January 1977, the French government bowed to pressure from the Arab world to release Abu Daoud, the mastermind of the 1972 Munich Olympic Massacre, in which eleven members of the Israeli Olympic Team had been taken hostage and killed. Using the excuse that the West Germans had not properly filled out the necessary forms to obtain his extradition, the French put Abu Daoud on a plane to Algeria. In the investigations following the Munich Olympic Massacre, the public also learned that German officials had known that neo-Nazi leader, Willi Pohl, had coordinated the massacre with Abu Daoud's Palestinian terrorist group, the Black September Organization, and that following the attack, Germany's Foreign Minister, Walter Scheel, had negotiated a deal in which he had agreed that Germany would make no further extradition requests if Black September would guarantee no future terrorist attacks on German soil.

Within this troubling political context, I put together a team to develop the concept of a center for Holocaust remembrance and education at YULA. Our mission was threefold: to honor the memory of the victims of the Holocaust; to teach the Holocaust's lessons to the next generation so it could confront ignorance, Holocaust denial, and revisionism; and to combat the unrelenting scourges of anti-Semitism, anti-Zionism, and racism of all kinds.

Our Holocaust center needed a name, and I knew from the start whose name it should bear. While there were thousands of people who had acted heroically during the Holocaust, there was one person who had responded to his people's tragedy, his family's losses, and his personal suffering by devoting the remainder of his life to seeking justice—Simon Wiesenthal.

Simon Wiesenthal was born in 1908 in Buczacz, Galicia, then part of the Austro-Hungarian Empire. He was an established architect in Lvov, Poland when Germany and Russia partitioned the country and the Red Army purged the city of its Jews. Wiesenthal's stepfather was arrested and died in prison, and his stepbrother was shot. He was reduced to working as a mechanic in a bedspring factory.

In July 1941, after the Germans invaded, he was lined up in a courtyard with other Jews to be shot, but was spared after the Nazi soldiers killed half the group, then left to attend a church service. He was held in the Janowska concentration camp outside Lvov before being sent to a forced labor camp.

Wiesenthal escaped from the camp in October 1943, but was recaptured in June 1944 and sent back to Janowska. In the final year of the war, he was among the few prisoners who survived a grueling forced trek westward through Poland, Germany, and Austria, with stops in the Plasgow, Gross-Rosen, Buchenwald, and Mauthausen concentration camps. By the time he was liberated from Mauthausen on May 5, 1945, he weighed ninety-seven pounds. Together with his wife, Cyla, with whom he was re-united after the war, he had lost eighty-nine family members.

While in the camps, Wiesenthal recorded details of Nazis involved in the atrocities he had witnessed. Just weeks after his liberation, he was organizing his notes and collecting evidence from others to build cases against ninety-one alleged Nazi war criminals for the War Crimes Section of the United States Army. He would continue this work for the next two years, while he headed a relief and welfare organization, the Jewish Central Committee of the United States Zone of Austria.

In 1947, Wiesenthal opened the Jewish Documentation Center, which was devoted exclusively to the search for Nazi war criminals.

In the early 1950s, Wiesenthal passed on information about the whereabouts of one of the primary organizers of the Holocaust, Adolf Eichmann, to the Israeli Consulate in Vienna and Israel's intelligence agency, the Mossad, which helped lead to Eichmann's capture in Argentina, and, later, his trial and execution in Israel.

Encouraged by Eichmann's capture, Wiesenthal intensified his efforts. In 1966, his investigative work led to the trial of sixteen former SS officers—nine of whom he had located—for participation in the extermination of the Jews in Lvov. In 1967, his sleuthing in Brazil led to the arrests of Franz Stangl, former commandant of the Treblinka and Sobibor death camps, and Gustav Franz Wagner, a former deputy commandant at Sobibor. Wiesenthal discovered Hermine Braunsteiner, a former guard at the Maidanek death camp, living in Queens, New York. Braunsteiner, in 1973, became the first Nazi war criminal extradited from the United States to Germany. Wiesenthal would go on to build criminal cases against more than one thousand former Nazis.

Simon Wiesenthal was often asked to explain why he had become a Nazi hunter. In a 1964 *New York Times Magazine* interview, he answered with a potent story:

> I once spent the Sabbath at the home of a former Mauthausen inmate who became a wealthy jewelry manufacturer after the war. After dinner, he asked me, "Simon, if you had gone back to building houses, you'd be a millionaire. Why didn't you?"
>
> I answered, "You're a religious man. You believe in God and life after death. I also believe. When we come to the other world and meet the millions of Jews who died in the camps and they ask us, "What have you done?" there will be many answers. You will say, "I became a jeweler." Another will say, "I smuggled coffee and American cigarettes." Still another will say, "I built houses," but I will say, "I have never forgotten you."

In August 1977, I gathered my nerve and called Simon Wiesenthal. To my surprise, his secretary immediately put him on the line.

"Mr. Wiesenthal, eleven years ago, after my wife and I visited the Mauthausen concentration camp, we stopped by your Documentation Center. We never expected to meet you. But you surprised us by spending a few moments with us when your secretary explained that we had come from Vancouver, Canada to see you. When I apologized for taking up your time, you said, 'I am always available for our people. If you ever need my advice, my door is open.' Mr. Wiesenthal, I need your advice. I am involved in an important project, and you are the only person who can help me with it. May I come to Vienna to discuss it with you?"

Wiesenthal replied in a deep voice, his English abraded by a heavy Polish accent. "Rabbi, the matter is so important that we can't discuss it on the phone? You need to come all the way to Vienna?"

"Yes, it's something I must discuss with you in person."

"Okay. If you must come, then come. I will make time for you."

While I was delighted that Simon Wiesenthal had agreed to meet me on such short notice, I was under no illusions that he would lend his name to our fledgling Holocaust center. I decided that I needed a businessman to accompany me to Vienna to assure Mr. Wiesenthal that our project was viable. I contacted Roland Arnall, a Holocaust survivor, who agreed to come along on the condition that we stop in Paris so he could show me the neighborhood in which he was born.

In Paris, Roland hired a driver to take us on a tour of the city's Jewish sites. After sightseeing, he asked the driver to take us to what he described as the city's best kosher restaurant. He pointed out the restaurant's front door from the car, and asked me to reserve a table at which he said he would join me in ten minutes.

I entered the lobby of the flamboyant restaurant and searched for someone who spoke English. "Is there a kosher restaurant here?" I asked.

"Kosher restaurant here?" a man incredulously responded with a French lilt to his voice. "I don't think *zees* is a kosher place!"

Only after I noticed the framed photographs of can-can girls decorating the lobby did I realize I was standing in the famous

Parisian cabaret, the Moulin Rouge, and that Roland had executed a flawless practical joke. Embarrassed by my gullibility, I ran outside to find Roland wiping tears of laughter from his cheeks with a silk handkerchief.

Mr. Wiesenthal's Jewish Documentation Center occupied a cramped, three-room office in a modern building on the site of the former Hotel Metropol, which the Gestapo had used as its Vienna headquarters. It had a staff of four, including Mr. Wiesenthal. When we arrived, he was waiting for us in the secretary's office.

Mr. Wiesenthal was a broad figure with large, penetrating eyes and a carefully groomed mustache. He had little patience for formalities. He greeted us with a compulsory smile, then ushered us into his office.

Binders and files lined floor-to-ceiling shelves like soldiers in tactical formation awaiting their next order. A map of Nazi-occupied Europe in muted shades of yellow and green dominated the room. Mr. Wiesenthal explained that he had deliberately hung the oversized map on the wall behind his desk to remind himself of the enormity of the undertaking he had assumed.

"You know how many camps the Nazis and their helpers ran?" Mr. Wiesenthal rhetorically asked us. "Tens of thousands!" The map you are looking at shows only the major concentration camps. So whenever I think I have accomplished something, I look at the map again and it tells me the truth—that whatever we are doing is absolutely nothing compared to the crimes that were committed."

With a sense of urgency, Mr. Wiesenthal moved abruptly to the point of our meeting.

"So Rabbi, tell me what is so important that you came all the way from Los Angeles to Vienna."

"Well," I responded. "Nearly six hundred thousand Jews live in Los Angeles, and yet the Jewish community is quite undeveloped. That's why we recently established Yeshiva University of Los Angeles in order to give young people a traditional Jewish education. But Los Angeles and America need more than a yeshiva. America is the greatest democracy in history, and a very secure place for Jews. Yet there is no major institution to perpetuate the memory of the six million. Mr. Wiesenthal, I recently visited a museum in LA where people come from all over America to learn about dinosaurs. In fact, there are a half dozen such places in America. But where can people go to learn about the Nazis? Who will teach them that thirty-two years after the Holocaust, anti-Semitism is still going strong? If we don't teach young people now, we will once again be caught unprepared, and history will repeat itself... I've come here Mr. Wiesenthal, because we want to create a Holocaust center in America, and we want to name it in your honor."

Roland interjected with a bit of his family history. He described to Mr. Wiesenthal how he was born in Paris in 1939 and was a little more than a year old when the city fell to the Nazis. When the Jewish deportations began, Roland explained, his family was loaded onto a truck and taken to the Drancy internment camp. "What my parents found most shocking was that our neighbors, who had been our friends for many years, cheered as we were dragged out of our apartment."

Roland then addressed the issue of our proposed Holocaust center. "Mr. Wiesenthal, what the rabbi is doing is essential for the next generation—for my children and other children who know almost nothing about these events. Having your name on our Center will make all the difference between its success and failure."

"Look," Simon answered. "This is for me very strange. What can I say? I am honored. I did not expect this. Nobody has ever come to Vienna to ask me for my name. Usually they come to give me the name of a Nazi they want me to hunt down. But you must understand. I am a Nazi hunter, not a teacher. I agree that what you want to do is absolutely right. But millions died and thousands like me survived. We were all in the camps together. Why pick only one name for your building?"

"Because, Mr. Wiesenthal," I responded. "You are the only man who never moved on. Instead, you stayed behind, looking at that map, day after day, spending every moment pursuing justice for the millions who were killed. Mr. Wiesenthal, all the survivors will agree that your name deserves to be on our building."

After a long pause, he responded. "Look, I must say, I like the idea. For years, whenever I have gone to America to speak, I have asked survivors why they don't create an institution to teach about the Holocaust. They have promised me many times they will do something. But still today there is absolutely nothing…. I like also that you are an activist who wants to speak out about anti-Semitism today. I have always said anybody can do research, but the question is what you do with the research. If you store it away like food in a freezer, it is rarely used. If you publish it in journals, it only reaches the intellectuals. Today, the fight against the haters must be taken to the public. After all, it is a fight to protect our children and grand-children and future generations against a repetition of those crimes…. Look, what can I tell you? I'm impressed. But I need to know more before I give you a final answer. I am going to send my lawyer and friend, Martin Rosen, to Los Angeles to meet with you. After that, I will let you know what I decide…. In the meantime, I will drive you back to your hotel."

Roland declined the offer of a ride, saying we would happily take a taxi. But Mr. Wiesenthal insisted, "I have to meet someone near your hotel, and it will be a good opportunity to get better acquainted with you."

Simon Wiesenthal drove a small, grey, timeworn car with manual transmission. Roland climbed into the front passenger seat, while I took my place in the back with the large design ren-derings of our Holocaust center stretched across my lap. The ride was like Mr. Wiesenthal's life: singular in its purpose, and beset with danger. Mr. Wiesenthal's arms flailed and his eyes darted as he stressed key points in our conversation. He zigzagged his way through the streets of Vienna, indifferent to traffic patterns and irate drivers forced to get out of his way. As he described his rocky relationship with Bruno Kreisky, the Jewish Chancellor of Austria and Nazi apologist, Mr. Wiesenthal nearly veered into a lane of oncoming traffic. Roland, who by now had turned a pale shade of green, desperately flung his arm into the back seat to signal me to stop talking in order to allow Mr. Wiesenthal to concentrate on his driving.

Finally, we arrived at the InterContinental Hotel, where we said our goodbyes, and Roland correctly interpreted my immediate look in his direction as a sign that I thought the ride was his Moulin Rouge moment.

A few weeks later, Martin Rosen visited me in Los Angeles. He had been among the US troops that had liberated the concentration camps at the end of World War II. Twenty years later, he had met Simon Wiesenthal, and over the years, had become his close friend and trusted advisor, particularly on American matters.

I showed Marty a balsa wood model we had prepared and made an exuberant pitch. I described the vital need for the Center, and emphasized how it would be the first major center of its kind in the United States. Although Marty was underwhelmed by our small model, he assured me that we had his support and he would encourage Mr. Wiesenthal to lend his name to the project.

On November 22, 1977, we opened the Simon Wiesenthal Center in a four thousand-square-foot space in the west wing of the Yeshiva University of Los Angeles building. The Center's primary exhibition told the story of the Holocaust in a series of square panels, each of which marked a year of Hitler's reign. Mr. Wiesenthal attended the inauguration and spoke about the terrible price the Jewish people had paid for survival:

> Most people have no idea how many Jews we have lost over the past two thousand years. Among the sixty million inhabitants of the Roman Empire, there were four million Jews, half a million of whom lived in ancient Israel, the rest in Italy, Spain and other parts of the Empire. At this same time, the British Isles held about one million people; today more than fifty million live there. If the Jews had been left to develop like the British, there would be two hundred million Jews in the world today. However, we are only fourteen million. Why? Because we are the leftovers of pogroms, inquisitions, and Hitler. It was not

only mass slaughter, but also forced baptisms and voluntary escape from Judaism, which took its toll on our numbers.

Whenever I speak, people tell me, "I have not lost anybody in the Holocaust; I am not a survivor." This is why I always tell my audiences that it is my firm belief that the Jews in America—whether they formerly had been living in Europe, whether they had lost relatives in the Holocaust or not—are all survivors. Every Jew alive today is a survivor! If Hitler had won the war, the first thing he would have said to the defeated nations is: "Give me your Jews!"—just as he had done all over Europe. And in each and every country, he would have found people ready to give up the Jews. It is only because Hitler lost the war that there are still Jews alive.

Our Center attracted a diverse audience. Not only did Holocaust survivors and their families come, as we had anticipated, but many Los Angeles public schools booked tours. The Center's themes seemed to resonate within and well beyond the Jewish community.

Hollywood personalities began to take notice, thanks, in part, to Jack Lerman and Johnnie Francis of the Eddie Cantor Charitable Foundation. They hosted a number of dinners to benefit the Center and reached out to celebrities, including Frank Sinatra. Frank read a newspaper article about us and asked his lawyer, Mickey Rudin, to get in touch with me. Soon after, the leader of the Rat Pack invited Malkie and me to his home in Rancho Mirage.

Frank and his lovely wife, Barbara, greeted us warmly at the entrance to "The Compound," as the Sinatras' expansive home on the seventeenth fairway of the Tamarisk Country Club was known. We sat together in the living room, where Frank explained his interest in helping our organization. "I regard Simon Wiesenthal as a hero, and believe that preserving the memory of the Holocaust is essential to our future well-being," he said.

Frank had invited his neighbor, Danny Schwartz, to join us, and had asked him to bring along his "Jewish telephone directory."

When Danny arrived, Frank joked, "I'm only an honorary member of the Jewish tribe, but you are a full-fledged member and should know all the best people." Then he turned to business, "So, tell me who you think we should approach to support the Center."

Danny suggested the generous Don Soffer, founder of Turnberry Associates, the real estate development firm that created the Miami suburb of Aventura. Frank immediately placed the call and made a persuasive pitch, in which he referred to me as "his rabbi." Malkie and I were tickled. He emphatically ended the conversation with, "I am sending down my rabbi, Rabbi Marvin Hier, to visit with you in a few weeks. I know you will join our cause."

When I arrived at Don's Miami office, concerned that he was put off by Frank's pressure, Don set me straight: "You don't have to thank me for agreeing to meet with you, Rabbi Hier. It doesn't happen every day that Frank Sinatra calls to ask for support of a worthwhile Jewish cause. And don't worry. Do you have any idea what good use I made of that call on the golf course?"

Don would become a major benefactor and trustee of the Simon Wiesenthal Center. Distinguished Floridians Stephen Levin, Herb Baum, Russell Galbut, and Ezra Katz, would later join the Board of Trustees and more than forty thousand residents of the Sunshine State would become members of the Center.

In October 1978, we welcomed Mr. Wiesenthal back to Los Angeles to celebrate his seventieth birthday. Esther Cohen arranged for him to go on a national speaking tour that culminated in an event attended by one thousand eight hundred people at the Los Angeles Bonaventure Hotel. Mr. Wiesenthal used the opportunity to remind the audience of the shock his generation felt when the Holocaust began, and of the vulnerability of Jews everywhere:

> We were so much in love with the technical and spiritual progress around us that we simply could not imagine that a country in which Jews lived together with the rest of the population could...overnight and suddenly re-emerge with the sheer brutality of organized crime....When we first heard about what was happening...our attitude was, "This could

only happen to the backward Jews in the East, but cosmopolitan and assimilated Jews have nothing to fear...." But when the Nazis became the masters of all of Europe, they invented a new slogan: "One can leave anything but Judaism." In other words, there was...no difference between the Jews in the East and the cosmopolitans and intellectuals [in the West]. They were all Jews. We must always remember that!

Then, in a triumphant moment, dozens of YULA students, Holocaust survivors, and dignitaries, including California Governor Jerry Brown, Los Angeles Mayor Tom Bradley, and Sam Belzberg, joined hands and danced in concentric circles. After having experienced years of darkness, the man who had become the conscience of the Holocaust lit up the room with his smile.

The poignant sight reminded me of the famous Talmudic story of Rabbi Haninah ben Teradion, who was murdered by the Romans for disregarding their ban on teaching Torah. The Talmud tells us that the Romans wrapped Rabbi Haninah in a Torah scroll and set it on fire. As the flames engulfed him, Rabbi Haninah's distraught disciples asked him what he saw. Rabbi Haninah told them, "The parchment is burning, but the letters are soaring upward."

Simon Wiesenthal experienced the unimaginable horrors of the Holocaust, but survived with a passion for justice. Bialystok, Minsk, Lodz, and other European cities had smoldered, but the sparks of those Jewish communities miraculously made their way to New York, Los Angeles, Toronto, London, and Jerusalem, where they ignited a new generation to again sing the songs of our ancestors.

The Simon Wiesenthal Center soon grew beyond a local Holocaust education center. Using her expertise in statistics, Malkie created a national direct-mail campaign modeled after the Democratic National Committee's that became the most successful campaign of any American Jewish organization, bringing us a constituency of more than four hundred thousand families. It was those smaller gifts from tens of thousands of donors from around the world that allowed the Center to expand into a true global human rights organization. We opened offices in key areas of the country to expand our donor base and to spread our educational activities.

Rhonda Barad then headed our New York office. The very capable Bobby Novak established and ran our Miami office with great distinction until his untimely death in 2007. We opened a Chicago office, now headed by Alison Pure-Slovin with the renowned philanthropists, Lester Crown and Judd Malkin, serving as Honorary Chairmen, and with the active participation of community leaders Sam Zell, Robert Hartman, Abraham Joseph Stern and Rivka Zell. We created a Canadian Friends of the Simon Wiesenthal Center organization based in Toronto that quickly developed a national presence under the direction of Sol Litman and Leo Adler, and later greatly expanded under the direction of Avi Benlolo.

At home, our sons Ari and Avi thrived too. After attending Jewish day schools in Los Angeles, Ari went off to a yeshiva in Israel, and then enlisted in the Israel Defense Forces, where he served as a tank driver on the Israel-Lebanon border. He returned to the US to study economics at Yeshiva University, and married Sandy Huberman from Vancouver. Avi attended YULA and Kerem Yeshiva, then moved to New York, where the legendary Ace Greenberg hired him as a stockbroker at Bear Stearns.

We were delighted when Avi decided to live with our brother- and sister-in-law, the Mermelsteins, in Borough Park, Brooklyn. We liked the idea of his being with family, and of his living in a vital Jewish neighborhood where he was sure to find a nice Jewish girl. But after three years and no news on the marriage front, Malkie thought, and I agreed, that the time had come for a little father-son talk.

When Avi came home for Rosh Hashanah, I took him to the Family Fitness Center on Pico Boulevard. We began our chat on the treadmills, then continued in the steam room. Leaning back on a slatted wooden bench, and closing my eyes in relaxation, I offered my fatherly advice. "Avi, Borough Park's gotta be a great place to meet a nice girl from a good family. Maybe if you haven't had any luck yet, you need to be a little more aggressive in looking for someone...." I continued to talk until the steam got to be too much for me. I walked toward the Jacuzzi, and noticed that Avi was already submerged.

"How long have you been here?" I exclaimed.

"I came in as soon as you went for your shvitz. It was too hot in there for me."

"*Oye a brach!*" (What a catastrophe!) "So who was I telling your whole life story and giving my advice on finding a wife to?"

A few minutes later, an Asian man came out of the steam room with a pensive look on his face. I wondered if he was planning his move to Borough Park to find himself a nice Jewish girl.

As the years passed and we advanced and expanded the mission of the Simon Wiesenthal Center, I was privileged to develop a close relationship with Simon. At times, he could be cantankerous and stubborn. But no one was so singularly devoted to the memory of the six million Jews murdered in the Holocaust as he was; no one so determined to seek justice on their behalf.

Simon undertook investigations despite the serious risk to him and his family. He received many death threats over the years. In 1982, after a bomb exploded outside his Vienna home, where he lived with his wife Cyla and their only child Paulinka, he was forced to have guards on duty at all times. Once, I asked him why he didn't set up an office in New York, where he might feel less threatened. He answered matter-of-factly, "A biologist studying malaria must live where the mosquitos live, so I have to live in Vienna where the former Nazis live."

He was audacious. Once, when waiting to meet him at Washington's Dulles Airport, I overheard a young man shouting obscenities, and then listened as Simon brazenly explained to airport security, "The man standing in front of me is a suspected Nazi war criminal whose name I have given to the Justice Department. The young man cursing me is his son."

When we were having tea in a Viennese hotel lobby, and I noticed that people at nearby tables were squirming in their chairs,

Simon explained, "Rabbi Hier, you are probably wondering why I talk so loudly. I do it deliberately, because everyone here knows me, and those over sixty-five can never look me in the eye. They are afraid that maybe I will look at them too closely and want to find out exactly what they were doing in 1941."

Simon was unafraid of stirring controversy. In 1975, he revealed that Freidrich Peter, the Chairman of Austria's Freedom Party, had been a member of the first ss infantry brigade, a murder squad that had killed three hundred and sixty thousand Jews in Eastern Europe in 1941. The accusation embroiled Simon in a storm of hideous allegations, investigations, lawsuits, and countersuits that would last beyond Peter's retirement from government in 1983, when members of all three of Austria's political parties gave him a standing ovation in Parliament for his service to the country.

Simon remained committed to his mission, even when criticized for not doing enough. In 1985, Simon refused to get involved in investigations by the World Jewish Congress into the Nazi past of Kurt Waldheim, the former Secretary General of the United Nations and President of Austria, on the grounds that there was insufficient evidence, because those who had made the accusations were no longer alive. His role, he insisted, was to find war criminals, not liars: "All Nazis are liars. But my work is to find those with blood on their hands who can be convicted." Although he came under criticism from many, including the Center (see Appendix 1), which at the least wanted Waldheim's name placed on a us government watch list to prevent him from entering the country, Simon maintained his position. He willfully endured the negative publicity, though it may have cost him the 1985 Nobel Peace Prize, an honor he richly deserved.

People everywhere admired Simon's courage and determination. In 1981, then-Mayor Dianne Feinstein, and her husband Richard Blum, invited Simon to attend the inauguration of the Moscone Center, the city's new convention center, at which Frank Sinatra was scheduled to perform. Frank opened the evening by saying, "In the entertainment industry, we present fictitious characters on the screen as a form of entertainment. But tonight I have the honor of introducing a real hero." He then sang his legendary "My Way," which he dedicated to Simon.

At a Wiesenthal Center dinner at which Simon was the guest of honor, Frank spoke in greater detail:

> You could not have selected an honoree I admire more than the man in whose name we gather tonight. I love Simon Wiesenthal with all my heart. I respect Simon Wiesenthal and I am proud to call him friend, and prouder still that he calls me friend. His life has compensated for all of those lives that were wasted. His dedication to his fellow man stands as a very definition of the word. His courage is written boldly across our history as no other man has before in the history of the world. His decency is engraved in our hearts, where it remains a symbol of man's capability of loving his fellow man.
>
> Simon is more than his brother's keeper, much more. He is his friend's keeper, and more than that, he is a stranger's keeper. And nowhere in the good Book does God ask more of His children. I've met an army of good people as I've stumbled through life, but none whose call to arms rivals Mr. Wiesenthal's…. Let me share with you this statement of truth. I would gladly give up every song I ever met to rest my head on the pillow of his accomplishments.

When Simon, Sam Belzberg, and I met with President Ronald Reagan in the Oval Office in February 1984, and Simon told the president how honored he was to meet him, President Reagan replied, "Sir, let me assure you, the honor is mine, not yours."

On August 9, 2000, President Bill Clinton bestowed America's highest civilian honor, the Medal of Freedom, upon Simon. Too frail to attend the White House ceremony, Simon asked me to accept the award on his behalf. In the presence of Congressmen, the diplomatic corps, and a Simon Wiesenthal Center delegation, headed by Sam Belzberg, President Clinton spoke movingly of Simon's accomplishments:

> "When millions were murdered, why was I allowed to live?" For more than half a century, Simon Wiesenthal has asked himself

this question again and again. To those who know his story, one of miraculous survival and of relentless pursuit of justice, the answer is apparent. From the unimaginable horrors of the Holocaust, only a few voices survived to bear witness, to hold the guilty accountable, to honor the memory of those who were killed. Only if we heed these brave voices can we build a bulwark of humanity against the hatred and indifference that is still all too prevalent in this world of ours.

Despite the numerous honors he received in his later years, Simon Wiesenthal maintained that there was nothing extraordinary about who he was. Speaking at the University of Vienna a few years before his death in 2005 at the age of ninety-six, he tearfully implored the students in the audience: "Do not turn me into a hero. I do not feel like a hero. In fifty years I have never forgotten even for a single day that I am a survivor..."

In February 1999, Simon called with a request that I help organize a celebration with a few friends in Vienna to mark his ninetieth birthday. Although he was born on December 31, we agreed to commemorate his birthday in June, when Vienna's weather would be more accommodating. "I have never asked anyone to celebrate my birthday, but I have one unfulfilled wish," he confided in me, "to have a party at the Imperial Hotel."

The Imperial Hotel was a city landmark of which the Viennese were duly proud. It had been built in 1863 as the Vienna residence of the Prince of Wurttemberg. Ten years later, it was converted into a hotel for the Universal Exhibition. It was an elegant building, with classic Viennese style.

But the Imperial also had an infamous past. Adolf Hitler worked there as a young man. During the Third Reich, he and ss Chief Heinrich Himmler had permanent suites, and built bunkers beneath the hotel to serve as their headquarters. Before the war, the hotel had been partly owned by Samuel Schallinger, a Jew who was forced to sell it in 1938, and who died at the Theresienstadt concentration camp in 1942.

"I want to make sure," Simon told me, "that all the taboos of the Third Reich are broken, and that the record of this hotel shows that Simon Wiesenthal celebrated his ninetieth birthday here."

On June 20, 1999, Simon, a small group of friends, Simon Wiesenthal Center trustees, senior staff, and I gathered in the opulent dining room of the Imperial Hotel. Monumental columns stood at attention. Marble figurines fixed cold stares upon us. Red brocade swags twisted atop massive windows like the curled lips of Goliath. As waiters served us an elegant kosher meal, a band we had hired played "*Mein Shtetala Belz*" (My Little Town Belz), a lullaby that evoked the innocent happiness of childhood.

With tears in his eyes, Simon gazed up at the elaborate crystal chandeliers that lit the room like six million stars in the night sky, leaned to me and whispered, "You see? Even the chandeliers are shaking because this is the first time they have heard such music.... Hitler is no longer here, but even in the Imperial, his favorite hotel, Jews are still alive and still singing."

Chapter Five

Justice, Justice Shall You Pursue

As the organization that carried the name of the world's most famous Nazi hunter, the Simon Wiesenthal Center made its first priority the search for and prosecution of former Nazi war criminals. The task was enormous. During the Nuremberg Trials, which ended in 1949, only one hundred and seventy seven Nazis had been prosecuted. The Allies and the Federal Republic of Germany, which tried thousands of alleged Nazi war criminals in the 1950s, eventually released all those who were convicted and serving sentences. Thousands of former Nazis, ss members, and Nazi collaborators were on the loose, while Holocaust survivors struggled to cope with their anguish and rebuild their lives.

The Nazi on the top of Simon's "most wanted" list was Josef Mengele, the physician and ss officer notorious for his selections for the gas chambers and his ghastly human experiments at Auschwitz. As trains delivered thousands of unsuspecting Jews to their final destination each day, the demented doctor greeted them not as a healer, but a beast stalking his prey. He inspected orphaned children, desperate teenagers, skeletal young women, and old men barely alive, then, with a smile or whistle and a quick flick of his hand, waved them off to the gas chambers. Unlike Heinrich Himmler, Adolf Eichmann, and other senior officials who coolly dispensed orders from distant offices, Mengele personally carried out lethal injections, shootings, beatings, and deadly experiments on twins, dwarfs, and pregnant women. He amputated limbs; injected eyes, spines, and brains with chemicals; shot children in order to perform autopsies on them; exposed healthy prisoners to diseases and extreme X-ray radiation; sterilized women; castrated men and drained the blood of children. Simon believed that Mengele—sadistic, sociopathic, anti-Semitic Mengele—personified the evil of the Third Reich more than any other Nazi.

After the war, the "Angel of Death," as he was known, expressed no remorse. He wrote in his diary in a carefree manner, "Wherever a joyous bird sings, he sings for another bird. Wherever a tiny star twinkles far away, it twinkles for another." But there were no joyous birds or twinkling stars at Auschwitz; only thousands of innocent men, women, and children, murdered by beasts disguised as human beings.

Mengele fled Auschwitz on January 17, 1945, shortly before the arrival of the Red Army. Assisted by a network of former ss members and Hitler's favorite bomber pilot, Hans-Ulrich Rudel, Mengele traveled to Genoa, Italy. In July 1949, he sailed to Argentina, where he lived in Buenos Aires, until fleeing to Paraguay in 1959, then Brazil in 1960. In spite of West Germany's extradition requests and the Mossad's clandestine operations, Mengele eluded capture.

In October 1984, it occurred to me that researchers looking for clues into Mengele's whereabouts had not yet searched us government archives, which likely included intelligence information that might prove useful. I discussed the matter with our counsel in Washington, Martin Mendelsohn, who formerly headed the United States Justice Department's Office of Special Investigations, and thought it was an excellent idea worth pursuing. Employing the Freedom of Information Act, the Wiesenthal Center requested all us government documents related to Josef Mengele. One month later, the American Army Intelligence and Security Command released the relevant declassified documents, which included a revelatory letter dated April 26, 1947 from Ben J. M. Gorby, a special agent of the us Counter-Intelligence Corps in Germany, to the commanding officer of a Counter-Intelligence Corps detachment in Vienna:

Headquarters
Counter Intelligence Corps Region V
970th Counter Intelligence Corps Detachment

26 April 1947

SUBJECT: Dr. MENGELE, FNU
TO: Commanding Officer
Hqs. 430th CIC Det., (VIENNA Detachment)
USFET, APO 777, U.S. Army

RE: Interrogation of Subject regarding removal of group of Jewish children from AUSCHWITZ Extermination camp in November 1944.

1. This office has received information that one Dr. MENGELE, FNU, former Oberarzt (chief medical Doctor) in AUSCHWITZ Extermination camp has been arrested in VIENNA.

2. Upon question by an Agent of this office the informant stated that to the best of his knowledge Dr. MENGELE was arrested in the U.S. Zone of Germany. Consequently, if this information is correct, your office should be informed of the arrest and of the present whereabouts of Subject.

3. Subject can be located and if an interrogation of Subject by CIC or upon request of CIC is possible, it is requested that he be interrogated with regard to the fate of a group of approximately 20 Jewish children who were removed by him from the AUSCHWITZ Camp in November 1944 and taken to an unknown place.

4. The fact of the removal of the Jewish children from AUSCHWITZ by Dr. MENGELE was confirmed to this office by the father of one of these children who lives in REGENSBURG. Other parents of children among that group of 20 are still alive and most eager to have news from or about their children.

5. Any information from your office, based on a thorough interrogation of Subject regarding the fate of the above mentioned children will be greatly appreciated by this office.

FOR THE COMMANDING OFFICER

BEN J.M. GORBY
Special Agent,
CIC Operations

This was the first document that had come to light suggesting that Josef Mengele, widely regarded as the most notorious German war criminal still at large, had been arrested by the United States Army after the war. This was astounding information. Had the US Army really had Mengele in its grasp? If so, how could it possibly have released him?

I knew that the Gorby letter could change the nature of the hunt for Josef Mengele. If made public, it would cause an outcry from the Jewish community and others who had suffered under the Nazis. The United States and other Western governments would be forced to join the efforts to bring Mengele to justice.

But that wasn't all. The released documents also included a letter dated June 26, 1962 from Major Buford F. McCharen Jr. of the 513th Intelligence Corps of the United States Army in Europe to G. M. Bailey, a Canadian visa-control officer in Cologne, West Germany. The letter was a response to a query concerning a "Joseph Menke" who had applied for a Canadian visa in Buenos Aires. Major McCharen attached an army intelligence report that suggested that Joseph Menke was a pseudonym for Josef Mengele. Yet there was no indication from the disclosed records that the American authorities ever followed up on the lead.

Equally disturbing was a memo informing us that four pages of documents relevant to the Mengele case had been withheld because they were considered potentially damaging to national security. I found this hard to believe and even harder to accept. I sent a letter to John Marsh, Jr., United States Secretary of the Army, appealing for the release of the documents.

While awaiting a response, we took the case to Washington, DC. Following a series of meetings with mid-level government officials that proved fruitless, Simon agreed that I should take the matter straight to the top. In a letter dated December 19, 1984, I appealed directly to President Ronald Reagan to launch an official investigation into the case of Josef Mengele. I pointed out that contrary to popular belief, and based on the Gorby letter, it appeared that the United States had, at one time, held Josef Mengele in custody. I requested a full-fledged investigation, including a thorough analysis of the withheld documents, to determine whether or not the United States had been involved in Mengele's capture and release.

President Reagan forwarded my letter to the Department of Defense, which passed it on to the General Counsel of the Department of the Army, who informed us that the Wiesenthal Center's request for the release of the withheld documents had been rejected. The letter claimed that all four documents were "properly withheld" and informed us that this constituted the Secretary of the Army's final action on the matter.

This was unacceptable to us. We convened press conferences in New York, Toronto, and Los Angeles in order to push President Reagan and Canadian Prime Minister Brian Mulroney to call for full investigations. On January 23, 1985, I told *The New York Times* that the documents created "reasonable doubt as to whether or not the US had a role in the case of Josef Mengele, and the only way the truth will surface is an official investigation by the US and Canadian governments…" And I went further, stating, "To think that two years after the Eichmann trial, Canadian and American intelligence could have arrested Mengele, and didn't, calls into question their entire commitment to the hunt for Nazi war criminals."

With the assistance of Dr. Willie Perl, an Austrian-born, Jewish-American lawyer and activist, the Wiesenthal Center located former special agent Gorby, who was now an attorney living in Tel Aviv. The Israeli police had already contacted Gorby and shown him the documents that carried his signature. Gorby confirmed that he had written the letter in 1947, when he was the Chief Operations Officer of the 970th Detachment of the Counter-Intelligence Corps, Region v, of the United States Army located in Regensburg, Germany. He told us, "There is no doubt that I considered my source of information that Mengele was arrested by the United States as fully trustworthy—for had I not thought so…. I would not have sent out such a memo to another detachment located in a foreign country (Austria), nor would I have sought and obtained permission to do so by my commanding officer, but rather I would have simply filed the memo internally."

A few days later, testimony provided by a former US Army private, Walter Kempthorne, bolstered our case. Now a fifty-nine-year-old retired engineer, Kempthorne told us that he had seen a man identified as Dr. Josef Mengele while assigned to guard duty at a Counter-Intelligence Corps prison for war criminals in the Rhineland in July 1945. Kempthorne recalled entering a building at the Idar-Oberstein prison camp, and seeing a male prisoner standing at attention before two guards. He said the man was red-faced, breathing heavily, and perspiring from exercise. Kempthorne recalled asking the guards what was going on, and one replied, "We're getting him in shape to get hung. This here is Mengele, the bastard that sterilized three thousand women at Auschwitz."

Locating Gorby and securing the Kempthorne testimony helped turn the tide. On February 6, 1985, the US Attorney General, William French Smith, announced that the US Department of Justice's Office of Special Investigations would undertake a full investigation in the case of Josef Mengele. The international media widely covered the story. I joined Senator Alfonse D'Amato, Congresswoman Elizabeth Holtzman, and Professor Allan Ryan to discuss the case on ABC's *This Week with David Brinkley*.

A week later, Senator Arlen Specter announced that a US Senate judiciary subcommittee that he chaired would begin inquiries into why Mengele had not been brought to justice, and asked me to testify. The big question, he recognized, was, "Why was Mengele allowed to get away?"

Senator D'Amato joined a Wiesenthal Center lawsuit to force the federal government to declassify the four withheld documents. D'Amato described the withholding as "absolutely absurd," and stated unequivocally that he thought Mengele was alive.

Given the high level of attention and activity, the news that came out of Sao Paolo, Brazil a few months later was shocking. Acting on a tip received by the West German prosecutor's office, Brazilian police had raided the house of Hans Sedlmeier, a lifelong friend of Mengele. Among other things, they found a letter from Wolfram and Liselotte Bosserts notifying Sedlmeier of Mengele's death. Apparently, while swimming near the Bosserts' home in the coastal resort of Bertioga on February 7, 1979, Mengele had suffered a stroke and drowned. He was buried in Embu das Artes under the name Wolfgang Gerhard, whose identification card he had used since 1971.

The police interrogated the Bosserts, who revealed the location of the grave. Forensic scientists, including Dr. Lukash, who was sent by the Center, exhumed the remains and confirmed that they were Mengele's. Mengele's son, Rolf, issued a statement on June 10 admitting that his father had died, and that the news had been kept quiet to protect the people who had sheltered him for so many years.

My first reactions to the news of Mengele's death were ones of frustration and futility. Despite our research, testimonies, press conferences, and lawsuits, Mengele had managed to live out his life without facing the consequences for having committed some of the most monstrous crimes in history.

But I realized that the recently announced US investigation, which coincided with an international hearing in Jerusalem at which twins and others who had survived Mengele's Auschwitz experiments provided moving testimony, had brought increased attention to the Mengele case, and prompted the Germans to redouble their efforts. Our work had, at least, led to a definitive answer in the case.

We also gained a small measure of satisfaction by learning that Mengele's final years had been tortured ones. Mengele's son told investigators that in his last years, his father had become a nervous recluse who lived in constant fear that his identity would be exposed. Whenever his son came to visit, Mengele cautioned Rolf to use public transportation and to blend in with the crowd to make sure he was not being followed. He nearly died of digestive failure caused by swallowing the hairs of his mustache, which he chewed constantly. At least our hunt had prevented Mengele from living a normal life.

For Holocaust survivors and others, the question of how the US Army could have held Mengele in custody and released him, remains troubling. Also disturbing is the fact that during Mengele's thirty-four years as a fugitive, no one turned him in. Despite the extensive newspaper coverage of his wartime activities and the rewards offered for his capture, Mengele evaded authorities with the help of a network of former ss members, family, and friends in Germany and South America.

Investigators who perused Mengele's letters after his death found one in which Mengele said he "wanted to stand before the Lord as a soldier and be buried with his arms to his side." I only hope that when Mengele faced his Creator, he was forced to replay a scene from Auschwitz that a Holocaust survivor, Agnes Zsolt, relates about her eleven-year-old daughter, Anne. Agnes had sent Anne to be hidden by a non-Jewish doctor. Searching for hidden Jews, Mengele discovered her hiding place. When he saw that her feet were covered with sores, he barked, "Look at you, you frog! Your feet are foul, reeking with pus! Up with you to the truck!" With that one abrupt command, young Anne's fate was sealed.

Each year, when I mark my birthday, which I unfortunately share with the Angel of Death, I remember Simon's determination and the Wiesenthal Center's perseverance to track him down. And I think about the families of Agnes Zsolt and of Mengele's other victims, whose suffering continues.

Despite the Mengele disappointment, the Wiesenthal Center continued its work pursuing former Nazis, which often involved navigating complex legal issues. Each case required thorough research into the suspect's involvement in the Holocaust, including drawing a fine line between his personal culpability and his role as a soldier following orders. Each country in which we worked had its own legal structure and limitations.

In 1979, we faced a particular legal problem when a West German statute of limitations on Nazi war crimes was set to expire. West Germany had twice previously recognized its responsibility to bring Nazi war criminals to justice by extending its statute of limitations on murder. But now, fierce battles were being waged in the Bundestag, the West German Parliament, and the three major political parties were divided over whether to revoke the statute, extend it once again, or let the extension expire, leaving many Nazi war criminals immune from prosecution.

Simon and I concurred that the Wiesenthal Center needed to address the issue head-on. We requested meetings with members of the West German Parliament, whom we would lobby to revoke the statute. We were pleased that the Simon Wiesenthal name provided the recognition we needed to gain access to the country's top political leaders. Within days of our contacting them, key members of Parliament and West German Chancellor Helmut Schmidt accepted our requests.

Rabbi Abraham Cooper and I organized a thirty-person delegation to spend four days in Bonn. We invited political and religious leaders whose experience might help this most important but delicate diplomatic effort. The President of Loyola College, Democratic Congressman Chris Dodd, Republican Congressman Bob Dornan, civil rights activist Bayard Rustin and several Holocaust survivors and Wiesenthal Center trustees joined our team.

On a clear morning in March 1979, we gathered in a meeting room in the Bundeshaus, a complex of stark white buildings overlooking the Rhine River that served as the seat of the West German Parliament. We were introduced to Franz-Ludwig Schenk Graf von Stauffenberg, an attorney, Member of Parliament, and son of Claus von Stauffenberg, the German army officer who on July 20, 1944 placed a bomb beneath a conference table in the Nazis' Eastern Front military headquarters in a courageous attempt to assassinate Adolf Hitler. The plot failed, and von Stauffenberg and many others involved in its planning were rounded up, tortured, and executed by firing squad.

Franz-Ludwig von Stauffenberg seemed pleased to meet us. Before our meeting officially got underway, he told us how much he admired Simon's work: "I have followed Mr. Wiesenthal's progress with various cases, and have great respect for him. I know my father would have been proud to know him," he said.

Hans Lederer was the first member of our delegation to speak. Hans was a German citizen who fought in the German army in World

War 1, miraculously survived the Holocaust, and continued to live in Germany after the war. He got right to the point, and minced no words: "Herr von Stauffenberg: Invoking a statute of limitations would not only reflect badly on the generation that supported Hitler. It would be a stain on the new Germany."

Von Stauffenberg had noble lineage, but sympathized with the attitude of common Germans. He explained: "I understand your position, and assure you that I support it. But many young Germans who took no part in Nazi crimes want to know why they must shoulder the burden for those who participated."

Other members of the Bundestag with whom we met throughout the day expressed similar reservations. They explained that if the statute of limitations were extended or revoked entirely, enabling prosecutions to continue, the Third Reich would cast an even longer shadow over the lives of ordinary citizens. They described how their constituents were eager to move beyond their country's terrible past, and viewed the statute as the final obstacle in their pursuit of normalcy.

Disheartened but persistent, we took our position to the next level. The following day, a tidy young staff member from the Office of the Chancellor ushered our delegation into an austere conference room. Chancellor Schmidt, a handsome, middle-aged man with thick dark hair elegantly swept across his forehead, entered the room. I introduced the members of our delegation, which now included Rabbi Arthur Schneier, rabbi of New York's Park East Synagogue, who had joined us for this key meeting.

Like von Stauffenberg, Chancellor Schmidt revealed that he had followed Simon's work with interest for many years, and that he fully supported what Simon was doing. Then, in a no-nonsense style, he articulated his willingness to help our cause: "The new Germany is eager to cooperate and assist in any way possible," he said.

I broadened the theme that Hans had introduced the day before, and discussed West Germany's future relationship with the United States: "Enforcing a statute of limitations would have grave consequences for West Germany's relationship with its most important ally, the United States," I began. "The law is not only an affront to American Jews, but an insult to the men and women who served in the US Army in order to rid the world of Nazism.... Those who murdered millions of people cannot be viewed as criminals for twenty-five years, then welcomed back to their communities as honorable citizens because they were clever enough to evade justice."

Chancellor Schmidt said that he respected my view, but wanted to make sure I understood the implications of revoking the statute of limitations. He insisted that no country had done more to attempt to bring former Nazis to justice than West Germany, but that prosecutions inevitably weighed on the next generation: "The issue is finding a way to bring justice to the victims of Nazism without blaming those who were too young to take part in the terrible crimes."

We understood the dilemma. We knew from the other side of the equation how children of Holocaust survivors were burdened by their parents' traumas. We recognized the need of young people to move forward. Nonetheless, we were horrified by the possibility that some of the worst war criminals in history could be allowed to continue with their lives without facing the consequences of their unspeakable actions.

We were relieved when on July 3, 1979, the West German Parliament voted to lift the statute of limitations by a vote of two hundred and fifty five to two hundred and twenty five, allowing the prosecution of murders, whether committed by suspected Nazi war criminals or others, to continue indefinitely. We were encouraged that our meetings in Bonn had been productive, that we had built bridges with top political leaders, and that our words had had an impact on Chancellor Schmidt, the Bundestag, and public opinion. It didn't hurt that a photograph of our meeting with Chancellor Schmidt had prominently appeared in *The New York Times* the day after our meeting.

Spurred on by the West German decision, and re-committed to the hunt for former Nazis following the Mengele case, the Simon Wiesenthal Center opened offices in Jerusalem and Buenos Aires in 1986 to strengthen its work tracking the post-war escape of Nazi war criminals and to coordinate international efforts to prosecute them.

We hired historian Dr. Efraim Zuroff to serve as the Center's chief Nazi hunter and to head up our Israel office, and Sergio Widder to run the Latin American office. We published lists of alleged Nazis yet to be arrested or charged, which caught the media's attention and helped Simon publicize several cases including those of concentration camp commandants Josef Schwammberger and Dinko Sakiá. We initiated Operation Last Chance, a campaign that offered financial rewards for information in Germany, Lithuania, Latvia, Estonia, Poland, Romania, Austria, Croatia, and Hungary. Over three decades, we would put pressure on European governments to open new cases and to prevent the closing of old ones. We would help locate more than three thousand Nazis.

There were many critics of our work. Some people feared we would spur anti-Semitism. Others asserted that we were misusing the court system to right the wrongs of history. Governments refused to cooperate. Efraim received death threats.

The line most often used against us was that we were, "dragging poor old men to court." Critics called us vengeful and vindictive. I preferred to think of us as committed to the pursuit of justice, and often reminded them that the old men with whom they sympathized had not taken into consideration the age of their victims when they had perpetrated their heinous crimes.

In 1989, some British journalists and public intellectuals condemned our efforts to have Antanas Gecevicius prosecuted. Gecevicius was a platoon commander of the infamous 12th Auxiliary Lithuanian Police Battalion, which, under German command, had massacred thousands of Jews in Lithuania and Belarus. Our research staff confirmed British press reports that Gecevicius was living in Scotland under the pseudonym Anthony Gecas. We presented our findings to Douglas Hurd, the United Kingdom's Home Secretary, who was responsible for immigration and citizenship, and requested that Gecas be extradited to stand trial in Lithuania.

The British War Crimes Commission undertook a fifteen-month inquiry to investigate the allegations against Gecas. At the time, Britain had no legal provisions for extraditing or prosecuting foreigners who had committed murders abroad before becoming

British citizens. But in 1991, Britain passed the War Crimes Act to enable such prosecutions to take place. We, and others close to the case, believed that Gecas's prosecution would soon follow.

But Scotland's Crown Counsel announced in February 1994 that it would not prosecute Gecas due to insufficient evidence. We were outraged. Many speculated that Britain's Secret Intelligence Service, for whom Gecas allegedly worked after the war, was protecting him. But Gecas was not the only suspected war criminal spared from prosecution. Investigations of three hundred others were similarly dropped. Since passage of the War Crimes Act, Britain has prosecuted only one suspect, Belorussian Nazi collaborator, Anthony Sawoniuk, who was convicted and sentenced to life imprisonment.

Several years later, when the issue of Gecas's extradition resurfaced, I was invited to appear on England's popular television show, *Good Morning Britain*, with a member of the House of Lords who articulated his opposition well: "You are pursuing individuals whose memories have lapsed and who are unable to mount credible defenses. Being punitive beyond the pale is not serving justice," he insisted. After the moderator sided with him, I unleashed a blunt response:

> You are making a blanket assumption that every man in his eighties suffers from memory loss. If that assumption were true, you should not continue to debate the great issues of the day in the House of Lords, since most members of the House of Lords are in their eighties. You are unwilling to close down the House of Lords because of the age of its members, but have no problem exonerating aging Nazi war criminals?!

The comment created such uproar in the British press, I thought the Brits would do to me what they didn't have the courage to do to Gecas: deport me.

By the early 1980s, it was clear that hunting former Nazis and operating a small Los Angeles Holocaust museum were not enough to combat the resurgence of anti-Semitism that the world, especially Europe, was experiencing. We needed to call attention to and denounce anti-Semitism in all its forms, from Holocaust denial, to neo-Nazi activity and political extremism. We needed to become a worldwide human-rights organization.

We opened a European office of the Simon Wiesenthal Center in Paris in the 1980s, and brought in Dr. Shimon Samuels, a renowned expert on anti-Semitism, to head it. Over the next several decades, the office would inform government leaders, the media, and local communities of neo-Nazi incidents, which would lead to the ban of neo-Nazi rallies in Spain, the cancellation of revisionist conferences in France, and the closure of neo-Nazi bank accounts in Sweden. It would protest the development of a convent and a disco on the site of the Auschwitz concentration camp. It would distribute educational materials to schools and universities, and monitor anti-Semitism and Holocaust denial in books, newspapers, and magazines.

Nowhere was the need for a human rights organization more apparent than in France. France's wartime record had been appalling. Following its capitulation to the Nazis in May 1940, the Vichy government had stripped three thousand Jews of their citizenship, restricted Jews from entering public service and becoming doctors, interned foreign Jews, and, in the summer of 1942, rounded up and deported eighty thousand Jews to the death camps.

I was familiar with many tragic stories of French Jewish families during the Holocaust because of several brave survivors who shared their memories with us. Robert Clary, formerly Robert Max Widerman, a French Holocaust survivor and American actor best known for his role as Corporal LeBeau in the popular television sitcom *Hogan's Heroes*, spoke many times at the Simon Wiesenthal Center about his experiences during the Holocaust.

It was a fantastic childhood. I came from a huge family—I was the fourteenth and last child. My father's name was Moishe, but he was called Maurice. My mother was Bella, the sweetest woman in the world. We loved our life, and Paris, and our neighborhood.

Then one day it all changed. The round-ups began. The first one I saw was absolutely frightening. I was fifteen years old. I had never seen such trouble, such hate from the French. The French policemen were thrilled to carry out the arrests and so were our non-Jewish neighbors. "Yeah," they yelled, "Take them away. Take the Jew bastards!"

Then, on September 23, 1942, it was our turn. It was after curfew, around 9:00 or 10:00 at night. Suddenly the buses arrived with the French police. All I remember from that night was the chaos in the apartment, the screaming and crying. "You have ten minutes to pack your belongings and come downstairs."

Robert Clary, his sister, and parents were sent by their fellow Frenchmen to the Drancy transit camp and put on a cattle car to the concentration camps. On the train ride east, Robert wrote a letter to his brother Jacques, which his mother dictated:

Dear Jacques,

We are writing to tell you we are on a train traveling toward Helene in the East…I am asking you in Mama's name that you take good care of yourself and Madeline…. We are in sealed cattle cars and frightful things are happening in them that I hope you will never see…. We have lots of courage and hope to come back alive to you…. I have only one wish: to be able to see all of you again one day soon…excuse my handwriting, but I am writing while the train is in motion. Mama kisses you and Golda…Papa, Ida, Jacques, the children and I think all about you.

P.S. Tell Madeline…to take out those ten sheets that are in the laundry store. Uncle is with us…warn his daughter… take care of the people who were not deported.

Robert survived three years in the Ottmuth, Blechhamer, Gross-Rosen, and Buchenwald concentration camps. Of the twelve members of his family who were sent to the camps, including his parents, he was the only one to survive. His prisoner number, A-5714, tattooed on his left forearm, remains a constant reminder.

After the war, anti-Semitic prejudices had lingered in France, and in the late 1970s and early 1980s, blatantly re-asserted themselves. In October 1980, a neo-Nazi group, the European Nationalist Fascists, claimed responsibility for setting off a bomb that killed four and injured twenty on the eve of Simchas Torah in front of the Rue Copernic Synagogue, a few minutes' walk from the Arc de Triomphe. Two other synagogues, two Jewish schools, and a Jewish war memorial were machine-gunned. The neo-Nazis and other extremists found a political home in the growing Front National Party led by Jean-Marie Le Pen.

Staff of our European office and those of us who periodically visited France experienced the new-old anti-Semitism firsthand. In the spring of 1988, following a meeting with French President François Mitterrand and his senior advisors at the Élysées Palace, I returned to my hotel to find Lydia Triantopoulos, the Wiesenthal Center's Public Relations Director, in tears. Lydia, who was fluent in French, had overheard a conversation between workers at the hotel's reception desk: "Can you believe those [expletive] Jews are back in Paris when I thought we had finally rid ourselves of them?"

A few days later, a middle-aged man in a stylish business suit intentionally stepped in front of me, shouting, while I was jogging in the city center. A young woman passing by, who realized I didn't understand French, explained that the gentleman was angry because I was disregarding the Grand Rabbi of France's instructions not to wear yarmulkas in public due to a recent spate of anti-Semitic attacks. I asked the woman to convey to my accoster: "I am not French. I am a rabbi visiting from America."

Even more irate, he shouted back, and she translated, "Would you wear that yarmulka in Washington?"

"Yes, Orthodox Jews wear yarmulkas everywhere in America," I said.

"I am also Jewish," he persisted. "But even if it is okay in America, this is Paris, where you should obey the wishes of the Grand Rabbi."

By the turn of the millennium, spurred on by a rapidly expanding immigrant Muslim population, French anti-Semitism took the form of anti-Zionism. In 2002, a year in which more than nine hundred individual anti-Semitic acts were committed in France, including the burning down of a synagogue and a Jewish school, we put together a Simon Wiesenthal Center delegation to meet with recently re-elected French President Jacques Chirac. In a grand salon in the Élysées Palace, President Chirac began by citing a self-congratulatory report that highlighted the French government's efforts to eradicate anti-Semitism. "Anti-Semitism is always a serious matter in France," he said. He then described a recent encounter he had with a Palestinian student living in France whom he had met on the presidential campaign trail:

"I shook the young man's hand, and asked him what he did for a living. The young man told me that he was studying at a university. I asked him what he planned to do when he graduated and returned to Palestine. The young man answered, 'Kill Jews.'

"'But why?' I asked. 'Have they done anything to you?'

"'Yes,' he answered. 'They have humiliated our people.'"

President Chirac told us he was so shaken by the encounter that he invited the man to lunch at the Élysées Palace to continue the conversation.

"We sat together at lunch and discussed the political situation in the Middle East. I don't believe I was able to change the young man's mind. It shows you how frustrated the Arabs are."

Taken aback by this comment, I exchanged glances with Sol Teichman, a Wiesenthal Center trustee, Los Angeles Jewish community leader, and Holocaust survivor, whose mother, three brothers, and sister had been gassed to death at Auschwitz. Rather than allow himself to be consumed by anger, Sol had directed his grief toward repairing the world. He often spoke at Wiesenthal Center events and urged listeners to do meaningful things with their lives. "I did not come away from those experiences with my faith in God and the goodness of man destroyed. On the contrary, I came away with a new conviction that if evil is so dark, then the forces of goodness must be that much brighter and more beautiful," he once said at an interfaith gathering in Bali.

I responded to President Chirac: "Mr. President. If there are people who have a reason to feel betrayed, they are the survivors of the Holocaust who lost everything while the world kept silent. Jews were not murdered in the Holocaust because they won too many wars. They were murdered because they were born Jews. But how did they channel their pent up feelings of humiliation? Did they blow up buses or planes? Did they strap themselves with suicide belts and detonate themselves inside cafes and schools in order to kill innocent people? No. They learned how to redirect their lives, to pick themselves up, and rebuild their families and communities, to contribute to the world without hatred, revenge or blame."

After leaving the presidential palace, we boarded a bus for a reception at the home of Baron David de Rothschild. As we arrived at the mansion, two members of our delegation arrived by cab. A group of passerby spotted their yarmulkas and shouted, "Jews, get out of France!"

In recent years, French anti-Semitism has found a new voice in comedian, actor, and provocateur, Dieudonné M'bala M'bala. In his hate-filled stand-up routines, which he performs at his Paris theater, Dieudonné describes Holocaust remembrance as "memorial pornography," and decries an overemphasis on the horrors of the Holocaust: "In France the Holocaust is like a dominant religion. It has replaced even Jesus Christ. We are obligated to accept this dogma and pray for it almost every night and teach it to our children..." He has appeared on stage and in videos with Holocaust denier Robert Faurisson, and has created and popularized the "quenelle," a hand gesture that mimics the Nazi salute.

A skit entitled *The Deported Jew* exemplifies Dieudonné's depravity. In it, Dieudonné plays a French citizen concerned that he has violated France's Holocaust remembrance law, while his sidekick, Jacky, plays a haggard Jew wearing a concentration camp uniform with an enlarged yellow star of David:

Dieudonné: Nobody should ignore the law! You think I'm happy with you coming in these pj's?

Jacky: What law?

Dieudonné: It's the law!!

Lady: I'll explain to him. You remember the Sarkozy directive on fifth graders? There was a second directive—and that one requires that you have a deported Jewish character in EVERY show, starting June 1, 2008. That's it—that's the law!

Jacky: But I didn't know…

Dieudonné: Yeah, because you're an idiot…that's how it is! So people don't forget! SO PEOPLE DON'T FORGET!!!

Jacky: I want to know what you're not supposed to forget!!!

Dieudonné: THAT JEWS HAVE SUFFERED!! THEY'VE SUFFERED!

Jacky: But…the Jews. They've suffered as much as anyone else.

Dieudonné: But it's the suffering of sufferings, Jacky! The one you cannot compare.

Jacky: You mean…

Dieudonné: It's all the way up, Jacky! Suffering higher than the universe, higher than God, Jacky!

Diedonné's shows and films spew anti-Semitism and anti-Zionism. He tells his many followers: "They [Jews] have organized all the wars and all the chaos on the planet. They were involved in the slave trade. We should know that ninety percent of the ships that transported slaves from the West Indies belonged to Jews and the majority of slave traders were Jews. Obviously Jews today are not responsible for what happened. But it is the reality and one we are not allowed to talk about."

The Simon Wiesenthal Center urged the French government to develop a strategy to prevent hate speech like Dieudonné's. In January 2014, we commended French Interior Minister Manuel Valls when he determined that performances considered racist or anti-Semitic could be banned by local officials. Towns throughout France soon canceled local appearances that were part of Dieudonné's scheduled national tour, and French authorities opened an investigation on grounds that Dieudonné had condoned terrorism by showing footage of the ISIS killing of US journalist James Foley.

Dieudonné is by no means a singular phenomenon. In a society that often chooses to hide its prejudices behind the banners of liberty and tolerance, he is one among many haters. In March 2012, twenty-three-year-old Muhammed Merah opened fire on the Ozar Hatorah Jewish day school in Toulouse, killing a rabbi and three children. Two months later, Mehdi Nemmouche, a twenty-nine-year-old French national of Algerian origin, fired at the Jewish Museum of Belgium in Brussels, killing four people.

Taking note of the dramatic rise in French anti-Semitic acts, we organized another Simon Wiesenthal Center delegation to travel to Paris in March 2014. This time, we met at the Élysée Palace with French President François Hollande, who had taken office in 2012. One of the leaders of France's Jewish community, Baron Eric de Rothschild, Member of the Canadian Parliament and former Canadian Justice Minister Irwin Cotler, and Wiesenthal Center benefactors Raphi and Rivka Nissel joined me and senior staff members, Rabbi Abraham Cooper, Rabbi Meyer May, Dr. Shimon Samuels, and Avi Benlolo.

President Hollande began, "The anti-Semitism we have all witnessed has no place in France. My government will leave no stone unturned in confronting it as we have done both in the attack on the school as well as the museum. As you know, the Jewish community of France has a long and impressive history in our country and my government is determined to see it strengthen and continue."

I thanked President Hollande for his friendship and support of Israel, and noted that this was our fourth meeting with a president of France. I described my view of the current situation, in which France's democratic values were being challenged both by far-right activists and extremist Islamic groups:

> It is our belief that one of the main reasons for the rise of anti-Semitism in France is the fact that the religious leadership of France's Muslim communities is part of the problem rather than part of the solution. As Simon Wiesenthal told President Mitterrand in this historic place, "The Nazi Holocaust could never have happened if not for the enablers: the clergy and teachers who waited in silence and fear, who lacked the courage to protest when their protests could have made a difference."
>
> Mr. President…French-born terrorists, like other terrorists, are not born with hate in their hearts. They are created by jihadists, teachers, and enablers, who inspire them…to become apostles of hate and violence…. Where are the ringing condemnations of jihadist terrorism from religious leaders on the streets of Europe?
>
> Mr. President, I declare with certainty that if, God forbid, a terrorist attack were to be carried out by Jews against innocent civilians, there would be wall-to-wall public condemnation by every Jewish leader in the world. No less should be expected from the spiritual leaders of the largest Muslim population in Europe.

My words proved tragically prophetic when, just a few months later, a Jewish Israeli, Yoseph Ben David, and two Jewish Israeli minors kidnapped and burned alive Mohammed Abu Khdeir, a sixteen-year-old Palestinian, as revenge for the Hamas kidnapping and murder of Jewish Israeli teenagers Naftali Frankel, Gilad Shaer, and Eyal Yifrach. Chief Rabbis and other leading Jewish religious figures around the world immediately joined major Jewish organizations, including the Simon Wiesenthal Center, in condemning the attack as an act of terror and demanding swift punishment of the perpetrators.

Post-World War II European anti-Semitism certainly has not been confined to France. Germany, the very country that allowed anti-Semitism to reach its most extreme expression, has had its share of post-war anti-Semitic incidents. To its credit, the German government has responded to such incidents with the utmost seriousness.

A notable example was in May 2013 when the Simon Wiesenthal Center received a tip that a monthly German pulp magazine, *Der Landser*, was publishing dangerously distorted World War II stories. *Der Landser*, which took its name from the colloquial term for a German soldier, advertised its stories as eyewitness accounts of heroic soldiers of the Wehrmacht, the German armed forces. It had a print circulation of sixty thousand, and was available for download on Amazon and iTunes.

Initially, we were skeptical that *Der Landser* was violating German laws that prohibited the use of Nazi symbols, the spread of right-wing ideology, and denial of the Holocaust, because the magazine had been in print since 1957, and was owned by the well-established Bauer Media Group, which operated in sixteen countries. We assumed that its stories were, as the magazine touted, simple adventure tales of Wehrmacht soldiers.

But when we perused back copies of the magazine on-line, and found illustrations of soldiers wearing Nazi ss uniforms, we realized we needed to fully investigate the matter. We asked Dr. Stefan Klemp, a German historian and journalist, to review the magazine, and to compare the stories, characters, and plots with historical events.

In July 2013, Dr. Klemp submitted a scathing report. According to his findings, *Der Landser* had published stories in its monthly "Heroes Column" about twenty-nine ss men, twenty-four of whom had served in units convicted of war crimes. Three were known Nazi war criminals: Hans Georg Otto Hermann Fegelein, a Waffen-ss general, member of Hitler's entourage, and brother-in-law of Eva Braun, whose units were responsible for the deaths of more than forty thousand Jews in the Soviet Union (Albert Speer had called him "one of the most disgusting people in Hitler's circle"); Gunther Anhalt, a high-ranking ss officer who commanded the ss's Second

Regiment when it murdered forty thousand Jews in the liquidation of the Jewish ghetto of Glebokie, Belarus in July 1943; and Anton Ameiser, an ss senior storm-unit leader.

Dr. Klemp described how *Der Landser's* stories glorified war and misrepresented Nazi Germany. He noted how the magazine failed to put events into the historical context of the Nazi era, or to mention war crimes perpetrated by German troops, anti-Semitism, or the repressive nature of the German government. He concluded that the magazine was seeking to "sanitize the Third Reich."

I wrote to Heribert Bertram, head of the Bauer Media Group, calling on him to discontinue publishing *Der Landser*:

> The Simon Wiesenthal Center believes that by presenting members of the Waffen ss, the infamous Totenkopf units, and Nazi war criminals as German heroes, *Der Landser* is desecrating the memory of the Holocaust, glorifying Nazism, and debasing the democratic values of post-World War II Germany.... Let us be clear. Those who fought under the banner of the ss were not some posse organized by a sheriff to restore law and order. Rather, they were haters, thugs, and murderers who almost destroyed all of Western Civilization. We have sent our report to the Minister of Justice and to the Minister of Interior calling for immediate investigations and action. The Simon Wiesenthal Center is urging you to immediately discontinue publishing and distributing *Der Landser*.

I also described in a letter to the German Minister of Justice how *Der Landser* had become a favorite publication of the new radical right and Islamist groups who viewed the Nazis as heroes. I believed this information would fall on receptive ears, given the results of two, recently issued, government-sponsored surveys that found that between 2011 and 2012, anti-Semitic incidents had risen in Germany by 10.6 percent, and that twenty percent of all Germans harbored anti-Semitic attitudes.

After receiving no response from the publisher, our Director of Public Relations, Avra Shapiro, put me in touch with Jack Ewing of *The New York Times*. On July 29, 2013, the *Times* reported that the German government was investigating the allegations, but that Bauer Media Group was undaunted because it had successfully staved off previous legal challenges: "German Interior Ministry officials said they took the Wiesenthal Center complaint 'very seriously' and would investigate. But in the meantime, companies that print and distribute *Der Landser* said they would continue doing so, noting that previous legal challenges had failed to find fault with the editorial stance of the magazine…"

I was quoted in the article as responding: "The way they interpret it, everyone in the Wehrmacht was just like in the American Army or the Canadian Army or the British Army…. They forget the most important point. People in this army were thugs and murderers who almost brought down Western Civilization."

Two months later, the Bauer Media Group announced that it was terminating publication of *Der Landser*. The company issued a statement in which it cited strategic business reasons for the decision. It denied any guilt, and claimed that a review by an outside lawyer had found that the magazine did not violate German law. *The New York Times* called the decision by Bauer, "a major victory for the Wiesenthal Center." With a measure of gratification, I told the *Times* reporter, Jack Ewing, that the Bauer Media Group "had no alternative given the overwhelming evidence."

Hungary is another country in which anti-Semitism flourishes. During the Nazis' rise to power, Hungary had been an all-too-willing partner. Just before Hitler's annexation of Austria in March 1938, Hungarian Prime Minister Kalman Daranyi returned from a visit with the Führer in Berlin enthusiastic about "solving" the Jewish problem.

> The Jewish problem does exist…to my mind…the Jewish elements living within Hungary play an unduly prominent part in…our economic life…. The number of Jews employed is considerably in excess of the ratio to the remainder of the population…. For justice to be rendered…the social disparities must

be...eliminated. And the influence of the Jewish element on the cultural and economic life of the country must be reduced to its proper proportions.

Just eight weeks after the Nazi invasion of Hungary in March 1944, more than four hundred thousand Jews were deported to Auschwitz-Birkenau. By the end of the war, nearly six hundred thousand Hungarian Jews had been murdered, thousands of them on the banks of the Danube by the Arrow Cross.

In recent years, Hungary's radical nationalist Jobbik Party has harked back to those dark days and reignited old-fashioned Hungarian anti-Semitism with hateful rhetoric. Jobbik's leaders argue that Jews pose a national security risk, and refuse to acknowledge Hungary's collaborative role in the Holocaust. In the Hungarian parliamentary elections of April 2014, the party secured a stunning twenty-one percent of the vote to make it the country's third largest political party—this, without prodding from the Gestapo or ss.

Jobbik's Foreign Affairs Chief Marton Gyongyosi is unapologetic: "Jews do not have the right to talk about what happened during the Second World War.... Me? Should I say sorry for this when seventy years later, I am still reminded on the hour, every hour about it? Let's get over it, for Christ's sake.... It has become a fantastic business to jiggle around with the numbers of dead Jews..."

Gyongyosi and Jobbik's other leading thugs are wholly uncreative in their anti-Semitism. They repeat the Nazis' old lies, and dress in paramilitary uniforms reminiscent of those worn by the Arrow Cross. Gyongyosi has called for a typical Nazi "tallying up" of Hungarian Jews: "I know how many people with Hungarian ancestry live in Israel, and how many Israeli Jews live in Hungary.... I think such a conflict makes it timely to tally up people of Jewish ancestry who live here, especially in the Hungarian Parliament and the Hungarian government, who, indeed, pose a national security risk to Hungary."

The only new anti-Semitic dimension in the Jobbik Party platform is anti-Zionism. In response to remarks made in 2007 by Israel's president, Shimon Peres, about Israeli investment in Hungary, Jobbik

Chairman Gabor Vona told a crowd gathered at an anti-Zionist rally in Budapest in March 2013, "The Israeli conquerors, these investors, should look for another country in the world for themselves because Hungary is not for sale." Gyongyosi claimed that Hungary was "subjugated to Zionism" and a "target of colonization."

In a 2012 survey conducted by Professor Andras Kovacs of Hungary's Central European University, twenty-one percent of the survey's respondents agreed that, "Jewish intellectuals control Hungary's press and cultural sphere." Twenty percent agreed that, "a secret Jewish network determines Hungary's political and economic affairs." Twelve percent believed that, "it would be best if Jews left the country."

Senior staff of the Wiesenthal Center have visited Hungary in recent years, and monitor Jobbik activities on an ongoing basis. In December 2011, we protested a pro-Iran demonstration organized by Jobbik at the US Embassy in Budapest, at which Jobbik's Gyongyosi said, "The Persian people and their leaders are considered pariahs in the eyes of the West, which serves Israeli interests. This is why we have solidarity with the peaceful nation of Iran and turn to her with an open heart."

In August 2013, we expressed our outrage to the Union of European Football Associations when a group of soccer fans held up a sign at a Budapest soccer match that read, "In memoriam Laszlo Csatary," referring to a Hungarian citizen who had deported more than fifteen thousand Jews to Auschwitz, and who had recently died, shortly after being indicted for war crimes. In response, the Jobbik party held a press conference at which Jobbik Member of Parliament Gyorgy Szilagyi accused the Wiesenthal Center of being a threat to Hungarian national security, and said that we "incite hatred and attack Hungary on a regular basis, systematically interfering in Hungarian domestic matters." Coming from Jobbik, I considered this a great compliment.

One of the people responsible for opening the floodgates of American anti-Zionism was US President Jimmy Carter. I first met President Carter in 1981 at a White House ceremony at which he presented

Simon Wiesenthal with the Congressional Gold Medal, the United States Congress's highest civilian award. At the ceremony, President Carter aptly paid tribute to Simon's work:

"His goal has not just been to see justice done, not to see criminals punished. His motive has not only been to seek revenge but to remember and to make certain that never again will such a crime against decency and civility and humanity be committed—never."

In response, Simon told President Carter and a distinguished audience about the small shred of hope to which he clung in the Mauthausen concentration camp: "A fellow inmate of mine and I sewed a Star of David on a tattered old shirt during the last days of the war. For us, it was a symbol of the survival of the Jewish people." He turned to President Carter and added, "That crumpled shirt with the Star of David insignia soon became the proud flag of Israel—a country whose very existence ensures us against the recurrence of another Holocaust."

Unfortunately, President Carter did not internalize Simon's message. Instead, over time, he revealed a deep, personal bias against Israel that he most clearly articulated in his 2006 book, *Palestine: Peace Not Apartheid*. There, he promulgated the hideous falsehood that Israel is an apartheid state, when in truth, it is the Middle East region's sole democracy, and promoted the self-defeating Arab narrative that Israel is to blame for all that is wrong in the Middle East.

In *Palestine: Peace Not Apartheid*, President Carter commits both acts of commission and omission. He plays into Arab manipulation of historical fact by extensively quoting Hafez al-Assad, former president and prime minister of Syria, who asserts that, "while Israel claimed the right to statehood in Palestine in 1948, because it was only recreating a nation demolished in ancient times, it rejected the recognition of a Palestinian state in the same area, the very place that generations of Palestinians, either Christian or Muslim, have inhabited continuously for thousands of years." President Carter leaves out the fact that the UN offered the Palestinians independence in 1947, but that the Arab leadership chose not to seize it, and instead declared war and suffered military defeat. He also ignores the fact that the Palestinians could have had an independent state at many points since then, had their leaders been willing to accept a Jewish state alongside it.

Despite the fact that *Palestine: Peace Not Apartheid* was an erroneous and distorted portrayal of the Israeli-Palestinian conflict, it was highly influential. Innocent readers, who trusted the opinion of a former president, Middle East peace negotiator, and winner of a Nobel Peace Prize, propelled the book onto *The New York Times* bestseller list.

We at the Simon Wiesenthal Center were less enthusiastic; in fact, we were outraged. We urged Simon Wiesenthal Center members to write to President Carter in protest. Over a period of several weeks, our indomitable and ever committed Communications Director Michele Alkin and Associate Director Felice Richter forwarded fifteen thousand letters to President Carter's office in Atlanta.

In response, on January 26, 2007, the former president of the United States sent me a curt and spiteful hand-written note that only confirmed my suspicions about him:

To Rabbi Marvin Hier,

I don't believe that Simon Wiesenthal would have resorted to falsehood and slander to raise funds.

Sincerely,
Jimmy Carter

I wrote back to President Carter:

Dear President Carter:

I believe that Simon Wiesenthal would have been as outraged by your book, *Palestine: Peace Not Apartheid*, as I was. I bought the book and carefully read it before forming any opinion on the matter. It is incredulous to me that, after your historic achievement of brokering peace between Israel and Egypt, you could write such a book.

Let me say, Mr. President, that I am not one who believes that Israel is infallible or incapable of serious errors of judgment. Countries, like human beings, are all fallible. But what is not present in your book is the fact that there never would have been a fence if the Palestinians would not have chosen terrorism and suicide attacks against innocent civilians as their chief tactics. No country, including our own, the United States of America, would act any differently. If we faced such attacks from our neighbors on a daily basis, we would be the first to put up a security fence. That is not apartheid, Mr. President, that is self-defense—the right of every country and every human being.

To his last breath, Simon Wiesenthal believed that the only reason there was no peace in the Middle East was because of Islamic extremists who refuse to compromise, not because of the State of Israel.

Sincerely,
Rabbi Marvin Hier

I never heard from President Carter again. But the apartheid label he maliciously affixed to Israel stuck. Before long, anti-Zionism gained momentum in the US among mainstream Americans. Israeli human rights violations were exaggerated, and, at times, fabricated. Arab terrorism was minimized and, not occasionally, willfully ignored. Many Americans readily internalized a distorted view of the Middle East reality.

The Simon Wiesenthal Center began to counteract the insidious and false claims being made against Israel with editorials in *The Washington Post*, *The Wall Street Journal*, *The Los Angeles Times*, and *The Miami Herald*. Rabbi Abraham Cooper began writing opinion pieces for Fox News, *The Huffington Post*, and other media outlets that turned to us for comment on current events in the Middle East.

In our ongoing work to defend Israel to the media, we emphasize historical context, the media's over-scrutinizing of Israeli actions, the impossible standard to which Israel is held, the hypocrisy of the

Arab world, and, whenever possible, the words of those trying to set a new course. Our message is based on several core beliefs:

Israel has a right to occupy land inhabited by those who call for and carry out attacks to bring about its destruction. At the end of World War II, the US, Britain, and France occupied Germany for ten years after Nazi Germany surrendered because of lingering security risks and political instability. Berlin remained an occupied military zone until 1990—forty-five years after World War II ended—even though the Third Reich was totally dismantled. Similarly, Israel must be allowed to occupy portions of the West Bank and Gaza, when necessary, to defend itself from its enemies, Hamas and Hezbollah.

Israel has a right to refuse to talk to those who seek to destroy it. The African-American community does not engage in dialogue with the Ku Klux Klan. Latinos do not sit down with Numbers USA. The US government will not meet with members of Al-Qaeda. So, too, Israel must be allowed to talk only with those governmental entities and organizations that accept its right to exist.

History must move forward. Spain was never given an opportunity to take back land lost in the Spanish-American War. Territories acquired after World War I and World War II were not negotiable or exchangeable later. Arab countries must bear the consequences of having launched and lost five wars against Israel.

The Arab world must not be allowed to make Israel its scapegoat. This point was made best by Abdulateef Al-Mulhim in the Saudi Arabian *Arab News* on October 6, 2012:

> On the anniversary of the 1973 War between the Arabs and the Israelis, many people in the Arab world are beginning to ask many questions about the past, present, and the future with regard to the Arab-Israeli conflict.... The questions now are: What was the real cost of these wars to the Arab world and its people? And the harder question that no Arab national wants to ask is: What was the real cost for not recognizing Israel in 1948 and why didn't the Arab states spend their assets on education, healthcare, and the infrastructures instead of wars? But, the hardest question that no Arab national wants

to hear is whether Israel is the real enemy of the Arab world and the Arab people…. The Arab world has many enemies and Israel should have been at the bottom of the list. The real enemies of the Arab world are corruption, lack of good education, lack of good health care, lack of freedom, lack of respect for the human lives and family; the Arab world had many dictators who used the Arab-Israeli conflict to suppress their own people. These dictators' atrocities against their own people are far worse than all the full-scale Arab-Israeli wars…

Israel is not an apartheid state. Boshra Khalaila, an Israeli-Arab who grew up in the village of Deir Hana in the Galilee, and graduated from Haifa University, had this to say when she spoke in Israel's defense at Israel Apartheid Week in South Africa in 2012:

I am married and doing a master's degree [in Tel Aviv]. I am a liberal, free woman, with all the rights that I could enjoy. I compare myself to other women my age in Jordan, the territories, Egypt, any Arab country. They don't have the rights that I have: freedom of expression, the right to vote. They are forced into marriage at a young age, and religious head covering, despite their own convictions. With me it's the opposite; I have everything.

In a Saudi radio interview, Khalaila asked her interviewer, "In Saudi Arabia, can a woman drive a car?"

"No," replied the interviewer.

"I can," she said. "Can a woman in Kuwait or Saudi Arabia meet a man and get to know him before getting married or is she forced into marriage at a young age?"

"No, she can't," said the interviewer.

"I can." said Khalaila.

Later, she described how she answered each of the interviewer's questions with her own, and how each time the interviewer was stunned into silence.

Many media outlets and human rights organizations are biased against Israel. Media and human rights organizations around the world condemned Israel for conducting Operation Pillar of Defense in Hamas-ruled Gaza in November 2012, despite the fact that Hamas had bombarded Israel with missiles for eight months before the operation began. The Simon Wiesenthal Center was the only major human rights organization that, one month earlier, publicized the fact that the Arab Lawyers Union, a confederation of bar associations and law societies from fifteen Arab countries, an observer of UNESCO, and a member of UN committees, gave its highest honor to Hanadi Jaradat, who, on October 4, 2003, blew herself up in a suicide attack in the Maxim restaurant in Haifa, killing twenty-one people and injuring fifty-one, including four children, an infant, and three Arabs. We were the only organization that called attention to a gathering of representatives of the Arab Lawyers Union at Jaradat's home in October 2012 at which the union presented an award to her family on the "sweet anniversary of her martyrdom," and the family described the pride they had in their daughter and what she had done in defense of Palestine.

It is this double standard toward Israel that I addressed when I was included among a group of leaders of Jewish organizations President Barack Obama invited to the White House in March 2013 to discuss his upcoming trip to Israel—his first as President of the United States. On the wide-ranging agenda were Iran's nuclear ambitions, the prospects for peace between Israel and the Palestinians, and the state of anti-Semitism worldwide. Among the other twenty invited guests were the Executive Vice Chairman of the Conference of Presidents of Major American Jewish Organizations, Malcolm Hoenlein; lawyer, author, and political commentator, Alan Dershowitz; President of the World Jewish Congress, Ronald Lauder; and representatives of AIPAC, the Anti-Defamation League, and the American Jewish Committee.

President Obama circled a conference table in the Roosevelt Room of the White House's West Wing to greet each of us individually. He took his seat, as Presidents Theodore and Franklin

Delano Roosevelt gazed out through gilded frames. With senior advisor, Valerie Jarrett, at his side, the President opened the session by encouraging each of us to speak frankly about the key issues as we saw them.

Malcolm Hoenlein and Ronald Lauder described the American Jewish community's distrust of Iran due to its track record of deception on the issue of nuclear capability. President Obama assured us of his administration's long-held policy that the United States would not permit Iran to acquire nuclear weapons. When the discussion moved to the topic of the Israeli-Palestinian conflict, I shared my skepticism about Israel making a deal with the Palestinians when the Palestinians themselves are so divided:

> Mr. President. Everyone supports a two-state solution. But the reality on the ground is a three-state situation with two competing Palestinian entities, one in Ramallah, and the other in Gaza. Hamas has not allowed President Abbas to visit his own people in Gaza in more than seven years. How can the Israeli public support making concessions to a Palestinian government that speaks with two opposite voices, one claiming it wants peace and the other firing thousands of rockets into Israel's heartland?

President Obama shook his ahead in agreement and said, "Rabbi, I fully agree with that, and understand why that would be a non-starter for Israel. The United States is not going to expect Israel to agree to make peace with those unprepared to recognize her existence."

In recent years, an international movement, the Boycott, Divestment and Sanctions (BDS) campaign, has emerged to delegitimize Israel. Established in 2005 by a group of Palestinian organizations, the global BDS campaign calls for putting economic and political pressure on Israel to end its occupation of Palestinian land, to grant full equality to Palestinian citizens, and to recognize the rights of Palestinian refugees displaced by the 1948 War of Independence. It has garnered support from a wide range of politicians, academics, artists, activists, and entertainers around the world, including UN Special Rapporteur Richard Falk, British physicist Stephen Hawking, South African bishop Desmond Tutu, and Pulitzer Prize-winning novelist Alice Walker.

Taken at face value, the stated goals of the BDS campaign sound legitimate, but behind them lie a sinister operation based on myths and falsehoods. In the Wiesenthal Center's numerous newspaper editorials, television interviews, and social media campaigns designed to counteract the BDS movement, we emphasize that: Israel's occupation of Palestinian-populated areas is the result of five wars launched by Israel's Arab neighbors who refused to accept the existence of a small Jewish state in their midst; Israel reluctantly built the security fence—more appropriately called the Hamas Wall—in response to a relentless wave of suicide attacks carried out by Hamas terrorists over the course of a decade; Israeli Arabs enjoy full rights of citizenship, including the right to vote, the right to public education, health care, welfare, and more—unlike the tens of millions of Arabs living in other countries in the Middle East; neighboring Arab countries have abandoned the plight of Palestinian refugees, and deliberately used them as pawns—unlike Israel, which embraced and absorbed seven hundred and fifty thousand Jewish refugees driven out of Arab countries in the 1950s.

What compels individuals and organizations like the Presbyterian Church USA, the Church of England, and the World Council of Churches that routinely ignore the most abysmal human rights violations of other countries to support the hypocritical BDS campaign? How can otherwise clear-thinking people back an agenda that calls for the expansion of democratic rights at the same time that it seeks to damage the only democratic country in the Middle East?

Alice Walker's 2013 book, *The Cushion in the Road*, provides some insight. In it, Walker expresses far less commitment to the betterment of the Palestinian people than condemnation of the Jewish people. She criticizes Jews, Jewish leaders, and Judaism. She decries Israel's successes, its ability to defend itself, and its adherence to humanistic and democratic values.

Walker fails to recognize that the Jewish commitment to life over death is the very basis of morality in the world. She is undaunted by the words of Osama bin Laden, who once boasted that the difference between Al-Qaeda and the US was that "we love death and the United States loves life," or those of Hassan Nasrallah, the leader of Hezbollah, who has said, "Each of us lives his days and nights hoping more than anything to be killed for the sake of Allah." She ignores the cult of death that is gaining traction in our world, and which, by definition, rejects morality in order to destroy.

Walker rejects the fundamental Jewish obligation to confront evil. She and other BDS supporters naively believe they can improve the Israeli-Palestinian conflict through love and understanding. But Jews are commanded both to, "love thy neighbor as thyself," and to "wipe out the memory of Amalek (evil) from under heaven." Judaism teaches that human beings have the capacity for both good and evil, and that we have a moral and social responsibility to root out evil so that goodness can flourish.

Walker's distaste for moral action extends to her critique of the president she most admires, Barack Obama. In response to his stated desire to assassinate Osama bin Laden, she writes: "Each time Obama has said we will kill Osama bin Laden, I have felt a testing of my confidence in his moral leadership…like millions of children around the globe who are taught, 'thou shalt not kill.' I am reacting, with disappointment and shock, that someone is blatantly declaring the intent to kill a specific person…." She adds, "We must all of us learn not to have enemies, but only confused adversaries who are ourselves in disguise."

Walker and other BDS supporters are certainly not the first to express weakness in the face of evil at crucial moments in history. In the 1930s, British Prime Minister Neville Chamberlain infamously appeased Hitler in order to avoid conflict. US Ambassador to the UK, Joseph Kennedy, concurred with the approach, as did a host of politicians and intellectuals.

Though he later modified his political pacifism, British philosopher, social critic, and recipient of the 1950 Nobel Prize in Literature, Bertrand Russell, believed in the 1930s that avoiding a full-scale world war was more important than defeating Hitler. In a letter dated May 23, 1937, Russell wrote:

> The general argument for pacification, as I see it, is that more harm is done by fighting than by submitting to injustice...if the Germans succeeded in sending an invading army to England, we should do best to treat them as visitors, give them quarters, and invite the Commander in Chief to dine with the Prime Minister. Such behaviour would completely baffle them. If, on the other hand, we fight them, we may win, or we may lose. If we lose, obviously no good has been done. If we win, we shall inevitably, during the struggle, acquire their bad qualities, and the world, at the end, will be no better off than if we had lost.

Richard W. Jencks, the one-time president of CBS/Broadcast Group, once recalled a lecture he attended in 1940 as a student at UCLA in which Russell argued that world peace, in the long run, would best be served by a Hitler victory in Europe.

Among world political leaders, only Winston Churchill actively opposed Hitler. He recognized the evil Hitler represented, and the foolishness of the appeasers and pacifists:

> After a boa constrictor has devoured its prey, it often has a considerable digestive spell.... It was so, after the Rhineland was forcibly occupied...now after Austria has been struck down... in a little while there may be another pause, then people will be saying, See how the alarmists have been confused. Europe has calmed down. It has blown over and the war scare has passed.... *The Times* will write a leading article to say how silly those people look, who on the morrow of the Austrian incorporation, raised a clamor for...action.... For five years, I have talked to the house on these matters. Not with very great

success, I have watched this famous island…descending the stairway which leads to a dark gulf. It is a fine, broad stairway at the beginning but after a bit, the carpet ends. A little further on, there are only flagstones, and a little farther on still, these break beneath your feet.

Most political leaders during World War II walked down that flagstone path. They refused to believe the carpet would end, and the stones would crumble beneath them. In the end, their path disintegrated altogether, and they enabled evil to march through the gates of Auschwitz.

Today's BDSers walk along a parallel path. They foolishly believe that all disputes can be settled by peaceful means, that there is no such thing as evil. They reject the challenge of striking a necessary balance between sympathy and responsibility, trust and realism. Their politics of moral avoidance threaten Jewish and Western values.

The BDSers one-state solution to the Israeli-Palestinian conflict would guarantee the destruction of Israel and imperil the Jewish future, as Walker, herself, readily admits:

I believe there must be a one-state settlement. Palestinians and Jews, who have lived together in peace in the past, must work together to make this a reality once again. This land (so soaked in Jewish and Palestinian blood, and with America's taxpayer dollars wasted on violence the majority of us would never, if we knew, support) must become, like South Africa, the secure and peaceful home of everyone who lives there. This will require that Palestinians, like Jews, have the right of return to their homes and their lands. Which will mean what Israelis most fear: Jews will be outnumbered and, instead of a Jewish state, there will be a Jewish, Muslim, Christian country, which is how Palestine functioned before the Europeans arrived. What is so awful about that?

What is so awful about that is the disingenuousness it represents. Israel is not South Africa. A Palestinian right of return is unfeasible. An Arab majority in Israel would never tolerate the practice of Judaism (look at what has happened to Jewish communities throughout the Arab world). The only way to protect religious and cultural freedoms in Israel is to allow Jews, with their long tradition of humanistic, liberal values, to continue to run the democratic country they established in 1948.

To bring attention to Walker's hypocrisy and that of the entire BDS movement, the Simon Wiesenthal Center included both the author and the movement on its 2013 list of "Top Ten Anti-Semitic/ Anti-Israel Slurs." We put the BDS movement in fourth place, following the Supreme Leader of Iran, Ali Hosseini Khamenei; the Prime Minister of Turkey, Recip Tayyip Erdogan; and United Nations Special Rapporteur, Richard Falk. We slotted Alice Walker in the number nine position, along with Max Blumenthal, author of *Goliath: Life and Loathing in Greater Israel*, for the poisonous pens they share.

One of the Simon Wiesenthal Center's recent battles encapsulates the international challenges we face. The primary battleground was Paris, but episodes took place in New York, Washington, DC, Los Angeles, and Jerusalem. The main player, ironically, was the organization established in the wake of World War II to promote international cooperation, the United Nations.

Ever since it cynically passed the "Zionism is Racism" resolution in 1975, the UN has been an organization that elicited skepticism from Jewish and human-rights organizations like ours. We knew it was capable of blatant hypocrisy and political manipulation. Because of this, we believed it essential to maintain our accreditation as a nongovernmental organization at the UN and at UNESCO, the UN agency that promotes international collaboration through education, science, and culture.

In November 2011, I lead a Wiesenthal Center delegation to Paris to meet with French Minister of Foreign Affairs, Alain Juppé, to discuss, yet again, a rise in the incidence of anti-Semitic acts in France. I had also scheduled a meeting with the Director-General of UNESCO, Irina Bokova. By chance, our meeting came on the heels of a UNESCO decision to accept Palestine as a full member state. Rabbi

May and Janice Prager attended this meeting with me. I could not sit down with the UNESCO Director-General without commenting on this counterproductive development:

"Madam Director-General," I began, "This one-sided decision is contrary to the position taken by the United Nations in New York, which has not granted Palestine full member status...this move is widely viewed by the Jewish community as biased..."

"We are not biased," Bokova responded briskly. "We are merely mirroring the view held by the majority of our member states."

"Then how come the UN has not acted in this way?" I asked.

Sensing that my argument was falling on deaf ears, I decided to move things in a more positive direction by introducing an idea we had been contemplating at the Wiesenthal Center:

"As you know, the Simon Wiesenthal Center has partnered with UNESCO many times in the past on joint exhibitions. Why not use this opportunity to launch a jointly sponsored exhibition on the three thousand five hundred-year-long relationship of the Jewish people to the land of Israel? This is just the time for UNESCO to say that the world should hear Israel's side of the story."

Bokova liked the idea, but was non-committal. She said she would give it further consideration, and get back to me.

Four months later, after a series of phone calls and visits between our own Dr. Shimon Samuels, Rabbi Abraham Cooper, and Bokova, UNESCO agreed to co-sponsor the exhibition. On March 22, 2012, Bokova visited us in Los Angeles, and, in the presence of thirty members of the diplomatic corps, including David Siegel, Consul General of Israel in Los Angeles, signed a mock-up of the exhibition's opening panel.

Our agreement with UNESCO was simple. We would finance the project and engage a scholar to develop the exhibition content. A UNESCO team would review the draft content and propose edits. Together, we would agree upon the final content, and set the dates that the exhibition would be mounted at UNESCO's Paris headquarters.

We hired Robert Wistrich, Professor of European and Jewish History at the Hebrew University of Jerusalem, who embraced the idea. Eight months later, he completed his draft. The exhibition would consist of twenty-four panels that presented an overview of Jewish life in the Middle East from biblical times to the present. The goal was to provide viewers with an understanding of the continuity of the Jewish presence in the land of Israel over 3,500 years, and the centrality of the land of Israel in the Jewish historical, spiritual, and national consciousness.

We submitted the draft to the UNESCO team for review. Professor Wistrich, Rabbi Cooper, who served as project manager, Dr. Samuels, and the UNESCO team met in Paris, where they agreed upon minor revisions and finalized the content. Both parties agreed upon the final exhibition title: *People, Book, Land: The 3,500 Year Relationship of the Jewish People to the Holy Land.*

In the meantime, Canada, Israel, and Montenegro accepted our invitations to co-sponsor the exhibition, and we formed an honorary committee consisting of Nobel Laureate Elie Wiesel, Member of the Canadian Parliament Irwin Colter, former United States Representative to the UN Esther Coopersmith, former Archbishop of Canterbury Lord George Carey, interfaith activist and Holocaust educator Father Patrick Desbois, and Algerian novelist Boualem Sansal.

The exhibition was scheduled to open on Monday, January 20, 2014. Hundreds of invitations to the opening were mailed. On Thursday, January 17, the panels were hung in the main exhibition hall at UNESCO's international headquarters in the Place de Fontenoy. All was in order.

Then suddenly, on Thursday evening, with patrons on route to Paris, Bokova's assistant, Dr. Eric Falt, informed Dr. Samuels that the exhibition had been cancelled. Ten minutes later, Falt was on the phone with me in Los Angeles delivering the same startling news: Director-General Bokova had capitulated to UNESCO's Arab Group, a consortium of twenty-two member states, including the Palestinian Authority, which had protested the exhibit.

"But why?" I asked, stunned by the decision. "What about our agreement?" Before I had a chance to press him about how the Director-General could violate a signed agreement, and why she wasn't the one calling me, he confessed, "It's out of my hands, Rabbi. I'm sending you the Arab Group letter."

Moments later, my fax machine spit out the repugnant document:

Madam Director General,

The Arab Group to UNESCO wishes to express its deep concern and strong disapproval regarding the planned exhibition at UNESCO, on January 21, 2014, *People, Book, Land: The 3,500 Year Relationship of the Jewish People to the Holy Land.*
    The very subject of the exhibition is eminently political, despite its seemingly harmless title.
    More importantly, the opponents to peace in Israel have made this issue one of their warhorses, and the publicity it would certainly get from a showing within UNESCO, the press campaign going with and following the exhibition, can only harm the ongoing peace negotiations, the constant efforts of Secretary of State John Kerry, and UNESCO's neutrality and objectivity.
    For all these reasons, out of worry that UNESCO's mission to unshakably support peace would be compromised, the Arab Group to UNESCO asks you, Madam Director General to cancel this exhibition.

Yours faithfully,
Abdulla Alneaimi
Delegate of the United Arab Emirates President Arab Group to UNESCO

UNESCO's decision to cancel the exhibition based on this twisted letter was outrageous. Did UNESCO honestly believe that our attempt to teach people about the historic connection between the Jewish people and the land of Israel would hinder US Secretary of State John Kerry's attempt to broker a peace agreement between Israel and the Palestinians? Was UNESCO, the organization that theoretically works to foster dialogue among cultures and peoples, censuring an accredited UN non-governmental organization with a twenty-year history of cooperation? Had UNESCO completely disregarded our agreement?

One week earlier, the US State Department had declined our invitation to join Canada, Israel, and Montenegro as an official sponsor of the exhibition. However, the State Department did not express any concern that the exhibition itself posed a threat to the Israeli-Palestinian peace process. In a letter addressed to Rabbi Cooper, Kelly Siekman, the State Department's Director of UNESCO Affairs, wrote: "At this sensitive juncture in the ongoing Middle East peace process, and after thoughtful consideration with review at the highest levels, we have made the decision that the United States will not be able to co-sponsor the current exhibit during its display at UNESCO headquarters..." We suspected that UNESCO's Arab Group had gotten wind of the State Department position and used it in formulating its calculated letter to the Director-General.

We would not accept this political manipulation. We informed the co-sponsoring governments, and fired off a letter to Director-General Bokova:

Madam Director-General:

As the person who came to Los Angeles to publicly put your signature on and launch this historic undertaking, we insist that you live up to your responsibilities and commitments as the co-organizer of this exhibition by overturning this naked political move that has no place in an institution whose mandate is defined by education, science, and culture—not politics.

Failure to do so would confirm to the world that UNESCO is the official address of the Arab narrative of the Middle East. We remember vividly how this exhibition began when we visited you in your office in Paris on the very day when UNESCO allowed the admission of "Palestine" as a full-fledged member. You know very well there were many who protested that political decision by UNESCO, but you went ahead anyway.

Now, however, even as our exhibition was being mounted in the UNESCO hall, you pulled the exhibition because of a protest launched by the Chairperson of the member states of the Arab Group to UNESCO. It seems then, that the UNESCO bureaucracy only takes action when the Arab world makes demands, but takes no action to defend an exhibition whose only purpose is to show the historic validity of the three thousand five hundred-year relationship of the Jewish people to its land.

Let's be clear. The Arab Group's protest is not over any particular content in the exhibition, but rather the very idea of it—that the Jewish people did not come to the Holy Land only after the Nazi Holocaust, but trace their historical and cultural roots in that land for three and a half millennia. If anything will derail hopes for peace and reconciliation among the people of the Middle East, it will be by surrendering to the forces of extremism and torpedoing the opening of this exhibition—jointly vetted and co-organized by UNESCO and the Simon Wiesenthal Center.

The Director-General immediately responded to our letter, holding firm to the decision:

In this very spirit, and having in mind the delicate phase that the peace negotiations are entering, I have no choice but to take seriously the concerns raised in the letter of the Chairperson of the Arab Group. This is all the more important, as the UNESCO Secretariat is beholden by its rules and regulations to consider fully the concerns raised by its Member States or any Regional Group regarding planned exhibitions or manifestations.

We immediately went into action. We contacted the White House Office of Public Liaison to apprise them of the situation, and to protest the US's failure to co-sponsor the exhibition. Our Public Relations Director, Avra Shapiro, informed the international press. We contacted the White House Office of Public Liaison to apprise them of the situation, and to protest the US's failure to co-sponsor the exhibition. Within hours, the story broke around the world. In a press statement,

Samantha Power, US Ambassador to the United Nations, and a close advisor to President Obama, harshly criticized UNESCO:

> UNESCO's decision is wrong and should be reversed. The United States has engaged at senior levels to urge UNESCO to allow this exhibit to proceed as soon as possible. UNESCO is supposed to be fostering discussion and interaction between civil society and member states, and organizations such as the Wiesenthal Center have a right to be heard and to contribute to UNESCO's mission.

Michele Alkin, our Director of Communications, was up late into the night drafting an emergency alert to our three hundred thousdand online activists around the world. The results came quickly.

Canada's Foreign Minister, the World Jewish Congress, the American Jewish Committee, and the Anti-Defamation League issued similar statements. Israel's Prime Minister Benjamin Netanyahu made the issue the first agenda item of his weekly cabinet meeting. Before the meeting, he briefed the Israeli press:

> UNESCO announced over the weekend that it was cancelling an exhibit that it had planned to hold in France on the connection between the Jewish people and the land of Israel. The explanation given was that it would harm the negotiations. It would not harm the negotiations. Negotiations are based on facts, on the truth, which is never harmful. But what does harm the negotiations is the automatic summoning of Israeli ambassadors in certain countries regarding matters of no substance, while significant violations by the Palestinian Authority pass without a response.
>
> The one-sided approach toward Israel does not advance peace—it pushes peace further away. It strengthens the refusal of the PA [Palestinian Authority] to make actual progress in the negotiations. We hope that this conduct by the PA changes. The one-sided and unfair attitude toward the State of Israel does not advance the diplomatic process.

I told the press:

> The Simon Wiesenthal Center welcomes Ambassador Samantha Power's statement condemning UNESCO's abrupt cancellation of the exhibition on the 3,500-year relationship of the Jewish people to the Holy Land due to a last minute protest by the twenty-two-nation Arab Group at UNESCO. The exhibition, two years in the making, was a joint project of UNESCO and the Simon Wiesenthal Center. The exhibition was already positioned in the UNESCO exhibit hall, and invitations were mailed out, when it was cancelled because the Arab Group claimed it would interfere with Secretary of State Kerry's Middle East mission. The fact that Ambassador Power issued her statement shows that the United States feels that the exhibition in no way interferes with Secretary Kerry's mission.

Meanwhile French public intellectual Bernard-Henri Levy weighed in against UNESCO with a sharp piece that ran in *The Huffington Post*:

> Never mind the insult delivered to the prestigious Simon Wiesenthal Center, here depicted as a den of troublemakers and saboteurs of peace.
>
> Never mind the grotesque reasoning by which a scholarly exhibition put together by experts from around the world becomes, since Israel is involved, an obstacle to "negotiation" and "peace...."
>
> One of the dramatic aspects of this affair is the pathetic self-image conveyed by an agency of the United Nations bowing—there's no other word for it—to a *diktat*....
>
> A final dramatic element is the conviction that peace, real peace—that is, the long-awaited reconciliation of two peoples with much in common but contending for the same land—lies in mutual recognition, in a joint willingness to entertain the reasoning of the other and understand its founding myths, and not in the intolerance, rejection, demonization, and historical and philosophical revisionism encouraged by the current deluded UNESCO.

Several weeks later, I received a phone call from Director-General Bokova informing me that the voice of the Simon Wiesenthal Center, along with those of honorable governments and organizations that joined our cause, including the US State Department, had been heard. *People, Book, Land: The 3,500 Year Relationship of the Jewish People to the Holy Land* would be re-scheduled to open on June 11, 2014, at UNESCO's Paris headquarters.

In recognition of the importance of the exhibition, French President François Hollande invited us to a reception in the Élysée Palace a few hours before the June 11th opening ceremony. We then joined 300 diplomats, dignitaries, and leaders of France's Jewish community at UNESCO headquarters for the ceremony.

In my remarks, I touched on the obstacles the Jewish state faces:

This is truly an historic occasion because it is the first time in the history of the United Nations through its educational and cultural arm, UNESCO, that the UN has co-sponsored an exhibit which outlines the historic raison d'etre for the UN decision to recognize a Jewish homeland in Palestine in 1947: the indisputable fact that the Jewish people have an uninterrupted three thousand five hundred-year relationship with the Holy Land.

This exhibit opens at a critical stage in the efforts to bring a just and viable peace to the Middle East, especially the people of Israel and the Palestinian people. But such a peace can only come when Israel's neighbors finally end their campaign to deny the Jewish people its national identity. No one can bypass this obstacle by pretending it doesn't exist. Peace is not a game like Monopoly where you can skip the inconvenient and proceed directly to Go.

The purpose of this exhibit is very clear: to put an end to the canard that a Jewish state came into being in 1948, not because Jews had any connection with the land of Israel, but because the world took pity on them as a result of the Holocaust.

This exhibit will educate the world by debunking myths with historic truth. Just like Egypt is a country with a four thousand-year footprint, so Israel, too, has that three thousand five hundred-year footprint in every nook and cranny of the land of Israel.

This is not only the belief of Jews, but a view shared by billions of people on the planet, who hold the Bible sacred. What we know from the Torah and the writings of the prophets, Christians know from their Old and New Testament.

They know it is no myth that Samson met Delilah near Gaza.

That it is no fable that the greatest of Israel's judges, Samuel, born in Ramah, crisscrossed the land of Israel and inaugurated her monarchy, installed her most famous kings: Saul and David. Samuel did not initiate this from Madrid or Amsterdam, but from the length and breadth of the land of Israel.

When the prophet Isaiah invoked, "What need have I, of all your sacrifices…devote yourselves to justice…uphold the rights of the orphan…defend the cause of the widow," he was not speaking from Paris, but from Jerusalem.

When the biblical Ruth, a non-Jew, born in ancient Moab spoke her, "Where you go, I will go. Your people shall be my people. Your God shall be my God." Those unforgettable words spoken to her mother-in-law were not intoned in London or Brussels, but from Bethlehem, not far from Rachel's tomb.

When the prophet, said, "Houses, fields, and vineyards will yet be bought in this land…. Soon will there be heard in the mountains of Judah and in the streets of Jerusalem, the voice of joy and gladness, the voice of the groom and the voice of the bride…" it was not the words of a foreign resident with an EU passport, but the words of Jeremiah speaking from the heart of Jerusalem.

In that land, Jews have built a dynamic and thriving civilization over thousands of years…. That land today is a world center for research in medicine and technology. A civilization built on the pillars of freedom and human dignity, where no one is compelled to worship a God, or vote for a particular party.

The State of Israel and the Jewish People respect the origins and followers of Christendom and Islam. The time has come for Israel's neighbors to end their attempted identity theft of the Jewish people's 3,500-year connection with the Holy Land.

As Sir Winston Churchill so eloquently told a delegation of Arab leaders in 1921, "It is manifestly right that the Jews, who are scattered all over the world, should have a national center and a National Home.... And where else could that be but in this land of Palestine, with which for more than three thousand years they have been intimately and profoundly associated?"

Today's battles against anti-Semitism, anti-Zionism, and other forms of racism are part of a larger war that must be waged against Islamic fundamentalism. The terrorist attacks on the headquarters of the *Charlie Hebdo* satirical magazine and the Hyper Cacher kosher supermarket in Paris in January 2015 were a wake-up call to the dangers we face. But while much has been written about the barbaric terrorists who darkened the City of Lights, very little has been said about the magnitude of the extremist Islamic threat.

One study provides some sense of scale. A 2013 Pew Research Center poll asked thirty eight thousand Muslims in thirty-nine countries whether attacks on civilians were justified. Seventy-eight percent responded that violence against civilians is never justified. This figure, which represents an overwhelming majority of Muslims who oppose terrorist tactics, could leave us complacent, like much of the world media, which continuously sends the message that jihadists do not speak for Islam. But these survey results also demonstrate that twenty-two percent of those polled support some form of violence against civilians. If we apply this figure to the world's Muslim population of more than one-and-a-half billion, we find that nearly three hundred and fifty million people are politically aligned with the jihadists. Even if we reduce this number by one hundred and fifty million from this survey, that would still leave two hundred million potential jihadists, a number equivalent to the population of the axis powers, (Nazi Germany, Japan, Italy, and Austria) at the beginning of World War II.

Will the West rise to defend itself against the threat that such a potent force of Islamic extremism represents? I am not certain. While the nearly four million-strong solidarity march in Paris following the January 2015 terrorist incidents was seminal, it did not override the fact that the French have overwhelmingly and repeatedly failed to take to the streets following terrorist attacks against Jews in recent years—despite the shadow cast by the Holocaust.

Western leaders displayed a similar indifference to threats against Jews when Hamas and Hezbollah smuggled tens of thousands of rockets into Gaza and Lebanon to build up their weapons arsenals against Israel. Only when Israel entered Gaza in the summer of 2014 to defend itself against those rockets hitting its population centers did world leaders rush to Jerusalem. And when they did, they pressured Israel to pull back.

Western leaders cannot defeat Islamic extremism on their own. Muslims leaders need to reclaim Islam from the extremists who have hijacked it. They must denounce violence and demand moderation.

In 1996, encouraged by Israel's Prime Minister Yitzhak Rabin, my colleague Rabbi Cooper and I visited Egypt's moderate, sometimes progressive, Sheikh Muhammad Sayyid Tantawy, the Grand Imam of Al-Azhar, considered then by many Muslims to be the highest authority in Sunni Islamic thought and jurisprudence. We asked Sheikh Tantawy to issue a *fatwa*, a legal opinion, against suicide bombing. Sheikh Tantawy assured me he would issue such a *fatwa*, and told Western and international audiences that Egypt condemned all attacks on civilians. But in 2002, at a reception for Arab Knesset Member Abd al-Wahhab Darawsheh he reversed his position by declaring that suicide operations and the murder of Israeli civilians, including women and children, not only were permitted, but should be intensified.

Few Muslim political or religious leaders have mustered the courage to speak out. A notable exception is Egypt's President Abdel Fattaha al-Sisi, who took a brave stand against extremism in January 2015. In the very mosque and university at which Sheikh Tantawy presided, President al-Sisi told his nation's most prestigious Muslim clerics that without reform, Islam had no future:

It's inconceivable that the thinking that we hold most sacred should cause the entire Islamic world to be a source of anxiety, danger, killing and destruction for the rest of the world. Impossible! ...I am not saying "religion" but "thinking"—that corpus of texts and ideas that we have sanctified over the centuries, to the point that departing from them has become almost impossible—is antagonizing the entire world.

Al-Sisi challenged the clergy: "I say, and repeat again, that we are in need of a religious revolution. You, imams, are responsible before Allah. The entire world.... I say it again: the entire world...is waiting for your next move..."

Indeed, the world is waiting. If a moderate Islam is to prevail, more Muslim leaders must speak the language of President al-Sisi, and Muslim clergy must translate their words into action.

President al-Sisi's words lingered in my mind when, three months later, I attended a meeting between President Obama and the heads of major American Jewish organizations at the White House. The meeting took place during a period of heightened tension in the history of American-Israeli relations. The US, Russia, China, France, the UK, and Germany (the "P5+1") and the European Union had just announced that they had reached an agreement on a framework deal with the Islamic Republic of Iran as part of the negotiations toward a comprehensive agreement on Iran's nuclear program. A month prior, Israeli Prime Minister Benjamin Netanyahu had boldly denounced the US negotiating position in a speech in the US House of Representatives. Meanwhile, following the failed US-led Israeli-Palestinian negotiations, Palestinian President Mahmoud Abbas was turning to the UN Security Council for unilateral recognition of a Palestinian state.

President Obama had requested we meet to discuss why he had endorsed the Iranian agreement, and why he believed the only solution to the Israeli-Palestinian impasse was a two-state scenario. He explained in detail why he believed the framework agreement was an important step in preventing Iran from obtaining a nuclear weapon and in making the US, its allies, and the world, safer.

When the time came for responses, I had two. First, I raised the issue of the failure of the world leaders involved in the Iranian negotiations to respond to the country's unabashed call for the destruction of Israel:

"Mr. President. Many world leaders will soon travel to Europe and China to commemorate the seventieth anniversary of the liberation of the Nazi concentration camps and the end of World War II. With respect, I must ask: What meaning does such an anniversary hold if none of the leaders currently involved in the most sensitive negotiations ever carried out between the P5+1 group and Iran is willing to repudiate statements made in the negotiations by Iran's supreme leader and by one of its most influential militia commanders that "erasing Israel off the map" is "non-negotiable"? What significance does the commemoration have if not one country—including the United States—is willing to denounce such statements?"

Second, I questioned who was to blame for the failure of the two-state solution to take hold:

"Mr. President. Why do the United States and other Western countries continue to claim that the obstacle to a two-state solution is Israel's unwillingness to withdraw from substantial portions of the West Bank, while they ignore the fact that Gaza is governed by a terrorist organization whose charter calls for the destruction of Israel? Mr. President, it is an indisputable fact that no Israeli government—whether Likud or Labor—could ever agree to a two-state solution as long as Gaza is governed by Hamas, because such a solution would, in fact, be a three-state solution."

The president reiterated his support for the framework deal, and I considered the irony that the day's proceedings were taking place in the White House's Roosevelt Room. With a portrait of FDR staring down at us, I thought back to the West's appeasement of Hitler in the 1930s, including President Roosevelt and Avery Brundage's decision to allow an American team to participate in rather than to boycott the 1936 Nazi-sponsored Summer Olympics in Berlin. Now, some eighty years later, we were appeasing the ayatollahs of Iran, the world's most dangerous sponsors of terror, who have been deliberately misleading the world for decades.

As I left the room, I glanced at the other portrait hanging above us, that of President Teddy Roosevelt, who had described his foreign policy approach with the adage, "speak softly, and carry a big stick." If we were not repudiating calls for the destruction of Israel, our ally, it seemed to me we were no longer carrying that big stick. In July 2015, when the President announced that they had reached an agreement with Iran, the Simon Wiesenthal Center placed an ad with a picture of the Ayatollah looking down on Congress in The Hill, a Washington, DC-based newspaper read by the President and members of Congress. Under the headline, "It's up to you now," the ad read: "What will we tell our grandchildren if Congress doesn't act? Even with a seat at the table, fanatics never act reasonably. Hitler didn't stop after Czechoslovakia Kim Jong-un continues to choose nukes over food. The Ayatollahs' fanatical theology will always trump reason and threaten the world."

Chapter Six

Goodwill Ambassadors

I t is an undeniable fact that the Jewish people is one of the world's most vulnerable peoples. Jews have experienced few periods in their three thousand five hundred-year-long history without discrimination or violent persecution. Pogroms, expulsions, and massacres are among the major touchstones of our collective past.

As the Simon Wiesenthal Center's reputation grew, we were increasingly in a position to attempt to alleviate this vulnerability by forging relationships with people of political influence around the world. Little by little, we expanded our organizational Rolodex so that by the 1980s, we were able to contribute to political dialogue at the highest levels in order to fight anti-Semitism, defend human rights, and promote ethnic and religious tolerance.

We decided to set out periodically from our Los Angeles head-quarters to initiate and nurture friendships with international political leaders. We would learn from brave dissidents, support politicians in places of conflict and transition, and come to know presidents, prime ministers, and kings. We would become goodwill ambassadors to political leaders in Europe, the Soviet Union, the Middle East, and the Far East. And we would have many good times along the way.

In the early 1980s, the most significant human rights issue affecting world Jewry was undoubtedly the struggle to free the Soviet Union's nearly three million Jews. Soviet Jews faced institutionalized anti-Semitism that prevented them from advancing in Soviet society, receiving religious educations, and engaging in Jewish life. Requests to emigrate were considered acts of betrayal. With the exception of the survival of the State of Israel, there was no more crucial issue facing the Jewish people.

The hatred and repression Soviet Jews faced was not a new phenomenon. In 1881, large-scale anti-Jewish riots had broken out in the Ukraine when Jews were falsely blamed for the assassination of Czar Alexander II. Similar pogroms had taken place in Kishinev in 1903, when Jews were accused of killing two Christian children in order to use their blood to prepare matzoh for the Passover holiday; the riots left forty-seven Jews dead, hundreds wounded, and houses and businesses looted and destroyed. Beginning in 1919 and continuing into the 1920s, Jewish properties and synagogues were seized and rabbis forced to resign their positions, as Communist laws forbid expressions of religion.

Stalin, whose anti-Semitism was reinforced by his anti-Westernism, followed the tradition. He accused Jews of being "not a living and active nation but something mystical intangible and super-natural," despite the fact that nearly six hundred thousand Jews had fought in the Soviet Army and nearly one hundred and fifty thousand had died for their country during World War II.

Soviet anti-Semitism reached new heights after 1948, when the USSR arrested and killed Yiddish writers and artists in a campaign against the "rootless cosmopolitans." In 1953, the government concocted the "Doctors' Plot," in which it accused prominent, predominantly Jewish Moscow doctors of conspiring to assassinate Soviet leaders, causing a wave of anti-Semitism and anti-Zionism that led to doctors and others being fired and arrested.

A brief respite came at the time of Israel's establishment, when Andrei Gromyko, the Soviet Permanent Representative to the United Nations, addressed the UN with words of support for the proposed Jewish state: "The fact that no Western European state has been able to ensure the defense of the elementary rights of the Jewish people...explains the aspirations of the Jews to establish their own state. It would be unjust... to deny the right of the Jewish people to realize this aspiration."

But by the late 1960s, when it became clear that Israel was firmly aligned with the United States and other Western powers, the Soviets reverted to their deeply rooted anti-Semitism. They imprisoned leaders of the Jewish movement, which was gaining strength, and denied tens of thousands of Soviet Jews emigration visas to Israel.

By then, however, a number of international Soviet-Jewish protest organizations had been established. Activists protested US performances by Soviet performers like the Bolshoi Ballet, staged marches, and lobbied Washington. They also encouraged American Jews to travel to the Soviet Union to visit and lend support to Jewish dissidents.

In June 1984, French President François Mitterrand was considering becoming the first Western leader to visit the Soviet Union since Konstantin Chrenenko had taken office. Mitterrand was under pressure not to go, because it was rumored that Soviet nuclear physicist and human rights activist, Andrei Sakharov, was dying from a hunger strike he initiated to protest the Soviets' refusal to let his wife, Yelena Bonner, travel to the US for medical treatment. We were intent on supporting President Mitterrand, and influencing him to press the Soviets to release Sakharov and Soviet Jewish dissident Anatoly Shcharansky (later Natan Sharansky) from internal exile.

We organized a mission that included a stop in Paris to meet with Mitterrand at the Élysée Palace.

I made my official remarks:

Our delegation has just come from Budapest, where we sought out a small street named in honor of a great hero of the Holocaust, Swedish diplomat Raoul Wallenberg, who saved tens of thousands of Jews from certain death by providing them with protective passports. While Wallenberg saved many others, he couldn't save himself. He was captured by the Soviets and disappeared into the Gulag.

Today, Mr. President, there are great men caught in the same predicament: Andrei Sakharov and Anatoly Shcharansky, who represent the voice of freedom that will not be silenced.... We hope that as you travel to the Soviet Union, you will take the opportunity to do all that you can on behalf of these two great people to see that the Soviets will not be able to do to them what they succeeded in doing to Raoul Wallenberg...and we hope that you will confront Secretary Konstantin Chernenko about the cultural genocide which characterizes official Soviet policy toward Jewish citizens...

Mitterrand went ahead with the state visit to Moscow, and pushed Chrenenko on the Sakharov case. He not only pointed out the worldwide concern over Sakharov and Bonner, he created a stir by abandoning diplomatic convention and raising the issue at a Kremlin banquet. Mitterrand mentioned Sakharov by name as an example of "people who are sometimes symbolic," and insisted, "Every protest must be made to ensure the freedom but also the life of these two people."

Chrenenko refused to discuss the case with Mitterrand. Following their meeting, a Soviet spokesman said some of Mitterrand's remarks showed the influence of "prejudices and stereotypes." But later, the Soviets acknowledged that Sakharov was alive and well. Mitterrand's pressure helped keep the issue of Sakharov's exile in the public eye. Two years later, Mikhail Gorbachev released Sakharov and Sharansky.

Also, in 1984, we decided to send a Simon Wiesenthal Center mission to the Soviet Union. Knowing that the Soviet authorities would prevent an organized group with a political agenda from entering the country, we presented the visit as a "Remembrance and Renewal Mission" to mark the fortieth anniversary of the end of World War II. We believed the Soviets would accept this program because they were well aware of the fact that they had suffered the greatest number of casualties of any country in the war, and portrayed themselves as those who had led the effort to defeat Hitler.

Our instincts proved correct. In January 1985, the Soviet Embassy in Washington, DC informed us that our participation in Soviet ceremonies marking the fortieth anniversary of the end of World War II had been approved. We put together a group of twenty-eight political figures, Holocaust survivors, and Wiesenthal Center supporters, including trustees Sam and Frances Belzberg, Bill and Barbara Belzberg, Larry Mizel and his son, future trustee, Cheston and Gary and Karen Winnick, and prepared for a May 1985 trip.

Before the mission got underway, Rabbi Abraham Cooper and I stopped in Luxembourg to participate in an official ceremony marking the fortieth anniversary of the war's end at the American Cemetery and Memorial near Luxembourg City. More than five thousand American soldiers are buried at the dignified, fifty-acre site. Most were killed in the Battle of the Bulge, the surprise attack on the Allied forces in which America suffered the greatest number of casualties of any battle in the war.

I took my place at the podium with solemn pride. An imposing limestone chapel loomed behind me, its warm gray hue blending with the cloud-covered sky. Thousands of indistinguishable white crosses spread out before me, reaching the horizon. Two enormous American flags rippled overhead.

I began my speech by noting the presence of each of the Allied Nations' ambassadors to Luxembourg. I paid tribute to the achievements of the Allied Forces during World War II, and honored the memory of the troops who sacrificed their lives to eradicate Nazi evil. I referenced President Ronald Reagan's controversial upcoming visit to the Kolmeshohe Cemetery at Bitburg, where nearly two thousand German soldiers, including forty-nine SS troops are buried. "Let there be no confusion between these ceremonies," I stated emphatically. "Those interred here fought and died to continue the principles of the Judeo-Christian civilization, while those buried at Bitburg did everything they could to end it."

The next evening, Rabbi Cooper and I attended Friday night services at the Great Synagogue of Luxembourg, a restrained 1950s edifice that had replaced an exuberant, onion-domed, Moorish-style building destroyed by the Nazis. From there, we walked to the home of Luxembourg's Chief Rabbi, Dr. Emmanuel Bulz, where we discussed the state of Soviet Jewry over a traditional Shabbos meal.

The discussion then shifted to the amount of influence American Jewry has in the United States. I explained how the influence had grown dramatically since the eve of World War II, when only a few Jewish leaders had any connection at all to President Roosevelt. Wanting to understand the relationship of Luxembourg's Jews to their leaders, but unsure how to pronounce the title of Luxembourg's head of state, I inadvertently turned a serious topic into a laughing matter. Spouting one of my classic malapropisms, I innocently asked, "Does the Jewish community have any influence on His Royal Highness, the Grand *Duck?*"

Desperately trying to maintain her composure, the Chief Rabbi's wife carefully admonished me, "We pronounce it *Duke*, not *Duck*, because His Royal Highness does not quack like a duck." Laughter erupted around the table. The Chief Rabbi laughed so hard I thought he might choke on his roast chicken.

Before flying to Moscow, the Wiesenthal Center's "Remembrance and Renewal Mission" visited the Bergen-Belsen concentration camp in northern Germany, where fifty thousand Jews, Czechs, Poles, anti-Nazi Christians, homosexuals, Roma and Sinti were murdered during World War II—among them, Anne Frank and her sister, Margot. Rabbi Leslie Hardman, who, at the age of thirty-two had served as the senior Jewish chaplain to the British Forces, and had entered Bergen-Belsen two days after its liberation, joined us. He recalled, "I tried to persuade the drivers of the army bulldozers pushing the dead bodies into pits to bury them with dignity.... If all the trees in the world turned into pens, all the waters in the oceans turned into ink and the heavens turned into paper, it would still be insufficient material to describe the horrors these people suffered under the ss. I struggled to bring comfort to the survivors, who were like the walking dead."

Rabbi Hardman's only respite from the unbearable suffering he encountered at Bergen-Belsen was a wedding ceremony he performed between a Jewish survivor and a British army sergeant.

"I held a tallis above the couple's heads as a makeshift *chuppah*, and, with tears in my eyes, recited the blessings, including the prophecy, 'Soon there will be heard in the cities of Judah and in the streets of Jerusalem, the voice of joy and gladness, the voice of the bridegroom and the voice of the bride.' At the time, those words felt like a tiny vindication from heaven."

We next journeyed to the Wannsee Villa in the suburbs of Berlin, where on January 20, 1942, ss General Reinhard Heydrich, Heinrich Himmler's chief aide and the man Adolf Hitler described as "the man with the iron heart," had gathered fourteen senior representatives of the Third Reich—eight of whom held PhDs—to present his "Final Solution to the Jewish Question." In the ninety-minute meeting, Heydrich used euphemisms like "reorganization" and "resettlement" to outline how the National Socialist Party would deport and murder Europe's eleven million Jews. I struggled to fathom the cold-blooded plot that had been agreed upon in this serene lakeside villa, with its lovely parquet floors and coffered ceilings. I thought about the millions of lives destroyed, the families devastated, and the obliteration of Jewish life in Europe.

Standing at the Wannsee Villa, I was also outraged anew by the results of a research project we had recently completed that demonstrated that Germany was providing hefty government benefits to the heirs of Nazi perpetrators. Through retirement funds, the War Victims Fund, and other government assistance programs, post-war Germany was supporting the wife of Hermann Goering, the second most powerful man in Nazi Germany, the wife of Julius Streicher, the founder and publisher of the vehemently anti-Semitic Nazi weekly, *Der Stuermer*, the family of Reinhard Heydrich, who had convened the Wannsee Conference, and countless others, as remuneration for their service to the Reich—despite the fact that that service involved murder on a scale never before witnessed in human history. I left the Wannsee Villa recommitted to our fight for justice.

We had been briefed for months on what to expect and whom to trust when we arrived in the Soviet Union. We had memorized pointers shared with us by those who had visited before: "Never get into a black cab stationed at the airport," its driver is likely to be a KGB agent. "If you ever doubt someone's KGB connection, ask him to pose for a picture."

But none of the briefings could have prepared us for what we experienced upon arrival at the Moscow International Airport. Airport personnel confiscated our luggage and a customs official whisked me away to a stuffy private office, where two beefy men smugly interrogated me in broken English:

"Why you have come to Moscow?"

"I am leading a tour group from the Simon Wiesenthal Center of Los Angeles. We are here for the fortieth anniversary of the end of World War II."

"You were here for thirtieth or thirty-fifth anniversaries?"

"No, we were not."

"So why you are here now?"

Without waiting for an answer, they continued to fire questions at me: "For who you are bringing this food? Why this medicine? Are you sure you are not opening hospital in Moscow?"

"We are not interested in opening a hospital. We are a Jewish group that keeps kosher, so we have brought our own food. The Soviet Embassy in Washington, DC has invited us to come."

With that, the intimidation came to an end, and a half-hour later, we cleared customs. The airport police seized a good portion of our food, but we were able to keep most of what was on the top of the refuseniks' wish lists: baby food, books, and medicine, including coagulant used for ritual circumcisions, which Malkie carried in her purse. I began to realize the courage it took the refuseniks to challenge this perverse political system.

On our first Shabbos in Moscow, we divided into groups of three and went to homes in different parts of the city. In each tiny apartment, we witnessed similar rituals: the closing of curtains before lighting Shabbos candles, the singing of Shabbos melodies in hushed tones, the serving of a few pieces of herring as a meal's main course. We experienced first-hand the scarcity, repression, and fear with which the dissidents lived their constrained lives.

Malkie and I were guests of Ilya Esses, a Jewish dissident who had been denied a visa to Israel since 1973. In his narrow apartment with drawn curtains and third-hand furniture, Ilya told us his story:

> My parents, Tzvi and Sonya, had traditional Jewish upbringings. They were forced to hide their religious backgrounds when the Communists took over. My father pretended to be an atheist. Only once, when I was seven years old, he allowed me to go to synagogue, for *Kol Nidrei*. He covered my face with his hat so nobody would recognize me. When we returned home, I kept asking my father why the Jews in the shul kept crying. Then, for the first time, my father told me about Jewish history....
>
> I studied mathematics and was admitted to the Soviet Academy of Sciences. In 1968, when I was studying in the Academy library, I came across Heinrich Graetz's *History of the Jews,* which changed my life. I took careful notes, and returned to the library again and again to read every volume in the series. I began teaching Jewish history to other Soviet Jews. I taught myself how to speak and read Hebrew. Eventually, my parents and many of my students received visas to go to Israel, but I did not.

I saw the pain and yearning in Ilya's eyes. I tried to encourage him by sharing my belief that the movement to free Soviet Jewry would rekindle a commitment to Judaism around the world:

> I want you to know that you are helping the Jewish people in a profound way. You are giving American Jews an opportunity to redeem themselves by doing for you what they failed to do for Jews during the Holocaust. When Jews around the world see how much you are willing to sacrifice just to read a Hebrew book, they will stop taking for granted their good fortune of being able to have Hebrew books in their homes. When they learn how you are unable to light Shabbos candles, conduct a Seder or build a *sukkah*, they will be inspired to make sure they light candles, host Seders and sit in *sukkahs*. So, thank

you—for what you are doing here and for what you are doing to rekindle Judaism in America and around the world.

The members of our mission were deeply moved by their encounters with the refuseniks. Each returned home more knowledgeable about Soviet Jewish life, and more connected to the Jewish people. As one member put it, "Going to the Soviet Union was a *real* Jewish education—the kind I never got in Hebrew school."

For me, hearing the refuseniks' stories first-hand substantiated the speeches I had been making on their behalf for years. The message I received from Ilya and the other brave Soviet Jews I met was similar to the theme of a story I had told at a midnight rally for Soviet Jewry attended by one thousand people in Vancouver in 1971.

An American Yiddish-speaking journalist visited Moscow's Central Synagogue. During the service, he leaned forward to ask a question of an old man draped in a long wool tallis sitting in front of him: *"Ich bin a schriber fun America un ich gei schriben vegan Russchie Yidden. Efsher vilt ir mir eppes zogen?"* (I am a writer from America and I am going to write about Soviet Jewry. Maybe you want to tell me something?) The old man turned toward him and answered:

"My family was slaughtered like cattle by the Nazis. My wife, four sisters, and two brothers…may they be at rest in the next world. We had one son, thank God. He married a Jewish girl and soon after, they had a son. They called him Valdenki. I can't tell you how much was added to my life when my grandson turned five and I began to take him to shul on Shabbos. Even the nightmares about my family and the Nazis stopped, because I had something to live for.

"Then one day, Valdenki's first-grade teacher found out he was going to synagogue with his grandfather. The teacher shouted, 'Stand up, Jew Vladenki!'

He shamed my grandson again and again for going to synagogue with me. His school friends joined in. My grandson was ashamed; he never went back to the synagogue again.

It's been nine years since Valdenki sat here beside me....
So if you want to tell the Jews of America something, tell them
to shake the world so that my Valdenki will one day be free
to live as a Jew, and Hitler will not have finished his task."

Our visit to the Soviet Union was one small effort within the larger
Soviet-Jewish protest movement that, by the late 1980s, was achieving
great success. Many Jews were being permitted to emigrate, and inside
the Soviet Union, a yeshiva was established for the first time since
the Communist Revolution of 1917. President Mikhail Gorbachev's
democratization gave greater freedom to anti-Semitic groups, which
further spurred Soviet Jews to seek emigration. By 1988, hundreds of
thousands of Jews were clamoring to leave, and in early 1990, more
than ten thousand Soviet Jews each month were allowed to emigrate
to Israel and the West.

Two years after our mission to the Soviet Union, we made a modest
attempt at Middle East diplomacy. We conceived a brief mission to
open a channel with King Hussein, the leader of Jordan, who had
ascended the throne in 1952 after his father's abdication, and who
looked to the United States as his most reliable ally. We made the
case to the Jordanian Embassy in Washington, DC that the American
Jewish community was the most important Jewish community outside of Israel, and that a respected American Jewish organization
like the Wiesenthal Center might be able to influence Arab-Jewish
relations.

A few months later, the Embassy informed us that the visit
had been approved. In March 1987—seven years before Israel and
Jordan signed a peace treaty—I led a three-day Wiesenthal Center
mission to Amman, the sprawling capital of Jordan, to meet with
King Hussein. Growing up in a tenement in New York City's Lower
East Side, I could never have imagined leading a Jewish delegation
across the Allenby Bridge to the palace of the Hashemite Kingdom
of Jordan. But there I was, crossing the Jordan River in the blazing
Middle East sun on my way to a meeting with the King.

General Ali Shukri, King Hussein's close personal advisor, greeted me and my colleagues, Rabbi Cooper and Rabbi May, under a coat of arms that embellished the arched entrance to the Raghadan Palace, the former home of King Abdullah, and one of the palaces used by King Hussein. General Shukri ushered us into a spacious waiting area with a colorful, high ceiling decorated with inscriptions in Arabic calligraphy. After a few minutes, we entered the adjoining Office of the Monarch, where King Hussein greeted us.

I reached out to shake the King's hand, and asked for permission to recite the traditional Jewish blessing for standing in the presence of a king. King Hussein seemed surprised by the request, but readily agreed. I began, "Blessed art Thou o Lord, King of the universe, who has given of Thy glory to mortal man."

I couldn't help but think that the "mortal man" standing opposite me represented a country that had been one of Israel's mortal enemies for the past forty years. In 1948, the Jordanian army had conquered Jerusalem's Old City and destroyed its ancient synagogues, desecrated Jewish gravestones on the Mount of Olives, and prevented Israelis from accessing the Western Wall, the remnant of the Temple that is Judaism's holiest site. In 1967 and 1973, Jordan's armies had collaborated, however reluctantly, with other Arab armies intent on annihilating the Jewish state in the Six Day War and the Yom Kippur War. I recited the blessing, knowing that Jewish law requires it be stated whether the king is a friend or a foe of the Jewish people.

King Hussein warmly welcomed each member of our mission to Jordan, and addressed us as a group: "We are delighted that you have come to visit our country. I know that wherever you will travel, you will receive a warm welcome from our people.... We must find a way for the children of Abraham to once again live together in peace and harmony as our ancestors lived before us." He then led us through the modest but impressive palace, enjoying his role as tour guide.

Over the next two days, we met with members of the cabinet and other government officials. We heard stories of the King's grandfather, King Abdullah, who was assassinated in July 1951 by a Palestinian extremist who feared the King was making peace with Israel. King Abdullah had been in Jerusalem to give a eulogy at the funeral of Riad Bey Al Solh, the assassinated former prime minister of Lebanon, with whom, it was rumored, he was pursuing a peace treaty with Israel, and to meet with Reuven Shiloah, Director of the Mossad. His grandson, the fifteen-year-old Prince Hussein, had been with him at Al-Aksa Mosque when he was shot. After the Six Day War, some believed the prince, who had by then become King Hussein, was unwilling to enter peace talks because of the memory of his grandfather's assassination and fear of his own.

Throughout our visit, King Hussein exuded kindness, generosity, and humility. He spoke passionately about his hopes for a new era, saying it was "time to remove the barriers of the past." He viewed our meeting as "an opportunity to reach out across the mistrust." By the time our visit was over, any mistrust we might have brought with us had faded. Members of our mission came away believing that before long, thanks in no small part to this charismatic leader, Israel and Jordan would reach a peace agreement.

In 1991, long before it had formal diplomatic relations with Israel, the Chinese government invited the Simon Wiesenthal Center on a historic mission. The Chinese had a long history of good relations with Jews. Many Chinese admired the Jewish people, and saw parallels between the persecution of Jews and the Western powers' domination of China. Shanghai had been a rare safe haven for Jewish refugees during the Holocaust. As victims of Hitler's Axis, China, it seemed, took an interest in an organization committed to memorializing the Holocaust.

Dr. Alfred Balitzer, a professor of government, Asia expert, and President Ronald Reagan's Special Ambassador to Brunei, helped organize our trip. We invited thirty Wiesenthal Center trustees, Holocaust survivors, and friends to take advantage of this unique opportunity to visit the most populous country in the world that was positioning itself to break out of its political isolation.

We landed at Hong Kong's teeming Kai Tak Airport, and boarded a connecting flight to Mainland China. We took off as scheduled. Three hours later, the pilot informed us that our plane could not land in Beijing because of fog and would have to be rerouted to Guangzhou, in southeast China. We took the news in stride.

But our patience ran out when we landed in Guangzhou and our pilot announced, "The aircraft's doors will now open, but you are forbidden to exit. You must wait for the arrival of immigration officials from Beijing." Expecting that Jews can sit still is optimistic under any circumstances, but asking them to remain in the seats of a plane whose doors are open is utterly futile. As the members of our group gathered their carry-ons, I informed the crew: "If we are not allowed to get off the plane within the next five minutes, we will be late for our dinner in Beijing with Qian Qichen, the Chinese Foreign Minister." Our status was immediately upgraded, and off we went.

When we learned that the baggage handlers, like the immigration officials, had not yet arrived in Guangzhou, we literally took matters into our own hands. It was an amusing sight: American and Canadian Jewish community leaders who had been promised a first-class trip were scavenging through boxes and crates in the belly of the plane in search of their designer suitcases. The frenzied scene reminded me of the Israelites preparing to leave Egypt, but I suspected the Israelites traveled with less baggage.

After the flight to Beijing, we arrived exhausted but enthusiastic at the Diaoyutai State Guesthouse, an enclave of villas and gardens for visiting foreign dignitaries and government officials in Beijing's Haidian District. We settled in and met our hosts, who greeted us warmly in a spacious meeting room in which a dozen yellow sofas had been arranged in a perfect semi-circle.

Foreign Minister Qichen, who in recent months had been revealing signs of interest in regional cooperation and economic development, spoke about the new China and its place in the world. He explained the Chinese people's interest in Jewish culture:

> A unique connection exists between the Chinese and the Jewish people. Our two peoples share the distinction of being among the oldest civilizations in the world. Even though China's Jewish community has always been quite small, we Chinese have an abiding fascination with Jewish history and culture.

I took the podium, and, after expressing my gratitude to the Foreign Minister and the other officials who made our trip possible, described one of the specific purposes of our mission: to request that the Chinese government televise *Genocide*, a documentary film that tells the story of the Holocaust, which the Simon Wiesenthal Center produced in 1980: "In addition to the connections that the Foreign Minister described, our two peoples share a more recent bond: the atrocities that Hitler and the Axis powers committed against us. It is imperative that we document and teach these historical events to the younger generation."

I also pressed for Chinese support of Israel: "While there are more than fifty Muslim states in the world, there is only one, very small Jewish state. If, heaven forbid, it is compromised, it will most certainly mean the end of Jewish civilization as we know it."

The Foreign Minister assured us that the world would not let that happen. Foreign Minister Qichen and a line of dark-suited government officials escorted us into a grand banquet room, where potted red orchids graced dining tables surrounded by bamboo chairs. We had given Foreign Ministry officials a crash course by telephone on preparing kosher food before we arrived, explaining the requirement of new pots and pans, supplying a list of kosher caterers, and assuring them that if the process was too cumbersome, we would be perfectly satisfied to eat fresh fruit. As we took our places, the Foreign Minister proudly announced through an interpreter, "Food is kosher!"

A team of waiters in starched white uniforms filed into the room, each balancing a floral soup tureen. With choreographed precision, they placed the tureens on the tables and lifted the lids, releasing poofs of steam that curled their way to the ceiling. An earthy smell filled the hall. I peeked into the broth to find cylinders of unidentifiable meat floating near the surface. Through the interpreter, the Foreign Minister declared, "Snake soup. Chinese delicacy. Symbol of wealth, bravery, and respect." I politely declined the soup, as did the rest of our mission, including those who did not usually keep kosher, but became instant members of the kosher club.

Confused but eager to please, the Foreign Minister clapped his hands, signaling the waiters to offer the next course, which, he assured me, had been specially prepared in new pots. I had the unfortunate task of having to inform him that it was not only the pots that mattered, but also the ingredients placed inside them.

After declining course after course, I spotted a waiter across the room bearing a large wooden bowl of tangerines. I quickly motioned to him to bring it over, and excitedly informed the foreign Minister, "Fruit is kosher!" The Foreign Minister clapped his hands once again, and conveyed abrupt instructions to the waiters, who, obediently delivered bowls of tangerines to every table. We could finally break our fast.

Our base of operations in Beijing was the luxurious, seven hundred-room China World Hotel. Out of respect to our mission and its dietary needs, our hosts insisted that we occupy an entire convention floor. We relished the expansive living quarters, wandered the hallways and meeting rooms of the cavernous China World Trade Center, and peered out at a dense flow of bicyclists peddling through the shadows of massive office buildings.

We began the next morning with a prayer service in the corner of a vast red-carpeted meeting room. I nonchalantly pulled a floral loveseat toward me to rest my open prayer book on its back cushion. From that day on, when we entered the meeting room each morning, we found thirty loveseats arranged in a precise rectangular grid. Our hosts apparently were keeping their eyes on us, and had gotten the impression that upholstered chairs were a key element of Jewish religious practice.

Looking to recover from our jetlag, we visited the enormous hotel spa before beginning our busy week. Alan Dalfen, a member of our mission who worked in the fitness industry, had noticed when we arrived at the hotel that the Jacuzzis were set at a cool sixty degrees, and had asked the manager if they could be re-set to a much higher temperature, "the way Americans like them."

In broken English, the eager-to-please manager assured him, "Worker re-set Jacuzzi 2:00 a.m. When group come in morning, water feel like America."

The next morning, we were delighted to find the Jacuzzis bubbling at a steamy 103 degrees. We lowered ourselves into the hot pools, closed our eyes and exhaled deeply. A moment later, an excited group of Japanese tourists arrived at the spa and excitedly jumped in to adjacent Jacuzzis, let out terrifying shrieks, and climbed out at lightning speed, threatening to sue the China World Hotel for second degree burns.

Over the course of the next week, we met with city officials and visited historic sights. We walked across vast Tiananmen Square, mindful that two years earlier, hundreds if not thousands of civilians were massacred there for participating in student-led pro-democracy demonstrations.

We meandered through the halls and courts of the Forbidden City, the home of Chinese emperors for almost five hundred years, which had become galleries for the innumerable paintings and objects in the imperial collection. We were probably among the only tourists ever to conduct an afternoon *mincha* prayer service at the most famous stretch of the Great Wall near Zhangjiakou.

By the time our week in China had come to an end, we had made important connections for the future, including with state officials who would eventually screen our film to millions of Chinese television viewers. The mission provided us with a glimpse of a vast country that would soon become a superpower. As my dear friends David and Fela Shapell reminded me many times after that unforgettable trip, "Our visit to China was the most exciting trip of our lives. We felt like we were present at the birth of a new world power."

In the early 1990s, the Middle East was in transition. In 1993, Israel and the Palestinian Liberation Organization signed the Oslo Accords, which gave the Palestinians the right to govern parts of the West Bank and the Gaza Strip. In 1994, the Israel-Jordan Peace Treaty was signed, making Jordan the second Arab country to normalize relations with Israel. A period of optimism ensued, and another trip to Amman seemed appropriate.

In February 1995, the Simon Wiesenthal Center organized a second mission to meet with King Hussein. This time, we formed a larger delegation of thirty rabbis, Holocaust survivors, and community leaders. Given our gastronomic experience in China, we made sure our Jordanian hosts imported kosher food from Israel.

We arrived at the Allenby Bridge by bus from Jerusalem, and crossed the Jordan River. A convoy of grey Mercedes limousines with royal insignias instead of license plates, appeared like a mirage in the treeless, desert landscape. Black-suited chauffeurs, silhouetted by the fiery afternoon sun, briskly loaded our luggage. We arrived promptly at the plush InterContinental Hotel in Amman's diplomatic district, where butlers were waiting to unpack our suitcases. "You are a guest of His Majesty, the King," my butler said, bowing his head. "You should not spend your time unpacking."

The next day, we met with King Hussein, General Shukri, and other army generals and senior members of the government, who updated us on political developments in the region. The King introduced us to his wife, the American-born, Princeton educated, Queen Noor, and his younger brother, Prince Hassan, who was the King's intended heir. Crown Prince Hassan would maintain cordial relations with many Jewish leaders in the years to come, and would become a friend and frequent guest of ours in Los Angeles.

To experience more of the country on this trip, we visited the ancient city of Jerash, nestled in a quiet valley thirty miles north of Amman. A Jordanian tour guide led us through the site's impressive Greco-Roman colonnaded streets, hilltop temples, theaters, plazas, and baths. The group advanced from ruin to ruin, fascinated by the site's multi-layered history.

With everyone's attention focused on Hadrian's arch, I snuck away to a makeshift market, where local vendors were arranging their wares on rickety wooden tables. Silver amulets and brass tea sets shone in the midday sun. A sinewy young man dusting off Middle Eastern drums agreed to swap his shirt for mine, and a mustached gentleman inhaling tobacco vapors through a glass-bottomed waterpipe consented to lend me his *kufiya*. I donned my disguise and situated myself behind a table arrayed with colorful beaded necklaces.

Not yet aware of my absence, the members of our group completed their archeological tour and made their way to the market. They scoured the stalls under broad-brimmed hats in search of the object of every Jew's deepest desire: a bargain.

"Two hundred dinar for these beautiful beads," one peddler shouted. "One hundred dinar for these!" shouted another.

"Fifty dinar!" I added to the mix.

The members of our group scurried to my table, despite their earlier pronouncements that the trip would be a learning experience, not a shopping expedition. Esther Liberman admired a long string of amber beads. Her husband, Jose, asked me, "Are these, here, fifty dinar?"

"Yes. Fifty dinar," I agreed.

"I'll give you forty," he said, in a solid attempt at Middle East negotiation.

"No," I said. "Sixty dinar!"

"What? The price has gone up?"

"Eighty dinar now," I announced.

"You are no businessman," Jose fumed, walking away. "Instead of making a sale, you're losing a customer."

Unable to contain myself any longer, I unwound my *kufiya* and yelled in Yiddish, "*Kum tzurick!*" (Come back!) As Jose turned white, I revealed my identity and quipped, "Jose, you have proven my theory: No Jew can resist a bargain—even in Jerash, Jordan!"

We ended our mission at the country's most-visited tourist site, the ancient Nabatean city of Petra, on the eastern flank of the Arava Valley, between the Dead Sea and the Gulf of Aqaba. We approached the site through a narrow gorge from the east. When we emerged from the darkness, we were astonished by what stood before us: the famous Al Khazneh "Treasury" building, an elaborate temple hewn into a rose-colored sandstone cliff.

We hiked to an amphitheater cut into the hillside and enclosed on three sides by mountain walls. Inspired by the theatrical setting, I decided a little shtick was in order. I approached a group of Arab teenagers and offered them ten dollars if they would speak to our group in Yiddish. I taught them the phrase, "*Vos macht a Yid?*" (So, how are the Jews?), which they sang as a chorus to the members of our group, who were so stunned and amused they thought the Messiah had arrived.

When we arrived back at our hotel in Amman, the butlers had already packed our suitcases. The king's limousines were at our disposal once again, and the chauffeurs drove us in royal style to the Allenby Bridge. We thanked them for their excellent service, and marched across the span.

Hours later, after arriving at Jerusalem's King David Hotel, I realized that the suit I had bought especially for the visit to Jordan was missing. I called Amman's InterContinental Hotel, where the manager promised me that the staff of his hotel was completely trustworthy, "I assure you the butlers of the InterContinental Hotel would not steal from a guest of His Majesty, the King." He suggested that the theft had occurred at the Allenby Bridge or in the King David Hotel. But since our suitcases never left our sight on the bridge and had been promptly delivered to our rooms at the King David, I could only surmise that a Jordanian house butler or hotel attendant was now walking the streets of Amman in an American rabbi's new blue suit and striped tie.

The friendship I developed with King Hussein beginning in 1987 would last twelve years, until his death in 1999. In addition to our two meetings in Amman, we would meet on four future occasions in the United States. On one of those occasions, a 1998 Simon Wiesenthal Center dinner in New York, chaired by Nelson and Claudia Peltz, the King was our guest of honor, and the recipient of the Center's Humanitarian Award before a large distinguished audience of politicians and businessmen. He cited the King's accomplishments as a uniquely effective leader who modernized his country as he pursued the paths of moderation and peace in the turbulent Middle East.

Unfortunately, the Middle East that King Hussein left behind was anything but moderate or peaceful. By the turn of the new millennium, Islamic fundamentalism had spread throughout the region and the world. Radical Islamist terrorism was taking its toll in Israel, Europe, and the Arab world.

In November 2004, King Abdullah II, who ascended the throne after the death of his father, King Hussein, continued his father's legacy by delivering a bold theological counter-attack on radical Islam known as the Amman Initiative. In it, he took an uncompromising stand against extremist interpretations of Islam, and reasserted moderate Islamic principles for guiding inter-Muslim and inter-faith relations.

The Simon Wiesenthal Center honored King Abdullah II for his courage in offering the Amman Initiative by presenting him with the Simon Wiesenthal Center Tolerance Award in June 2005. Rabbi Cooper, Rabbi May, and I led a group of forty-five participants to Amman for the presentation ceremony.

We gathered in the Throne Hall of Raghadan Palace, an oval chamber in which the reigning monarch performs official ceremonial duties. In this room in March 1956, King Hussein had dismissed the British commander of the Arab Legion to bring Jordan under full Arab authority. We fixed our eyes on a polished desk flanked by the flags of Jordan and the Hashemite Kingdom, and awaited the King's entry.

Suddenly, a commotion erupted at the back of the room. We were told that television crews setting up cameras to film the presentation ceremony were angered by a last minute press embargo requiring them to leave. A senior official explained, "You know we also have our security concerns. When a major Jewish organization gives an award to the King, His Majesty's security forces must carefully consider whether airing the event on television might wake up extremist elements within the Muslim Brotherhood and endanger his security."

When the tumult died down, King Abdullah entered the room, took his place behind the desk, and motioned for me to begin:

> Today we are pleased to again return to Jordan for the purpose of conferring upon you, Your Majesty, the Simon Wiesenthal Center's 2005 Tolerance Award, presented in recognition of your courage in opposition to the forces of evil, the disciples of terrorism and suicide attacks, fanaticism and anti-Semitism, who are the enemies of mankind...
>
> In acting as a force for moderation at such a critical time in human history, you have taken to heart the painful legacy that the twentieth century, with its wars, genocides, and the Holocaust, has imparted to us, that:

Nothing enduring was ever created by hate.
No future was ever made brighter by tyranny,
No faith was ever strengthened by fanaticism.

As Albert Einstein cautioned, "The world is a dangerous place. Not because of the people who are evil; but because of the people who don't do anything about it."

A few months later, in September 2005, when King Abdullah learned of Simon Wiesenthal's death, he wrote me a beautiful, hand-written letter:

My Dear Friend:

Her Majesty Queen Rania and I learned with regret of Mr. Simon Wiesenthal's passing, and wanted to write to you to convey our sincere condolences, and to say how deeply sorry we were at hearing the news.

As you well know, my family's association with Simon Wiesenthal has been long standing. In June of this year, I was honoured to receive the Simon Wiesenthal Center's Tolerance Award—the silver shofar, which symbolizes hope for universal peace; and, I will remember how my father, His Late Majesty King Hussein, recounted how he was deeply moved during his visit to the Center in Los Angeles in 1995.

Simon Wiesenthal will always be remembered as a special man; one who sought to bring justice to some of the most horrific crimes of our times; a man who called for tolerance and understanding, and who will certainly be remembered by all.

Kindly convey Her Majesty Queen Rania's and my deep sympathies to Mr. Wiesenthal's daughter and her family. We hope and pray that God will give you all the strength to accept his will.

Yours Always,
Abdullah

Several months later, Nelson Peltz invited Rabbi Cooper, Rabbi May, and me to join him on a trip to the United Arab Emirates. On our way, we stopped in London for an introductory lunch with Sheikh Mohammed bin Rashid Al Maktoum, Vice President and Prime Minister of the Emirates, and the constitutional monarch of Dubai, the country's most populous emirate and city. After giving us a tour of his opulent house and grounds, Sheikh Mohammed escorted us into a formal dining room. A plump man in a white lab coat, who I assumed was present to attend to a medical need, awaited our arrival. But Sheikh Mohammed soon corrected my mistaken impression: "Rabbi Hier. We have consulted with the Office of the Chief Rabbi to ensure that your meal in my home is kosher." The Sheikh had hired a *mashgiach*.

The next surprise came when Sheikh Mohammed introduced us to his second wife, Princess Haya bint Al Hussein, the daughter of King Hussein of Jordan. The princess told us that she remembered visiting the Museum of Tolerance in Los Angeles as a teenager, when her father delivered a speech there. "I remember the visit well," she said. "It made a deep impression on His Majesty."

In Dubai, we met with savvy political leaders and businessmen with whom we discovered political affinities. We shared concerns over a recent swell in international terrorist incidents, and the threat of a nuclear Iran. They explained that the Emerati people feel vulnerable, because they are on the front lines, with Iran a mere two hundred miles northeast on the eastern rim of the Persian Gulf.

We were wowed by Mohamed Alabbar, a global entrepreneur, top advisor to Sheikh Mohammed and Founder and Chairman of Emaar Properties, one of the largest real estate development companies in the Middle East, which developed the Burj Khalifa, the tallest building in the world, and the Dubai Mall, the world's largest shopping mall. Mohamed was a key player in the transformation of Dubai from a sandy Bedouin outpost to a regional financial hub and international tourist hotspot. He was a young, dynamic visionary who articulated his belief that Arabs and Jews must learn to end their conflict and live together in peace.

At the presidential palace in the capital, Abu Dahbi, Crown Prince Sheikh Khalifa voiced his opposition to Iran acquiring nuclear weapons. When our meeting concluded, and we were running late, he lent us his private helicopter so we would arrive at Dubai International Airport on time for our flight home.

Our mission to the United Arab Emirates introduced us to a progressive piece of the Arab world. Our hosts were hospitable and respectful, free of the rancor of the Middle East. My son, Avi, who had become Director of the Simon Wiesenthal Center's Leadership Missions, developed a close relationship with Mohamed Alabbar. Over the next five years, Avi organized three additional missions to Dubai. Each time, Mohamed hosted us in the exquisite Armani Hotel Dubai.

On each mission, Jewish community leaders from the US, Canada, and other parts of the world were amazed by the extraordinary hospitality. Hotel staff held up signs in the lobby directing us to daily *minyans*. The Armani's Executive Chef worked hand-in-hand with a kosher caterer from Beverly Hills' La Gondola Restaurant we brought with us from Los Angeles to prepare the hotel kitchen to receive kosher food that was flown in from London and New York. Those who regularly wore yarmulkas, did so freely.

Once, when Avi arrived a day early to prepare for a mission and an airport attendant warned him to remove his yarmulka as a security precaution, the ruler of Dubai himself rectified the situation. That evening, Mohamed Alabbar called Avi with the message that His Highness Sheikh Mohammed was very sorry for the incident and wanted Avi to feel at ease wearing his yarmulka. The next day, Sheikh Mohammed personally apologized.

On our most recent Dubai mission in March 2014, we took a magnificent luncheon cruise. As our sleek yacht smoothed out of the harbor past clusters of fantastic skyscrapers and wound through an astonishing collection of artificial islands in the shape of a mega palm tree, I thought I heard a familiar tune. Sure enough, a band brought on board by our Arab hosts was playing Chassidic melodies. We formed a circle and danced as the yacht skimmed the waters of the oil-rich Persian Gulf.

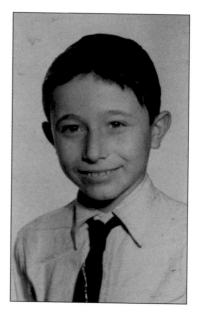

On New York's Lower East Side

As a student at the Rabbi Shlomo Kluger Yeshiva

Rabbi Aharon Kotler speaking in the *beis midrash* of the Rabbi Jacob Joseph Yeshiva

At the Catskill's West End Country Club

In the *chasen's* (groom's) room at my wedding; seated, left to right: Rav Mendel Kravitz, me, and Rav Shmuel Dovid Warshavchik; standing: Malkie's father, Harry Levine, and my father, Jack Hier

The *chasen's tish* (groom's reception); seated, left to right: Rav Yitzchok Tendler, Rav Yankele Flantzgraben, Rav Hersh Ginzberg, Rav Mendel Kravitz, and me; standing: Rav Yehuda Kurnzer and our parents, Jack and Rose Hier, and Harry and Hanna Levine

My parents escorting me down the aisle

The married couple

On the bimah of Congregation Schara Tzedeck, Vancouver

Dedicating a new Torah with the Siegel family; Abrasha Wosk is fourth from the right

Kelly Cohen enjoying kiddush

Teaching teens in Vancouver

Speaking at a Schara Tzedeck NCSY event; Reb Velvel Schuster and Reverend Bernard Leibowitz are to my left

Beis medrash at Yeshiva University of Los Angeles

First meeting with Simon Wiesenthal (center) and Roland Arnall (right) at Mr. Wiesenthal's Vienna office

Dancing with Simon Wiesenthal (left), California Governor Jerry Brown (center) and Los Angeles Mayor Tom Bradley (right) at a Wiesenthal Center National Tribute Dinner at Los Angeles' Bonaventure Hotel

With Simon Wiesenthal (center) and Senator Ted Kennedy (left) when the senator received the Wiesenthal Center's Humanitarian Award at New York's Waldorf Astoria Hotel

Celebrating Simon Wiesenthal's 90th birthday at Vienna's Imperial Hotel

With President Bill Clinton and First Lady Hillary Rodham Clinton at the ceremony honoring
Simon Wiesenthal with the Presidential Medal of Freedom

My son Ari serving as a tank driver in the Israel Defense Forces

Rabbi Meyer May (left), Rabbi Abraham Cooper (center) and I meeting with Israeli Prime Minister Yitzhak Rabin

Israeli Foreign Minister Shimon Peres with Gordon Diamond in Jerusalem

Israeli Foreign Minister Shimon Peres with Leslie Diamond in Jerusalem

Sasson Tiram.

With Israeli President Shimon Peres and Nelson Peltz in Jerusalem

With Chinese Foreign Minister Qian Qichen in Beijing

Pretending to be a peddler in Jerash, Jordan

Greeting Jordan's King Hussein at a Wiesenthal Center Tribute Dinner in his honor in New York

A Wiesenthal Center delegation meeting with French President François Hollande at the Élysée Palace. Joining me were: Eric de Rothschild, Rabbi Abraham Cooper, Rabbi Meyer May, Avi Benlolo, Irwin Cotler, Dr. Shimon and Graciela Samuels, Rivka and Raphy Nissel and Graham Morris

Wiesenthal Center delegation attending an event at Lord Jacob Rothschild's London home; front row, left to right: Syd Belzberg, Joanne Belzberg, Stacy Widelitz, Dawn Arnall, Lord Jacob Rothschild, me, Laura Huberfeld, Murray Huberfeld, Avi Hier and Jorge Rosenblut; middle row: Malkie Hier, Lee Samson, Anne Samson, Rabbi Meyer May, Margaret Nichols, George Feldenkreis and Rick Trank; back row: Annette Blum, Gloria Brandes, Janice Prager, Rabbi Abraham Cooper and Alan Stern

170

Wiesenthal Center Leadership Mission to Poland participants at the entrance to Auschwitz; left to right: Larry Mizel, Cheston Mizel, Rabbi Abraham Cooper, Leslie Diamond, Avi Hier, Annie Hier, Murray Laulicht, Linda Laulicht, Ron Abrams, me, Malkie Hier, Raphael Nissel, Herb Baum, Timothy Brodlieb, Karen Baum, Janice Prager, Rabbi Meyer May, Suri Stern, Ken Brodlieb, Joe Stern, Efraim Zuroff, Gordon Diamond, Shereen Pollak, Michael Pollak, Linda Levy and Herb Buchwald

With German Chancellor Angela Merkel and Los Angeles Mayor Antonio Villaraigosa at Los Angeles' Getty Center

171

With Malkie and Canadian Prime Minister Stephen Harper at a Canadian Friends of the
Simon Wiesenthal Center event in Toronto

With Jordan's King Abdullah II in Amman

At the London home of the Ruler of Dubai, Sheikh Mohammed bin Rashid Al Maktoum;
left to right: Nelson Peltz, Sheikh Mohammed, me and Princess Haya bint Al Hussein

With UNESCO's Director-General Irina Bokova at the Museum of Tolerance in Los Angeles

173

Meeting with the Secretary General during the Gaza War; left to right: Mark Weitzman, me, Secretary-General Ban Ki-Moon, Rabbi Abraham Cooper and Rabbi Meyer May

Presenting a Medal of Valor to Lassana Bathily, a Muslim clerk who saved many lives in the terrorist attack at the Hyper Cacher kosher supermarket in Paris

With former UK Prime Minister and Middle East Envoy for the UN, the European Union, the US and Russia, Tony Blair

Meeting with President Barack Obama with the leaders of major Jewish
organizations at the White House

Chapter Seven

Vatican Visits

I n April 1983, I stood, captivated, as a mid-sized figure with thinning white hair and deeply set eyes entered the stately Hall of the Popes in the Vatican's Apostolic Palace. He smiled broadly, locked eyes with me momentarily, and glided past in a shimmering white silk cassock.

He was Pope John Paul II, the venerated leader of the world's 700 million Catholics. A poet, theologian, and philosopher, he had been elected five years earlier as the first non-Italian pope in more than 450 years. Like all popes, he was, according to Christian tradition, the successor to Saint Peter, the rock upon which the Church was built, and the keeper of the keys to heaven.

We had come to the Vatican for a private audience with Pope John Paul II following a Simon Wiesenthal Center mission to mark the fortieth anniversary of the Warsaw ghetto uprising. We had walked the cobblestone streets of Warsaw and passed through the infamous entrance gate at Auschwitz. Now we stood before the former Polish cardinal, eager to hear his thoughts on the future of Jewish-Christian relations.

We believed this was precisely the moment to attempt to forge a relationship with the Vatican. We knew that Pope John Paul II was open to interfaith dialogue more than any pope who had preceded him. We knew that as a personal witness to Jewish suffering under the Nazis, he would be sympathetic to Holocaust survivors bound together by the name Simon Wiesenthal.

As a guest of the Pope, I was invited to make opening remarks. Pope John Paul slowly extended his arm, signaling me to begin:

> The Simon Wiesenthal Center delegation has come here today directly from Krakow, Auschwitz, and Warsaw, where we walked the streets of what once was the most vital Jewish community in the world.... Streets once full of students and scholars, philosophers, and peddlers. Streets where the voices of children could be heard everywhere. But they are all gone now, taken in broad daylight to the crematoria by fellow human beings.
>
> Among us here today are those who were themselves victims, who saw their fathers and mothers, their brothers and sisters, offered up on the altar of hatred and fanaticism... murdered by others, most of them believers, who frequently invoked the name of their God....
>
> We come here today hoping to hear from you, the beloved spiritual leader of seven hundred million Christians, a clear and unequivocal message to all that this scourge in all its manifestations violates the basic creed to which all men of faith must aspire.

The Pope redirected his gaze toward the audience, and spoke in English, one of the more than ten languages in which he was fluent:

> I am very pleased to welcome you to the Vatican today, and in this way to further the continuing religious dialogue between Judaism and the Catholic Church. Such meetings as ours deepen bonds of friendship and trust, and help us to appreciate more fully the richness of our common heritage.... I am happy

that your itinerary included a visit to Poland to commemorate the fortieth anniversary of the Warsaw Ghetto Uprising. Just recently, speaking of that horrible and tragic event of history, I said it was a desperate cry for the right of life, for liberty, and for the salvation of human dignity...

Pope John Paul descended the stairs of his throne and approached us. He spoke with each member of our delegation, taking extra time with Holocaust survivors, David and Rosa Orzen, to whom he spoke in his native Polish. At once, he conveyed worldliness and transcendence.

Moved by his words of reconciliation, Ira Lipman, a Simon Wiesenthal Center trustee, spoke for all of us when he said, "Your Holiness. If you continue this approach of befriending and reaching out to the Jewish people, you will surely become one of the greatest popes in history."

Pope John Paul II, born Karol Jozef Wojtyla, brought a new perspective on interfaith relations to the Church, in part, because he had grown up among Jews. He was born in 1920, thirty miles southwest of Krakow in Wadowice, Poland, a town of ten thousand Catholics and two thousand Jews; some of his closest friends where Jewish. Throughout his childhood, he shared meals and celebrated religious festivals with Jewish neighbors. He would long remember the deep impression a *Kol Nidrei* service he had attended as a youth in the Wadowice Synagogue had made upon him.

Wojtyla was a compassionate young man, troubled by the anti-Semitism that enveloped his world. He was one of a small few who accompanied Ginka Beer, a Jewish friend, to a train station when she left the University of Krakow Medical School for Palestine in 1935. He would later recall how he stood overcome with emotion, unable to speak, as she boarded the train.

Wojtyla did not know at the time that Beer would be one of the fortunate Jews of Wadowice. Her mother and many of the future pope's friends and their families would fall victim to the Nazi occupation of Poland that began in September 1939. Most would be murdered at Auschwitz, where years earlier, Wojtyla's closest friend, Jerzy Kluger, had taken him to play at his uncle's distillery.

Wojtyla faced his own dangers from the Nazi occupation. When the Gestapo rounded up more than eight thousand men and boys in an attempt to quell an uprising in Krakow on "Black Sunday," August 6, 1944, he hid in the basement of his uncle's house, then escaped to the Archbishop's Palace.

As a result of these experiences, Wojtyla developed a profound empathy for Jews. He showed signs of respect even as a young priest, when he refused to baptize Stanley Berger, a Polish-Jewish boy who had been sent by his parents to hide in the home of a Polish-Christian family during the war. The future pope claimed that the child should be raised in the faith of his birth parents, not as a Catholic.

Wojtyla's perspective was radically different from that of the Church of his youth. During Wojtyla's formative years, Pope Pius XII, formerly Cardinal Eugenio Pacelli, headed the Church through the lowest period in its long and turbulent history with the Jewish people. Despite being one of the world leaders best informed of Nazi atrocities, the cautious pontiff issued ambiguous encyclicals, provided minimal diplomatic aid, and insisted on Vatican neutrality.

While serving for more than twenty years as the Vatican's diplomatic representative to Germany before becoming pope, Pacelli had formed a distinctly prejudiced opinion of Jews, as he described in a personal letter:

> In the midst of all this, a gang of young women of dubious appearance, Jews like all the rest of them, [were] hanging around in all the offices with lecherous demeanor and suggestive smiles. The boss of this female rabble was Levian's mistress, a young Russian woman, a Jew and a divorcee, who was in charge.... This Levian is a young man of about thirty or thirty-five, also Russian and a Jew. Pale, dirty, with drugged eyes, hoarse voice, vulgar, repulsive, with a face that is both intelligent and sly.

As pope, Pius xii failed to aid the Nazis' helpless victims. He refrained from protesting the deportation of Jews from Germany, France, and the Scandinavian countries. He did not intervene when the Nazis began their "euthanasia" program to murder the mentally and physically disabled. In June 1941, when informed that Hitler had double-crossed Stalin and attacked the Soviet Union, Pius xii rushed to his private chapel to say novena prayers for the swift victory of the Führer and his armies.

Though Pope Pius xii sheltered some Jews in his summer residence in Castel Gadolfo, and in convents in Rome and other Italian cities, he did not intervene on October 18, 1943, when the Nazis raided the Jewish ghetto in Rome, forcing more than a thousand Jewish men, women and children out of their homes and into trucks—some just a few hundred yards from the Vatican's walls. The Jews prayed and called out to the Pope in desperation. Pius promised to do all he could to help, but after threatening to launch an official protest, rescinded his opposition, causing Nazi Germany's Ambassador to the Holy See, Baron Ernst von Weizacker, to cable Berlin:

> The Pope, although under pressure from all sides, has not permitted himself to be pushed into a demonstrative censure of the deportation of the Jews of Rome...he has...done everything possible even in this delicate matter in order not to strain relations with the German government and the German authorities in Rome...

When World War ii finally ended in May 1945, one-third of the world's eighteen million Jews had been murdered. Pope Pius xii never called into action the vast network of cardinals, bishops, and priests at his disposal throughout Christian Europe to intercede. He never condemned the Nazis or protested the deportation and murder of Europe's Jews. He never expressed—even in a private letter or secret dispatch—shock or disapproval of Nazi atrocities.

Defenders of Pope Pius xii claim that his passivity resulted from his commitment to the preservation of the Church, and fear that public protest would intensify the Nazi's oppressive actions. But in the midst of the Holocaust, the Church showed no fear in expressing forceful opposition to the establishment of a Jewish state in Palestine. In a letter to President Franklin Roosevelt dated June 22, 1943, the Apostolic Delegate to Washington, DC, Amleto Giovanni Cicognani, bluntly voiced the Church's objections:

> Catholics the world over are piously devoted to this country, hallowed as it was by the presence of the Redeemer and esteemed as it is as the cradle of Christianity. If the greater part of Palestine is given to the Jewish people, this would be a severe blow to the religious attachment of Catholics to this land. To have the Jewish people in the majority would be to interfere with the peaceful exercise of these rights in the Holy Land already vested in Catholics.
>
> It is true that at one time Palestine was inhabited by the Hebrew Race, but there is no axiom in history to substantiate the necessity of a people returning to a country they left nineteen centuries before.
>
> If a "Hebrew Home" is desired, it would not be too difficult to find a more fitting territory than Palestine.

The Vatican's response to the Holocaust might have been entirely different had Pope Pius XII's predecessor, Pope Pius XI, lived a few years longer. The more aggressive and outspoken Pius XI objected to Mussolini and Hitler's manipulations, and sought a vehicle for protest, despite his anti-Semitic leanings. Pope Pius XI found that vehicle in John LaFarge, an American Jesuit priest, whose book, *The Race Question and the Negro,* had captured his imagination. After meeting LaFarge at a general audience, the Pope bypassed his senior advisors and LaFarge's superiors to ask him to draft an encyclical against racism and anti-Semitism. Pius XI requested that LaFarge's document be "a bulwark against the madness" that was spreading throughout Europe. He told LaFarge, "Write it as if you were the Pope," and swore him to secrecy.

LaFarge completed a one-hundred page draft of the *Humani Generis Unitas* (*On the Unity of the Human Race*) in late September 1938, just as Germany, the UK, France and Italy appeased Hitler by signing the Munich Pact.

Members of the Vatican hierarchy opposed to the encyclical's message and angered by the Pope's disregard of protocol, delayed delivering the document to the Pope until January 21, 1939. Three weeks later, on February 10, 1939, Pius XI died of a heart attack. According to Cardinal Eugène Tisserant, a prominent French cardinal, the encyclical was on the Pope's desk at the time of his death.

Pope Pius XI's successor, Pope Pius XII, never released the document in his nearly twenty-year papacy. The "Lost Encyclical" remained a secret until 1972, when the *National Catholic Reporter* discovered it among LaFarge's papers, which had been bequeathed to them after his death in 1963. In 1995, the document was first published in French, and in 1997, in English.

Although the draft encyclical contained anti-Jewish sentiment and criticized Jews for not acknowledging Jesus Christ as the true messiah, it emphatically condemned racism and anti-Semitism:

It is further increased when it becomes clear that the struggle for racial purity ends by being uniquely the struggle against the Jews. Save for its systematic cruelty, this struggle is no different in true motives and methods from persecutions everywhere carried out against the Jews since antiquity. These persecutions have been censured by the Holy See on more than one occasion, but especially when they have worn the mantle of Christianity.

As a result of such persecution, millions of persons are deprived of the most elementary rights and privileges against violence and robbery, exposed to every form of insult and public degradation, innocent persons are treated as criminals though they have scrupulously obeyed the law of their native land. Even those who in time of war fought bravely for their country are treated as traitors, and the children of those who laid down their lives in their country's behalf are branded as outlaws by the very fact of their parentage...

> In the case of the Jews, this flagrant denial of human rights sends many thousands of helpless persons out over the face of the earth without any resources. Wandering from frontier to frontier, they are a burden to humanity and to themselves.

Had Pope Pius XI been able to disseminate the "Lost Encyclical" in 1939, he could have prompted the development of a widespread Christian opposition movement to hinder Hitler's plans. Instead, the Church remained quiet on the issue of anti-Semitism, and silent as six million Jews were murdered.

A shift in Church thinking about interfaith relations did not occur until the death of Pope Pius XII, and the ascendancy of Cardinal Angelo Giuseppe Roncalli as Pope John XXIII in 1958. His concern for the Jewish people was clear from his actions as nuncio (Vatican representative) to Turkey, Greece, Bulgaria and France during the Holocaust. In 1944, Roncalli participated in "Operation Baptism," which saved the lives of thousands of Hungarian Jews by issuing them baptismal certificates, immigration certificates and visas. After being denied Vatican support, he turned to Boris III of Bulgaria and the Red Cross to help save the lives of thousands of Slovakian Jews who had been deported to Bulgaria. After the war, he reportedly ignored a Vatican directive that called for baptized Jewish orphans to remain with Christian families rather than to return to their families of origin or to Jewish communities.

Pope John XXIII changed Catholic liturgy to reflect his enlightened attitude toward the Jewish people. In the prayer for the conversion of the Jews, he removed the Latin *perfidis* (faithless). And in 1959, just three months after becoming Pope, he made the bold decision to convene the Second Vatican Council, also known as Vatican II, to address relations between the Church and the modern world. It was "time to open the windows of the Church to let in some fresh air," he said.

Pope John XXIII called for the drafting of a declaration on the Church's relationship to the Jewish people that was the genesis of the *Nostra Aetate* (*In Our Age*) declaration, a document presented at Vatican II after John XXIII's death that represented a monumental shift in perspective toward the Jews in Roman Catholic thought. On anti-Semitism, the document declared: "The Church, mindful of the patrimony she shares with the Jews, and moved not by political reasons, but by the gospels' spiritual love, decries hatred, persecutions, [and] displays of anti-Semitism directed against Jews at any time and by anyone."

The declaration passed by a vote of 2,221 to 88 at Vatican II, and was promulgated on October 28, 1965 by John XXIII's successor, Pope Paul VI. *Nostra Aetate* paved the way for a greater openness in the relationship between the Church and the larger religious world.

But no one advanced the cause of interfaith reconciliation more than Pope John Paul II. In 1979, just one year into his papacy, John Paul II made a historic visit to Auschwitz, where he prayed for his childhood friends who had been killed by the Nazis. As he stood opposite inscriptions bearing the names of the countries whose citizens had been murdered, he stated:

> I kneel before all the inscriptions bearing the memory of the victims in their languages.... In particular, I pause...before the inscription in Hebrew. This inscription awakens the memory of the people whose sons and daughters were intended for total extermination.... It is not permissible for anyone to pass by this inscription with indifference....

In 1986, three years after our Vatican meeting, John Paul II became the first pope to make an official papal visit to a synagogue. At the Great Synagogue of Rome, he embraced Rome's Chief Rabbi, Elio Toaff, and described Jews as the "elder brothers" of Christians.

Pope John Paul II also altered the course of Church history when, in 1994, he became the first pope to establish formal diplomatic relations between the Holy See, the Vatican's ecclesiastical jurisdiction, and the State of Israel. The Vatican appointed an apostolic nuncio to

Israel and Israel appointed an ambassador to the Vatican, normalizing a relationship that had been anything but normal. By establishing diplomatic ties, the Pope acknowledged Israel's significance to the Jewish people; it was a defining moment in Catholic-Jewish relations.

Pope John Paul II followed up this critical development with a visit to Israel in March 2000 as part of the Second Millennium celebrations. The contrasts between his trip and that of Pope Paul VI, who, in 1964, had made the first papal visit to the Holy Land in two thousand years, were striking.

In 1964, Pope Paul toured Christian sites in East Jerusalem, which was then under Jordanian control, but declined to enter West Jerusalem and to visit Judaism's holiest site, the Western Wall. Israeli dignitaries, including Prime Minister Levi Eshkol and President Zalman Shazar, were forced to greet him in Meggido, the Greek Armageddon eighty miles north of the capital. During the visit, he never once uttered the words "Jew" or "Israel." When, upon his return to Rome, he sent a thank you letter to President Shazar, he omitted Shazar's title, and addressed the letter to Tel Aviv rather than to the president's official residence in Jerusalem.

In 2000, Pope John Paul II visited Israel's capital, Jerusalem, where he met with religious and political Jewish leaders, including Ashkenazi Chief Rabbi Yisrael Meir Lau, Sephardi Chief Rabbi Eliyahu Bakshi-Doron, President Ezer Weizman, and Prime Minister Ehud Barak. When the Israeli national anthem, *"Hatikvah,"* was played, the Pope stood respectfully and saluted, bringing tears to many in the audience. He visited Yad Vashem, Israel's national Holocaust memorial, where in the presence of survivors of Hitler's death camps, he said:

> We wish to remember for a purpose, to ensure that never again will evil prevail as it did for the millions of innocent victims of Nazism. As the Bishop of Rome and successor of the Apostle Peter, I assure the Jewish people that the Catholic Church... is deeply saddened by the hatred, acts of persecution, and displays of anti-Semitism directed against the Jews by Christians at any time and in any place.

He added that there were "no words strong enough to deplore the terrible tragedy of the Holocaust."

The Pope made history by visiting the Western Wall, where he placed a note in a crevice of an ancient stone asking for forgiveness. "God of our fathers," it said, "You chose Abraham and his descendants to bring Your name to the nations. We are deeply saddened by the behavior of those who, in the course of history, have caused these children of Yours to suffer, and asking Your forgiveness we wish to commit ourselves to genuine brotherhood with the people of the Covenant."

In 2003, three years after the Pope's historic visit to Israel, and twenty years after our first meeting, I returned to the Vatican with a small delegation of Simon Wiesenthal Center trustees for a second private audience. This time, our purpose was to present Pope John Paul II with the Wiesenthal Center's highest honor, our Humanitarian Award.

We were invited into the Pope's private library. Antique bookcases lined sienna walls. A great Persian rug stretched down the length of the room and led our eyes to the slouching figure of Pope John Paul II, aged and ill. A massive oil painting depicting Christ's ascension to heaven dominated the wall behind him, and sadly juxtaposed the Pope's surrender to gravity.

Despite his poor condition, the Pope welcomed us back to the Vatican: "I would like to hear directly from you whether my efforts at Catholic-Jewish reconciliation have made a difference," he said in a frail voice. I told the Pope that we had come to honor him on the twenty-fifth year of his papacy, because his efforts had indeed made a difference. I reviewed his achievements, including his many "firsts": first pope to visit Auschwitz, to institute a permanent Vatican Holocaust Remembrance Day, to visit a synagogue, to recognize Israel, to seek forgiveness for wrongdoing against the Jewish people. "For all of these milestones," I said, "We present you with our highest honor, our Humanitarian Award, symbolized by this silver menorah whose inscription reads: "Presented to His Holiness, Pope John Paul II, for his lifelong friendship with the Jewish people. December 1, 2003, 6th Kislev 5764."

Ira Lipman reminded the Pope that during the first Wiesenthal Center audience twenty years earlier, Ira had predicted that His Holiness would go down in history as one of the great popes if he continued to embark on a course of reconciliation. "You have done it," he told a smiling John Paul. "You have done it."

Before leaving, I showed Pope John Paul II a photograph of a site in Jerusalem we had recently acquired on which to build a Museum of Tolerance. The Pope rubbed his hands across the image, as if bestowing his blessing upon it.

We at the Simon Wiesenthal Center did not always agree with Pope John Paul II. We opposed his meeting with Austrian President Kurt Waldheim in 1987, his nomination of Pope Pius XII for sainthood in 1990, and his signing of a joint covenant with Yasser Arafat in 2000 that called for Jerusalem to be declared an international city. The Simon Wiesenthal Center was among his harshest critics when Pope John Paul II allowed Carmelite nuns to operate a convent in a converted Nazi storehouse building at Auschwitz.

Nonetheless, the accomplishments of Pope John Paul II in the realm of Jewish-Catholic relations were remarkable. He took a more benevolent, nuanced approach toward the Jewish people, and advocated more vehemently for Jewish-Catholic reconciliation than any pope before him. And he implemented concrete changes for the good that have had lasting effects.

The election of a new pope has always elicited enormous speculation. When the shoes to be filled were those of the exceptional John Paul II, who died in 2005, public interest ran especially high. But few were surprised when the white smoke blew from the Sistine Chapel's tiny chimney and the Cardinal Protodeacon announced from the central balcony of St. Peter's Basilica that the new pope would be Joseph Ratzinger, one of the Church's most prominent theologians and one of Pope John Paul II's closest confidants.

Joseph Ratzinger was born in Bavaria, Germany, into a family that bitterly opposed the Nazis. In 1941, Ratzinger was unwillingly conscripted into the Hitler Youth. In 1943, he was drafted into the German anti-aircraft corps responsible for protecting German industry from allied attacks. He trained in the German infantry, but deserted his post as the Allied front drew near. He was interned in a prisoner of war camp for several months before being released at the end of the war.

Given Ratzinger's German heritage and conservative views, some Jews were apprehensive about his election, and feared a reversal in the progress made by John Paul II. But Ratzinger, who took the name Pope Benedict XVI, quickly demonstrated his commitment to continuing the legacy of John Paul II. He included in his first official trip, a visit to Germany, a stop at the Cologne Synagogue to "reaffirm that I intend to continue with great vigor on the path towards improved relations and friendship with the Jewish people..." In his synagogue speech, Pope Benedict said:

> The Catholic Church is committed—and I affirm this again today—to tolerance, respect, friendship and peace between all peoples, cultures and religions, and...in the twentieth century, in the darkest period of German and European history, an insane racist ideology, born of neo-paganism, gave rise to the attempt, planned and systematically carried out by the regime, to exterminate European Jewry.... The terrible events of that time must never cease to rouse consciences, to resolve conflicts, to inspire the building of peace.

While he said relations had improved much in recent years, he added: "Much still remains to be done. We must come to know one another much more and much better."

I had the honor of coming to know him better when the Wiesenthal Center had a private audience with Pope Benedict XVI on November 14, 2005. Our forty-member delegation of staff, trustees, and friends met the Pope in the Apostolic Palace's Hall of the Popes, the very room in which we had first been introduced to Pope John Paul II. Pope Benedict XVI sat in an intricately carved chair, his red leather loafers peeking out beneath his white cassock.

In my speech, I highlighted the need to combat religious fanaticism:

> Your Holiness.... Today the greatest threat to mankind comes not from secularists and atheists, but from religious fanatics and zealots. Today those who help recruit and inspire terrorists to murder innocent civilians by promising them a place in heaven are not ungodly political leaders, but fundamentalist Immans and Mullahs who claim obedience to their creator.
>
> Today, the President of Iran, a religious man who prays five times a day, has re-enacted the words of Adolf Hitler and openly called for the obliteration of the State of Israel in violation of the United Nations Charter without any General Assembly condemnation—showing the determination of these fanatics and the failure of the civilized world to deal with them...

Pope Benedict responded by reaffirming the Church's commitment to interfaith dialogue: "After a difficult and painful history, relations between our two communities are presently taking a new, more positive, direction. We must continue to advance along the path of mutual respect and dialogue, inspired by our shared spiritual heritage...in the service of the human family."

The Pope spoke with each member of our group individually. Trustee Murray Huberfeld told the pontiff that his visit to the Vatican was particularly meaningful, because his parents, Pinchus and Rae Huberfeld, were Holocaust survivors and that his mother was saved by a Christian family who hid her during the war. I was relieved and pleased when Pope Benedict told me that he considered my call for a coalition of moderates "crucial to the future wellbeing of mankind."

Many in our group held out prayer beads they had bought for non-Jewish friends that they wanted the Pope to bless. There were so many, I was afraid the Pope would think we were all converting to Catholicism. But Pope Benedict was experienced and efficient: he asked one of his aides to gather the beads in a single bag, over which he recited a collective blessing.

We ended our visit with an official tour of the renowned Sistine Chapel. We craned our necks toward the barrel-vaulted ceiling as a guide explained Michelangelo's method of painting his iconic fresco, Creation of Adam. A half-hour later, on the bus leaving Rome, we realized we were missing Shimon Samuels. My phone rang: "Rabbi Hier. It's me, Shimon. I'm sorry I lost you! I was so taken by the Sistine Chapel, I lost track of time, and before I knew it, I was locked inside for noon mass!" We doubled back to the Vatican, and rescued our wandering Jew.

Pope Benedict XVI lacked his predecessor's vision and charisma, and, like the popes before him, made decisions the Wiesenthal Center opposed. We protested his support of Pius XII's canonization. We condemned his lifting the excommunication of Bishop Richard Williamson, a convicted Holocaust denier. We were appalled when he condemned terrorist attacks in Europe and Egypt, but failed to acknowledge attacks against Israel.

But Pope Benedict deserves praise for maintaining the strides made by the Church in the area of Jewish-Catholic relations since the Holocaust. During a trip to Israel, Pope Benedict assured the audience at Jerusalem's *Heichal Shlomo*, the seat of Israel's Chief Rabbinate, "Today I have the opportunity to repeat that the Catholic Church is irrevocably committed to the path chosen at the Second Vatican Council for a genuine and lasting reconciliation between Christians and Jews."

He recognized the significance of the Holocaust in Jewish consciousness, stating at Yad Vashem:

I have come to stand in silence.... To honor the memory of the millions of Jews killed in the horrific tragedy of the *Shoah*. They lost their lives, but they will never lose their names. May the names of these victims never perish! May their suffering never be denied, belittled or forgotten! And may people of goodwill remain vigilant in rooting out from the heart of man anything that could lead to tragedies like this!

Pope Benedict's most important contribution to the Jewish-Christian relationship was a book he published in 2011 on the life and teachings of Jesus Christ. In *Jesus of Nazareth: Holy Week*, the second volume in a three-volume series, the Pope placed blame for Jesus's crucifixion on select individuals rather than the Jewish people as a whole. He wrote:

> Now we must ask who exactly were Jesus's accusers? Who insisted that he be condemned to death...according to John it was simply "the Jews." But John's use of this expression does not in any way indicate—as the modern reader might suppose—the people of Israel in general...after all John himself was ethnically a Jew, as were Jesus, and all his followers. The entire early Christian community was made up of Jews.

With this statement, Pope Benedict XVI reversed two thousand years of church history.

Pope Benedict's reign was short-lived. In 2013, the pontiff shockingly announced his resignation—the first resignation of the papacy in nearly six hundred years. At the same time, the Church found itself embroiled in sex scandals that were causing parishioners to lose trust in the institution. The appointment of an effective leader was crucial.

On March 13, 2013, the second day of the papal conclave, the white smoke blew, and the announcement was made that Cardinal Jorge Mario Bergoglio of Buenos Aires, Argentina would become pope—the first pope ever from Latin America, the region with the largest Catholic population in the world. Known for living modestly, using public transportation and visiting the poor, he chose the name Francis in honor of Saint Francis of Assisi.

Pope Francis immediately captivated the world with his unassuming personality. Unlike Pope John Paul II, who was known for grand gestures, and Pope Benedict XVI, who was dubbed the "Prada Pope" by the Italian media because of his custom-made slippers and other expensive tastes, Francis exuded simplicity and informality. Minutes after the election results were declared, the master of ceremonies offered the new pope a traditional red cape trimmed with ermine. "No thank you, Monsignor," Pope Francis is reported to have replied. "You put it on instead. Carnival time is over!"

He announced that he would live in a three-room suite in the Vatican guesthouse rather than in the spacious papal apartments in the Apostolic Palace. He turned down the bulletproof, glass-enclosed Popemobile the pontiff had used since Pope John Paul II was shot in 1981, opting instead for an open-air jeep that he frequently left to greet crowds, causing nightmares for his security detail.

Reports from Argentina of Bergoglio's warm relationship with the Jewish community were encouraging. He was known to visit synagogues on Rosh Hashanah and Chanukah. He was the first public figure to condemn the July 1994 bombing of the Argentine Israelite Mutual Association building in Buenos Aires, Argentina's deadliest bombing, which killed eighty-five people and injured hundreds.

On October 24, 2013, just seven months into Pope Francis's papacy, I led a sixty-member Simon Wiesenthal Center delegation that included Holocaust survivors, Christians, and a prominent Muslim to the Vatican for a private audience. We were among the first Jewish organizations Pope Francis invited.

Before our Vatican visit, we held a historic Simon Wiesenthal Center Board of Trustees meeting in Rome's Villa Miani. It was only the second time in the organization's thirty-eight-year history that we held a board meeting outside the US. Trustees Larry A. Mizel, Dawn Arnall, Alan Casden, Gordon and Leslie Diamond, George Feldenkreis, Judah Hertz, Stuart Isen, Jimmy Lustig, Jack Nagel, Martin Rosen, Lee Samson, Ed Snider, Don Soffer, Jaime Sohacheski, Marc Utay, Gary Winnick and Rosalie Zalis attended, and trustees Syd Belzberg, Jonathan Dolgen, Steven Ghysels, Sid Sheinberg and Burt Sugarman participated via teleconference.

As I looked around the meeting room, I was struck by the development of our board, from an initial dozen members in our early days, to a group now fifty-four members strong, all of them exceptional corporate leaders and philanthropists. In the coming years, equally talented and committed younger people, including Marc Utay, Peter Lowy, Murray Huberfeld, Howard Friedman, Brett Ratner, Jay

Snider, Steve Ghysels, Cheston D. Mizel, Steve Robinson and James Packer would infuse the board with new energy.

When we arrived for the audience, Vatican officials led us into Clementine Hall, a magnificent sixteenth-century space within the Apostolic Palace. I recognized the frescoed hall as the chamber in which the body of Pope John Paul II had been laid before being ceremonially carried across St. Peter's Square. When Pope Francis arrived forty minutes late, he exhibited exceptional humility by bowing his head and repeating, "Pardon, pardon, pardon." He walked to the front of the hall, positioned himself in a white high-back armchair, and nodded for me to begin my remarks.

I spoke about the continuing threats to Middle East peace from terrorists and rogue nations like Iran:

> There is no greater virtue in Judaism than peace or "*shalom.*" Peace dominates our prayers. Peace, *shalom*, is one of the names of the Almighty Himself…. Peace is attainable…only if one is willing to make changes…. There are some nations that can't compromise. That's what Chamberlain forgot in 1938 when he returned from Munich with his "Peace in our time." Only Churchill understood who Hitler really was. If not for him, today's audience with Your Holiness and a delegation from the Simon Wiesenthal Center could never have taken place. As Rabbi Joseph B. Soloveitchik writes in *Fate and Destiny*, "Evil is an undeniable fact. It exists. I will neither deny it or camouflage it…" Evil existed during the time of Moses as it did in the time of Jesus and as it does in our own time.

Turning to the resurgence of anti-Semitism, I said:

> Seventy-five years after the infamous Kristallnacht pogrom, a poll commissioned by the respected Ebert Foundation estimates that 150 million Europeans still harbor anti-Jewish sentiment. Your Holiness, we know that we have you as an ally in our struggles against anti-Semitism, and we want to reiterate to you that you have an ally in the Simon Wiesenthal Center in

your struggle to secure the rights of religious minorities everywhere, especially endangered historic Christian communities in Egypt, Iraq and beyond.

And finally:

> [We] are delighted that Your Holiness has accepted an invitation to visit Israel next year—the spiritual center of the Jewish people, where Jews, Christians and Muslims are free to practice their faith and to express their opinions without fear or repression. May your presence there help all those committed to a lasting Middle East peace, to finally recognize the existence of a Jewish state alongside her twenty-three Arab neighbors.

Unlike Popes John Paul II and Benedict XVI, Pope Francis stood to make his remarks. He began by expressing his gratitude to the Wiesenthal Center for the respect it showed him and his predecessors.

> These meetings are a concrete sign of the respect and esteem, which you have for the Bishops of Rome, for which I am grateful. They are likewise an expression of the appreciation of the Pope for the task to which you have dedicated yourselves: to combat every form of racism, intolerance and anti-Semitism, to keep alive the memory of the *Shoah*, and to promote mutual understanding through education and commitment to the good of society.

Pope Francis called for confronting intolerance:

> In these last few weeks, I have reaffirmed on more than one occasion the Church's condemnation of all forms of anti-Semitism. Today I wish to emphasize that the problem of intolerance must be confronted in all its forms: wherever any minority is persecuted and marginalized because of its religious convictions or ethnic identity, the wellbeing of society as a

whole is endangered and each one of us must feel affected.... Let us combine our efforts in promoting a culture of encounter, respect, understanding, and mutual forgiveness.

He concluded by urging us to continue our work: "I encourage you to continue to pass on to the young the importance of working together to reject walls and build bridges between our cultures and our faith traditions. May we go forward with trust, courage and hope! *Shalom!*"

Larry Mizel, the Simon Wiesenthal Center Chairman of the Board, presented Pope Francis with a stone-carved menorah to commemorate the occasion. I introduced each member of our group, and observed Pope Francis's remarkable ability to make each person standing before him feel as if he were the most important person in the world. When Jack Nagel, accompanied by his wife Gitta, told the pontiff that he had survived Auschwitz, Pope Francis intuitively placed his hands on Jack's shoulders, and kept them there until their conversation ended. When Esther and Jose Liberman relayed that a French Catholic family had hidden Esther and her mother during the war, Pope Francis listened intently, noticeably humbled by this story of Christian charity. The Pope spent a few moments with Mohamed Alabbar, who delivered a private message from the leaders of the United Arab Emirates.

We came away from our meeting optimistic about the future of Catholic-Jewish relations, as long as they are in the hands of Pope Francis. His sincerity, warmth and vision of inclusion made a powerful impact upon us. We unanimously agreed that this pope had the potential to create a legacy as important as that of John Paul II.

In May 2014, shortly after US Secretary of State John Kerry's efforts to broker a two-state solution between Israel and the Palestinians failed, Pope Francis demonstrated shrewd diplomatic skills on a trip to Israel and the West Bank. Though he maintained that he had no political agenda, the Pope's packed itinerary, which included more than thirty events over three days, emphasized his sympathy for the suffering on both sides of the conflict.

The most controversial aspect of the tour from the Israeli perspective was Pope Francis's stop in Bethlehem at the security barrier Israel erected following a relentless campaign of Palestinian suicide bombings. The pontiff prayed at a section of the cement wall that had been spray-painted with graffiti reading "Free Palestine" and comparing Bethlehem to the Jewish ghetto in Warsaw during the Holocaust. This unfortunate choice of location was disturbing, as the comparison between Bethlehem and the Warsaw ghetto was completely unfounded.

But Pope Francis's visit also included meetings with Israel's Prime Minister Benjamin Netanyahu, its President Shimon Peres, and its Chief Rabbis, and stops at the Western Wall and Yad Vashem. There, the Pope laid a wreath in the Hall of Remembrance, met with six Holocaust survivors, whose hands he kissed, and delivered an emotional homily.

Before leaving, Pope Francis wrote in the Yad Vashem guest book: "With shame for what man, who was created in the image of God, was able to do; with shame for the fact that man made himself the owner of evil; with shame that man made himself into God and sacrificed his brothers." He signed his note: "Never again!! Never again!! Francis."

The most significant event of Pope Francis's trip was a visit to the tomb of Theodor Herzl, one of the founders of Zionism and the primary advocate for the creation of Israel. When he laid a wreath at Herzl's grave, he became the first pope in history to acknowledge Zionism as the legitimate national movement of the Jewish people. It was a hopeful moment in the unfolding story of Jewish-Christian relations.

At this writing, Pope Francis's papacy is young, and controversies are inevitable. The most likely future dispute will be the granting of sainthood status to Pius XII, the pope during the Holocaust. In 1990, Pope John Paul II nominated Pope Pius XII for sainthood. In 2009, Pope Benedict set him further down the path by declaring him "venerable." The final recommendation for full-fledged sainthood will likely fall to Pope Francis, who has defended Pius by stating that his role in the Holocaust must be understood within the context of his time. Should Pope Francis recommend sainthood, he will place a challenge before the Jewish-Catholic alliance that he and his recent predecessors have worked hard to cultivate (See Appendix 2).

But Pope Francis's papacy also represents great possibility. In a June 2014 interview in Spain's *La Vanguardia* newspaper, Pope Francis went further even than Pope John Paul II in saying that "inside every Christian is a Jew." This directness, combined with Pope Francis's humility and diplomatic prowess could make for one of the most effective papacies in history. Time will tell.

Chapter Eight

When Grand Street Meets Hollywood

W hen we established the Simon Wiesenthal Center, we knew we needed to create different vehicles to deliver our message to different audiences. Newspaper editorials, letter-writing campaigns, and traditional museum exhibits spoke to the older generation. If we were to teach young people the lessons of history, we needed to engage them in a more visceral way.

Like it or not, we needed to harness the technology that was shaping the younger generation. So, like other museums in the late 1970s, we committed ourselves to creating what, for its time, was a high-tech museum experience: a multi-media exhibit projected by eighteen slide projectors onto a single screen.

While at work on the exhibit one afternoon in January 1979, a visitor came to see me. Tall and slim, with a friendly face framed by cropped, jet-black hair, Fay Kanin had come at the suggestion of a mutual friend. I showed her through our modest museum, and explained our new exhibit concept. She listened attentively, then gave me her astute feedback: "I am impressed with the exhibit content, but skeptical about the format. Why be a slave to eighteen slide projectors? Why not make a film?"

New to Hollywood, I innocently asked, "So, what other media projects have you worked on?"

I had no idea that the woman giving me advice was a successful screenwriter, playwright and producer, who was half of the husband-and-wife team that had written the Clark Gable-Doris Day comedy, *Teacher's Pet*, and many Emmy Award-winning television movies.

Fay turned to me with a mildly patronizing smile and said, "Rabbi, I've had to put a lot of projects on hold in order to take on my newest assignment. Maybe you haven't heard. I have just been named the president of the Academy of Motion Picture Arts and Sciences."

No further details of Ms. Kanin's resume were needed. I decided to scrap the slide projector project, and begin to think about a film.

I had long been enthralled by the movies. As a child, I had spent many happy afternoons in the Lower East Side's movie theaters watching my favorite screen cowboys. Later, I was captivated by Clark Gable, Katharine Hepburn, Gary Cooper, Bette Davis, Cary Grant, and Rita Hayworth. Now I was living in Los Angeles, home of the movie industry, where I had an opportunity to turn an old interest into a new challenge.

The truth was, a documentary film was a promising medium for telling the story of the Holocaust to a wide audience. Through film, we could share personal stories of Holocaust victims and perpetrators as well as teach the larger historical context in which the Holocaust took place. Intrigued, I took the next step of finding a director.

My first choice was Saul Bass, the renowned graphic designer and filmmaker who had worked with Hollywood greats Alfred Hitchcock, Otto Preminger, and Stanley Kubrick. Saul was excited by the idea, but had to decline because of a demanding schedule that included designing the graphics for the upcoming Academy Awards. He recommended that I get in touch with his design director, Arnold Schwartzman.

A few days later, Arnold and I met to discuss the project. I described what I hoped to accomplish with the film. Arnold outlined his career, including his impressive, recent work with Saul, and shared some of his personal background with me: "As a child in England, I lived through the Blitz. I will never forget the bombing, the destruction, the terror of it all."

That clinched it. I recognized that Arnold's personal experience of the devastations of war was an asset that would help shape his vision of the film. I offered Arnold the position, and he accepted. We were on our way.

We developed a budget and discussed writers. We engaged Oxford University historian Martin Gilbert, renowned for his biographical work on Winston Churchill and his scholarship on the Holocaust, to produce a historical outline as a framework for the film. With diligence and creativity, Arnold scoured film archives and conducted interviews with Holocaust survivors, including an especially poignant one with Simon Wiesenthal at the Western Wall. I developed personal stories of Holocaust perpetrators and victims, and wrote an introduction to debunk the myth that Jews went to their deaths like "sheep to the slaughter":

> People often ask, "Why did the Jews go like sheep to the slaughter?" Sheep to the slaughter? How can they know what it was like, crowded together in a way that even animals are not treated…weakened by months of hardship and hunger…locked up in sealed wagons, without food, weapons, without friends knowing that if even one escaped the Nazis, who was there that would welcome them? Who cared? Who would lift a finger?

We agreed on a single, all-encompassing word as the title: *Genocide*.

But as Arnold worked on the final cuts, we realized something was missing. The film was dramatic and compelling, but it might not have broad enough appeal. After weeks of consideration, it came to us: we needed actors with immediately recognizable voices to narrate the film—a male narrator for the historical narrative and a female narrator for the personal stories.

For the male voice, we decided to ask Orson Welles. For the female voice, I knew immediately that I wanted Elizabeth Taylor. But how could I approach Elizabeth Taylor, the world's most famous female movie star? And how could I muster enough chutzpah to ask her to donate her time to help the Simon Wiesenthal Center make a film?

Fortunately, the Wiesenthal Center had a relationship with Elizabeth's then-husband, US Senator John Warner. He and I had worked together on a number of projects, including the German statute of limitations on Nazi war crimes issue. I sent Senator Warner the script, and waited to see if anything would come of it.

Within days, Senator Warner called me: "Rabbi, Elizabeth and I have a clear division of labor," he said. "I take care of the government business, and she takes care of the movie business. However, since you and I have worked together in the past, I'll do you a favor. Instead of sending the script through Liz's agent, I'll put it on her nightstand, and leave the rest to her."

A week later, Senator Warner called me back with the thrilling news that his wife was interested in the project. "The bad news, Rabbi, is that you owe me a night's sleep: the moment Liz started reading the script she couldn't stop crying."

The following week, a "Mrs. Warner" called my office. Initially baffled by the name, my secretary soon realized who was on the other end of the line, and excitedly put the call through. Elizabeth was enthusiastic and direct: "Rabbi, I was very moved by the script you sent me. I would be happy to narrate the film, but I have some questions. Are you free for lunch today?"

Startled by the pace at which things were moving, I hadn't yet considered where I would hold a meeting with one of the world's most famous celebrities. I quickly began to think, "Let's see…the kosher restaurant won't work…its tables are so close together, all of Jewish LA will know about my newest plans by the end of the day…. Where else can we…?"

Elizabeth jumped in. "How about the Polo Lounge?"

"Of course," I replied, too embarrassed to admit that I had never heard of it. "Let's meet at one o'clock," I said.

I rushed to my secretary: "Do you know a restaurant called the Polo Lounge?"

Flabbergasted by my ignorance, she explained, "The Polo Lounge is THE hot dining spot for Hollywood stars and dealmakers. Everyone knows it's in the Beverly Hills Hotel."

I called the restaurant and foolishly explained, "My name is Rabbi Marvin Hier. I am an Orthodox rabbi who will be having lunch today with Elizabeth Taylor. I can only eat a fruit plate, but she can order whatever she wants. I'll foot the bill."

The maître de listened patiently until I asked for "a nice table for two." Then he put an end to my blathering: "Don't worry, Rabbi, Elizabeth Taylor has a table of her own. It will be ready for her when she gets here."

I arrived early and was escorted across an elegant pink and green dining room to a semi-circular banquette facing the hotel gardens. I snuck peeks at guests at adjacent tables until Elizabeth sauntered in, fifteen minutes late. Instantly, all eyes were upon her, including those of a gaggle of tourists who had gotten wind of her arrival, and were pressing their faces against the garden window. I introduced myself and pointed out that we "had company."

Elizabeth casually looked out and waved to the crowd. I joked, "Elizabeth, you probably think they're all here to get a glimpse of you, but I think they're wondering what an Orthodox rabbi is doing having lunch at the Polo Lounge."

I tried to take in the scene in which I, implausibly, was a central character. Next to me sat the glamorous Elizabeth Taylor. Around us, waiters swarmed, filling our glasses, adjusting and re-adjusting our silverware. I thought back to my days as a Catskills waiter, and decided it was far more pleasurable to be a guest than an employee—especially with this service.

We discussed the film over Elizabeth's salad and my melon slices. In contrast to her steamy screen persona, Elizabeth was gracious and unassuming. "Rabbi," she said, "I am very impressed with the script. I would be pleased to narrate your film. The only thing is, we would need to record it in London, where I will be filming over the next few months."

Trying to contain my exhilaration, I replied with forced non-chalance, "Thank you, Elizabeth. I'm sure we'll have no problem working out the travel details."

As if we were old pals, Elizabeth went on, "Rabbi, do you have a car?" "Sure," I answered, a bit taken aback.

"Would you mind giving me a ride to my dentist?"

I nearly fell off my chair. "Of course. Wait right here. I'll be back for you in a few minutes."

At top speed, I ran to my car, which was parked two blocks down Sunset Boulevard, because I had been too embarrassed by its unkempt state to relinquish it to the hotel valet. In a frenzy, I threw books in the trunk, pushed papers under the seats, and swept crumbs out the doors before driving back to the Beverly Hills Hotel.

As I accompanied Elizabeth through the lobby, an elderly man spotted us and blurted out, "Oh my God, that's Liz Taylor!" His wife concurred, "You're right, that's her! Isn't she beautiful?" then added, "But I wonder what she sees in him?!"

In the fall of 1981, Arnold and I traveled to London to record Elizabeth's narration for *Genocide*. I instructed a driver to collect me from my hotel first thing in the morning and take me to London's famous kosher eatery, Bloom's Restaurant, to buy a couple of sandwiches to get me through what I anticipated would be a long work day. Next, we picked up Elizabeth at the Savoy Hotel. When we reached the recording studio complex, I entered the main building while Elizabeth waited in the car.

"Good morning. I'm Rabbi Marvin Hier from the Simon Wiesenthal Center in Los Angeles. I'm here with Elizabeth Taylor who is recording a documentary for us. Can you tell me which studio we'll be in?"

"Elizabeth Taylor?" asked the man at the desk in astonishment. "We have no such appointment scheduled."

"That can't be!" I blurted out. "The director of the film, Arnold Schwartzman, is here waiting for us, isn't he?"

Without waiting for an answer, I phoned Arnold, who answered in a huff: "Rabbi, where are you? We're already late!"

After our own version of "Who's on First," Arnold and I deduced that my driver had mistakenly delivered me to a music recording studio run by sound engineer John Wood in Chelsea instead of John Wood Studios, a film recording studio operated by a different John Wood, in Soho. I had the unpleasant task of returning to the car to inform the grand dame of cinema that we had to retrace our forty-minute route through London traffic. "There goes our film," I thought to myself.

Elizabeth pursed her lips and peered out the window in aggravation. But after a few minutes of tense silence, she piped up, "Rabbi, what smells so delicious?"

"Kosher salt beef sandwiches," I replied.

"Well, aren't you going to share the wealth?"

I removed one of the sandwiches from its soggy paper bag, and passed it to Elizabeth. She relished the greasy delicacy, then volunteered to finish half of my sandwich, which I had been too nervous to eat. By the time the feast was over, we had arrived at the right studio, and Elizabeth Taylor, well nourished by Bloom's kosher salt beef, recorded an unforgettable film narration.

The premiere of *Genocide* was scheduled for January 17, 1982 at the Kennedy Center in Washington, DC. Frank Sinatra, now a Wiesenthal Center trustee, accepted my invitation to chair the event. Elizabeth agreed to attend.

As the date approached, Frank called me, concerned: "You know Rabbi, the Kennedy Center event is in the middle of the winter. The weather will be miserable, and people won't want to stay out late, so we need to start on time. I know Liz, and she is late for everything. Rabbi, there are only two ways to deal with this: either you call her or I call her."

I agreed to take charge, and put my best diplomatic skills to the test as I phoned Elizabeth. "As you know, Elizabeth, Frank is chairing the event. He is very concerned about starting on time, especially since we have scheduled a press conference with Simon Wiesenthal before we screen the film. Frank would appreciate it very much if you would come on time."

Hollywood figures placed bets on whether or not Elizabeth Taylor would accede to Frank Sinatra's wishes. Much to my surprise and relief, she did. Elizabeth arrived at 7:30 pm sharp, right as our press conference got underway. Later in the evening, Frank whispered to me, "It was her earliest arrival ever."

The premiere was an overwhelming success. Nearly two thousand guests filled the Kennedy Center's shimmering Concert Hall, including Simon, who flew in from Vienna. *The New York Times* quoted me describing the film's objective:

> I hope this will help younger people to see the event [the Holocaust] as something not apart from them.... If preventative medicine is the best form of medicine, then the time to remind ourselves of the Holocaust is before a society gets too sick.... There are films that are seasonal. This is a film for all seasons.... This is a call from the victims of Hitler's "Final Solution," a warning to all generations that indifference and silence to the events around us may be hazardous to the continuity of human civilization.

Days later, at an early morning press conference at the Samuel Goldwyn Theatre in Beverly Hills, the Academy of Motion Picture Arts and Sciences announced the nominations for the Fifty-Fourth Annual Academy Awards. To my complete surprise, among the nominees for Best Documentary Feature was *Genocide*. Arnold and I marveled at our good fortune. Family, friends and colleagues from around the world called to offer their congratulations.

On March 29, 1982, Malkie and I arrived at the Dorothy Chandler Pavilion in Los Angeles for the Academy Awards ceremony. The paparazzi were not nearly as interested in our walk down the red carpet as they were in those of Meryl Streep and Jane Fonda, but the pre-ceremony ritual was exciting nonetheless. We had a hard time believing that we—two Orthodox Jews from New York City's Lower East Side and Borough Park—were mingling with Hollywood's polished movie stars.

Conversations inevitably revolved around which film would win the Oscar for the year's Best Picture. The competition was stiff: *On Golden Pond, Raiders of the Lost Ark, Reds,* and the long shot, *Chariots of Fire.* Malkie and I made our predictions, but our thoughts were fixated on our own, slightly less exalted category.

Fay Kanin, who had set me on the movie-making path two years earlier, took the stage. She praised the array of films produced that year, and introduced the event's host, Johnny Carson, who opened the ceremony with a trademark monologue.

I fidgeted as the winners were announced for Best Supporting Actress and Best Visual Effects. I tried to remain patient through the movie clips and speeches. But it was difficult to maintain my composure. Like anyone who is nominated for an Oscar, I wanted to win.

Finally, Carson called upon husband-and-wife actors, Richard Benjamin and Paula Prentiss, to present the Oscar for Best Documentary Feature. The nominated films included excellent documentaries about Cuba, El Salvador and Dr. Helen Caldicott. Ken Burns's first film, *Brooklyn Bridge,* rounded out the list. I waited for what seemed like an eternity for the presenters to open the envelope.

Finally, I heard the magical words, "The Oscar for Best Documentary Feature goes to…*Genocide.*" I flashed Malkie a big grin then rushed to the stage with Arnold. At the podium, Arnold thanked the production team, and I, gripping my golden statuette, added, "…special thanks to the Board of Trustees of the Simon Wiesenthal Center and of Yeshiva University of Los Angeles for making this film possible, and to Simon Wiesenthal, who stood alone all these years so that the world would not forget…." To make the most of my prime-time opportunity, I concluded, "This film is dedicated to the memory of the victims of the Holocaust. They have no graves, but their memory will live to the end of time. Thank you."

Genocide was the first documentary on the Holocaust to win an Academy Award, and I, the first rabbi. Who would have thought that Marvin "Moishe" Hier, a *yeshiva bocher* from the Lower East Side, would hold such an honor?

After the awards, Malkie and I were whisked away to the Board of Governor's Ball at the Beverly Hilton. While other guests feasted on French gourmet fare, the master chef amused us by personally presenting us with two fruit plates. Dozens of voting members of the Academy congratulated us on our "important film."

When we finally arrived home after the ball, our phone was ringing off the hook. Our son Ari, who didn't have a television in his Yeshiva University dormitory in New York, excitedly relayed how his friends had schlepped him to a local bar to watch the Oscars, and how the bartender had provided a round of drinks on the house when he yelled, "That's my father who just won!"

Soon after, a group of yeshiva students burst into our home, singing and dancing. As we danced arm in arm, I realized that many of these boys were the grandchildren of Holocaust survivors. Stories like those of their families would now be shared with millions of people, Jews and non-Jews, around the world, as *Genocide* would receive international distribution.

The next day, I received a call from Elizabeth Taylor, and a congratulatory letter from Fay Kanin, which included an invitation to become a member of the Academy of Motion Picture Arts and Sciences. Other Hollywood figures, professional colleagues and friends also called.

But the most gratifying call came from my mother: "Moishe," she began, "Do you remember that snooty lady who could never be bothered saying hello to me in shul? I just saw her in the park, and you'll never believe what she said to me, she said, 'Raisel Hier I want you to know that the whole neighborhood is talking about you! I can't tell you how proud we are to know the mother of the first rabbi in history to win an Academy Award.' Moishe, when she told me that, I felt like the richest lady on the Lower East Side."

Gradually, the thrill of having received the entertainment industry's highest accolade for my very first film began to wane. There was work to be done at the Simon Wiesenthal Center and Yeshiva University of Los Angeles. But a few weeks later, there was more Oscar-related excitement when my secretary interrupted a morning meeting at the yeshiva with a distressing announcement. "Rabbi Hier…I'm so sorry…someone has…broken into your office…and…stolen your Academy Award!"

I ran to my office, and sure enough, the Oscar's place of honor, high atop the center shelf of my bookcase, was vacant. I thought, "Instead of being the first rabbi to win an Oscar, I'm going to be the first shlemiel ever to have lost one!" Malkie tried to reassure me, without much success, that the statuette would somehow turn up.

That evening, despite being in no mood for a party, I attended the yeshiva's Purim festivities. Just like my friends and I had done back in our yeshiva days, the students prepared a Purim shpiel. But unlike our impersonations, spoofs and other low-tech comedy routines, they presented an animated short film they had created about the hidden treasures of our yeshiva's study hall.

As soon as the film's first frame was projected onto the screen, the case of the missing Oscar was solved. There it was, an animated version of the most recognizable trophy in the world, tiptoeing out of my office, down the corridor, and into the *beis medrash*, where it climbed onto a shelf alongside worn Talmud tractates. The image wonderfully illustrated the improbable trajectory of my life, from *yeshiva bocher* to Hollywood producer, and delivered an amusing message: if you want to win an Academy Award, you better first learn some Talmud.

In gratitude for her generous work on *Genocide*, the Simon Wiesenthal Center planned to honor Elizabeth Taylor at a Sunday dinner at the Beverly Hilton Hotel. More than 1,000 guests were expected to arrive from all over the country. But at 7:15 am the morning of the dinner, my home phone rang. I immediately recognized Elizabeth's distraught voice: "Rabbi, I apologize for calling you so early in the morning, but I wanted to get a hold of you first thing, because I know this will come as something of a shock…I have to cancel tonight's dinner."

"Elizabeth, what's happened? Are you all right?"

"Well yes, I'm fine," she assured me, "But Rabbi, that shlemiel of a husband of mine forgot to send the clothes for tonight's dinner that I specifically arranged for him to bring on our plane. I have nothing to wear, and I will not be publicly embarrassed."

As a trained rabbi, I knew how to answer all kinds of complicated questions related to marriage. But now I was out of my league. I tried a little common sense: "Elizabeth, I don't know anything about women's clothes, but I'm sure you can buy another dress. This is Los Angeles, after all."

"Rabbi, it's Sunday. None of the stores are open."

"There has to be something we can do. You know, Simon is going to be at the dinner, and he will be terribly disappointed if you cancel." I carefully ventured further. "How about I ask one of our trustees to see about getting a store opened for you? Is there a particular store that you like?"

"Well, I might have some luck at Giorgio, if it were open," she replied.

I immediately called Bill Belzberg, who said he knew Fred Hayman, the owner of Giorgio's. Bill called Fred, whose wife relayed the news that Fred had just left for a jog in Rancho Park. Ever resourceful, Bill called on a few of his buddies, who changed into their jogging suits and set out on the mission. A half-hour later, they found Fred, who was amused by the tale, and readily agreed to open his store. We shuttled Elizabeth to Giorgio's, where, thank God, she found a dress to her liking.

That night, before a standing-room-only audience that included many of the leading lights of the entertainment industry, I told the story of a rabbi, a movie star and a missing dress. Elizabeth doubled over in laughter. But when the time came for her to take the stage, Elizabeth Taylor, the consummate actress, collected herself, and spoke passionately about our film:

> I stand before you with mixed emotions: humbled that you have seen fit to bestow this unique honor on me, and yet, at the same time, so very sad, because it brings back into focus

that tragic epic in human history, when death became so ordinary, torture was so trite, and silence so pronounced. When the tears of children gushed forth like running streams. When leaders forgot to lead. When few cared. When men and women forgot that they were formed in the image of God.

I am often tempted to speculate how fortunate I am to have escaped the horror, to have been spared the anguish. But when I think about it deeply, I realize I did not escape unscathed. None of us did. We were all, in a sense, there, hovering above the gates of Auschwitz, trying to shield ourselves from the magnetic pull of its destructive force that wanted to do us all in, Jew and Christian, black and white. It wanted everything we possessed and cherished: our Van Goghs, our Rembrandts, our Tennysons, our Freuds and our Einsteins.

When I read the script for the Simon Wiesenthal Center's film, I could see the victims before my eyes, their voices speaking to me. "Tell our story," they said to me. "Nay, not for our sake, for we are long gone. But for yours so you may live."

I have tried so very hard to tell their agony and their heroism, and I hope millions of people will see and hear their profound message...

Let me just say to the enemies of our people, wherever they may be, we say in the words of one of the victims, "*Mir velen zey uberleben*" (We shall outlive them). And to the friends of mankind, wherever they may be, "*Chazak v'amatz!*" (Be strong and brave!) Remember that in the final analysis, they that sow in tears shall yet reap in joy.

Film had proven a powerful medium for our message, and I interpreted our success with *Genocide* as a sign that I should stick with it. In 1982, we established Moriah Films, a film division of the Simon Wiesenthal Center. We chose the name from the mountain upon which, according to Jewish tradition, Abraham was called to sacrifice his son Isaac and where King Solomon built his Temple. Moriah was the place where Jews had made their entrance onto the world stage.

In keeping with the mission of the Wiesenthal Center, we set out to create a film library devoted to the Jewish experience and to contemporary human rights issues. Based on our experiences with Orson Welles and Elizabeth Taylor, we would ask Hollywood's leading actors to donate their talent to provide narrations. Through film, we hoped to teach audiences around the world about epic historical events, and inspire them to lead lives of moral clarity.

Several years later, Wiesenthal Center trustees Jeffrey Katzenberg, then co-founder of DreamWorks SKG, and now CEO of DreamWorks Animation, and Ron Meyer, then President of Universal Studios, and now Vice Chairman of NBC Universal, provided some much-needed advice. They concurred that since Moriah was going to produce documentaries on a regular basis, it should build its own film and video production studio to enable an in-house crew to produce films from beginning to end, and a sound studio to record narrations, edit music, create sound effects, and mix films. We soon found a donor and proudly named the production studio in honor of Pearl Resnick, an ardent and loyal supporter, and her late husband Jack.

We hired the multi-talented writer and producer, Richard Trank, to serve as Moriah's Executive Producer. Rick put together an outstanding crew of writers, photography and lighting specialists, art directors, and sound engineers, and developed a network of researchers around the world that would help Moriah create compelling films of historical depth and accuracy. Over the next several decades, Rick and I would write and produce more than a dozen films.

In our next three films, we explored aspects of World War II and the Holocaust. In *Echoes That Remain* (1991), we combined archival photographs and film footage with live action sequences shot on location in Czechoslovakia, Hungary, Poland, and Romania to depict Eastern European Jewish communities before the Holocaust. We released *Liberation* (1995), a panoramic sweep of World War II, to coincide with the fiftieth anniversary of VE Day. In *The Long Way Home* (1997), we wove together historical narrative, interviews, anecdotes, and personal recollections to examine the world's indifference toward and unwillingness to help Jewish refugees after World War II.

We believed critics and audiences alike would be particularly moved by this tragic, little known story. With the help of Ira Lipman, a long-time friend and trustee of the Wiesenthal Center, we planned a grand premiere at New York City's Radio City Music Hall. That November evening in 1997, as I walked up West 50th Street toward the Art Deco landmark, I felt a jolt of excitement when I saw the title of our film lighting up the legendary theater's famous marquee. Inside, the atmosphere was equally electrifying: more than five thousand people had come to see our film.

The Long Way Home was screened at the Sundance Film Festival and received numerous awards. *The Los Angeles Times* called it "superb" and "masterful," and Siskel and Ebert gave it the all-important "two thumbs up." Showtime Cable Networks acquired it for television broadcast.

In January 1998, the Academy of Motion Pictures announced the nominees for the Seventieth Annual Academy Awards and *The Long Way Home* was among them. Though sixteen years had passed since *Genocide* had earned an Oscar, I assumed the Academy's nominating committee would be reluctant to name us winners a second time, and was more than satisfied with having been nominated.

On March 23, 1998, I dusted off my tuxedo and, with Malkie at my side, made my way to the Academy Awards ceremony at the Shrine Auditorium in Los Angeles. Having been through the Oscar experience once before, and by now having many friends and acquaintances in the entertainment industry, I was slightly more at ease than the first time around. I enjoyed the shmoozing and spectacle of the annual extravaganza.

When the curtain went up, Master of Ceremonies Billy Crystal, perched on the bow of the Titanic in honor of the year's anticipated Best Picture winner, sang a delightful medley that poked fun at the evening's major nominees. After his close friend, Robin Williams, accepted the Oscar for Best Supporting Actor for his role in *Good Will Hunting*, Crystal introduced Robert DeNiro to present the award for Best Documentary Feature. DeNiro read the nominees: *4 Little Girls* by Spike Lee and Sam Pollard, *Ayn Rand: A Sense of Life* by Michael Paxton, *Colors Straight Up* by Michêle Ohayon and Julia Schachter, *Waco: The Rules of Engagement* by Dan Gifford and William Gazecki, and our film, *The Long Way Home.*

My heart raced as DeNiro opened the envelope. "The Oscar for Best Documentary Feature goes to... *The Long Way Home!*"

Astounded, Producer Rick Trank, Writer/Director Mark Jonathan Harris and I made our way to the stage. I thanked the Academy, the Board of Trustees of the Simon Wiesenthal Center and the patrons and benefactors of Moriah Films, and concluded, "This is for the survivors of the Holocaust who walked away from the ashes, rebuilt their lives, and helped create the State of Israel. May God bless them."

Backstage, I passed Walter Matthau and Jack Lemmon, who were presenting awards later in the evening. Lemmon took one look at me holding my Oscar and wise-cracked, "Walter, they must have changed the rules. Once upon a time, you had to go to a good acting school to win an Oscar. Now it seems you have to go to a good yeshiva."

Meanwhile, on stage, Crystal had the audience in stitches with an improvised *schtick*: "Wow, what an evening! First my best friend wins an Oscar, and now my rabbi wins one.... Who else wants one? You over there: you want one? C'mon up!"

Friends and acquaintances from around the world called to congratulate me. My good friend and six-time Academy Award winner Arthur Cohn, who had been in the audience, called. Billy Crystal called, too. He told me that he had received a call from the rabbi of his synagogue after the awards ceremony. "Billy," he said, "In our temple, you tell everybody I'm your rabbi. How come in front of six hundred million people, you say Marvin Hier is your rabbi?"

The Moriah name was now known. Our films were being screened in theaters and broadcast on television and cable stations throughout the world. Thanks to the Wiesenthal Center's dedicated development team, headed by Executive Director Rabbi Meyer May, National Director of Development Janice Prager and Bobby Novak, we expanded our donor base around the world. The Canadian Friends of the Simon Wiesenthal Center provided ongoing support. Wiesenthal Center trustee and benefactor Lee Samson and his wife Anne, whom Malkie and I had known from our Vancouver days, attracted new donors and corporate sponsors and chaired four outstanding film premieres. The indefatigable Rosalie Zalis, a Wiesenthal Center trustee for more than thirty years, brought thousands of people to see our films and raised millions of dollars when she, along with her husband Dr. Ed Zalis, chaired ten premieres at the Academy of Motion Picture Arts and Sciences and the Directors Guild of America theaters in Los Angeles.

Our success was made possible, in large part, by Jeffrey Katzenberg and Ron Meyer, who bolstered Moriah by helping us secure A-list celebrities to narrate and provide the voices for our films. Over the next fifteen years, our cache of esteemed narrators would include: Elizabeth Taylor, Orson Welles, Sir Ben Kingsley, Patrick Stewart, Morgan Freeman, Sandra Bullock, Edward Asner, Anne Bancroft, Michael Douglas, Richard Dreyfuss, Brooke Shields, Kevin Costner, Nicole Kidman, Dustin Hoffman, Christoph Waltz, Whoopi Goldberg, and Leonard Nimoy.

In 2006, we needed a top-caliber narrator for a film that held special meaning for us, *I Have Never Forgotten You: The Life and Legacy of Simon Wiesenthal*. Simon had passed away in September 2005. Soon after, we embarked on a film that featured interviews with longtime associates, government leaders, friends and family members, many of whom had never discussed their relationship to Simon on camera before.

A few months into the project, the Simon Wiesenthal Center honored media magnate Rupert Murdoch with its Humanitarian Award at a tribute dinner held at New York City's Waldorf Astoria Hotel and chaired by the Co-Chairman of our Board of Trustees, Nelson Peltz and his wife Claudia. Special guest, fellow Australian, and Academy Award-winning actress Nicole Kidman presented the award with great charm, especially when she quipped, "I think my father and your father, Mr. Murdoch, were probably the only Zionists in all of Australia."

I realized then that Nicole's Australian accent could nicely offset the harrowing stories of Simon's life. At the end of the evening, I asked her if she would narrate the film, and she graciously accepted.

Several months later, Rick Trank and I flew to Nashville to record the narration in a studio not far from Nicole's home. Despite not feeling well, Nicole worked with us for three hours. We were more than satisfied with the results, but Nicole was not. She sent a message to our office the next day telling me that her cold had prevented her from giving the narration her best effort and asked, "Can we re-record it? Simon Wiesenthal and the story of the Holocaust are so important that I want to do my best." We couldn't argue with that. Still in Nashville, Rick returned to the studio to re-record the session.

Dustin Hoffman approached his work with Moriah with similar perfectionism when he narrated our 2009 documentary, *Against the Tide*, which examined the failure of American Jewry and the Roosevelt Administration to rescue Europe's Jews during World War II. Dustin was fascinated by the film's protagonist, Peter Bergson, who had dedicated his life to saving Jews after having read a newspaper article about Nazi atrocities. Dustin was especially intrigued by the fact that Bergson had been more successful gaining support for his cause with non-Jewish members of Congress and Hollywood personalities than with leaders of mainstream Jewish organizations.

Rather than record the narration in the typical two or three hours, Dustin spent an entire day on the set, experimenting with different voices in order to best capture Bergson's character. In the end, he gave a stellar performance that contributed to the Documentary Channel naming the film one of the top premieres of the year. At breaks in the recording, Dustin shared some of his family story: "My father rejected religion entirely. Among other things, he didn't allow me to have a bar mitzvah.... So, Rabbi Hier, is it too late?"

"It's never too late for a bar mitzvah," I replied.

I don't think Dustin followed through on the idea, but if he ever does, I'm sure he'll read his lines from the Torah flawlessly.

In 2012, Murray Huberfeld, a friend and Wiesenthal Center trustee who, along with his wife Laura, chaired many Moriah Films screenings in Jerusalem, sent me a copy of *The Prime Ministers*, a remarkable, insider account of Israeli politics written by Yehuda Avner, a speechwriter and advisor to five Israeli prime ministers. As soon as I read the book, I knew I wanted to turn it into a film, and I wanted Sandra Bullock to provide the voice of Israel's only female prime minister, Golda Meir. The year before, I had tried to interest Sandra in narrating *It Is No Dream: The Life of Theodor Herzl*, but she had declined, stating that she thought the film needed a male voice.

This time, I did some research, and discovered that Sandra had something in common with Golda: her mother, like Golda, had become a schoolteacher after immigrating to America. I discussed the coincidence and the project with Sandra, who liked the script and agreed to juggle her busy schedule to fit us in.

A few weeks later, Rick and I met Sandra at Jeffrey Katzenberg's DreamWorks Animation sound studio offices in Burbank. Sandra convincingly portrayed the tough, straight-talking Golda, but was missing some of her grandmotherly warmth. I suggested that she read a few lines in Yiddish, the way Golda might have, "You speak German, right? Yiddish is so close to German, you can do it."

I proceeded to give Sandra a brief lesson in Yiddish pronunciation, reciting, and having her repeat, one sentence at a time. She did beautifully. We continued recording, and Sandra delivered many well-pronounced Yiddish lines, including Golda's famous remark to the fifty thousand Soviet Jews who came to greet her when she visited Moscow as Israel's ambassador to the Soviet Union in 1948, "*Ich bin gekuman danken eich vos ihr zent geblibin yidden*" (I have come to thank you all for remaining Jews).

At a break in the recording session, Sandra told me why she had accepted the role as the voice of Golda Meir: "When I first looked at Golda's picture, I saw a strong resemblance to my grandmother. I felt an affinity between them. I saw this as a sign from someone out there to take on the role."

Over the years, several Hollywood actors became devoted supporters of Moriah Films. They publicly expressed their commitment to Moriah, and repeatedly volunteered their talents to narrate our films.

Michael Douglas never turned us down. Like his father, veteran film star Kirk Douglas, Michael greatly admired Simon Wiesenthal. In 1989, Kirk had been disappointed when HBO had passed him over for the lead role in its television movie, *The Murderers Among Us: The Simon Wiesenthal Story*. Rick and I first worked with Michael on *In Search of Peace*, a film that explored the origins of the Middle East political conflict that we produced following the collapse of the Camp David Summit in 2000. He provided a stirring narration that greatly contributed to the film's critical acclaim.

In 2001, in gratitude for his narration and his support for the Wiesenthal Center, we honored Michael with a Humanitarian Award at our National Tribute Dinner in Beverly Hills. At the award ceremony, Michael spoke movingly about Simon, whom he called "a man who stood up for humanity in its darkest hour and dedicated his entire life to the pursuit of justice."

In 2013, Michael enthusiastically agreed to provide the voice of Israeli Prime Minister Yitzhak Rabin in *The Prime Ministers*. Despite short notice, he re-arranged his schedule, arrived at the New York recording studio fully prepared, and gave a wonderful performance in a record half-hour. I got the impression that the experience of providing Rabin's voice was special for Michael. When the recording session was over, he confirmed my suspicions. "It was as if I was reliving great events in Jewish history," he told me.

Sir Ben Kingsley has never refused a request to help Moriah. He provided brilliant narrations for several Moriah films, including *Winston Churchill: Walking with Destiny*, in which we examined why Winston Churchill's legacy remains relevant in the twenty-first century, and why his leadership remains an inspiration to contemporary political leaders. Ben attended the premiere of *Walking with Destiny*, which we held on May 10, 2010 to coincide with the seventieth anniversary of the day Winston Churchill had been summoned to Buckingham Palace, handed the reins of power, and had remarked that he believed he was, "walking with destiny."

The premiere took place at the official residence of the US Ambassador to the UK, Winfield House, a neo-Georgian mansion in central London's Regent's Park. US Ambassador to the UK, Louis Susman, and his wife, Marjorie, were our hosts. Nearly two hundred guests attended, including the Dutch and Belgian Ambassadors to the UK, Sir Martin Gilbert, and a granddaughter and great-grandson of Sir Winston Churchill.

Before the screening, we awarded Ben the Simon Wiesenthal Center's Distinguished Service Award for his continuing contributions to Moriah Films. He warmed the hearts of the assembled guests when he remarked, "For me, this moment is very special, because it joins together two of my lifelong heroes.... When I was a young boy, I grew up memorizing many of Winston Churchill's wartime speeches that I have now had the privilege of narrating in this remarkable film. Later in life, I had the privilege of portraying Simon Wiesenthal in the television film, *The Murderers Among Us*. So tonight, my two life heroes are here in this room among all of us."

We turned to Ben the following year to narrate another Moriah bio-pic, *It Is No Dream: The Life of Theodor Herzl*. Unlike many Hollywood actors for whom Zionism was too thorny an issue, he readily accepted. When asked why he volunteered his time for Moriah Films, Ben told the Associated Press, "I love narrating the material. It's enlightening, passionate, mature and deals with the ravages of the twentieth century in a very articulate way that hopefully will reach the eyes and ears of young minds who will see the lessons of history and not ignore them."

Only once did we have difficulty finding an actor to read a part in a Moriah film. In October 2011, despite having had Ben provide the overall film narration, having secured funding from Herzl admirers and Los Angeles Jewish community leaders Jack and Rita Sinder, and having scheduled a premiere to take place in just three weeks' time, we lacked a top-rate actor to provide the voice of Theodor Herzl in *It Is No Dream*.

Around the same time, I participated in an event at the Academy of Motion Picture Arts and Sciences to mark the fiftieth anniversary of the acclaimed 1961 dramatic film, *Judgment at Nuremberg*. I shared the stage with Maximilian Schell, one of the stars of the film, and Karen Sharpe, the widow of its director, Stanley Sharpe. Television and radio host Larry King moderated the discussion.

As I sipped a club soda at the pre-event reception, a dashing young man with a high forehead and trim beard hobbled over on crutches and asked with a mild German accent, "Are you Rabbi Hier?"

"Yes, I am."

"Do you still need someone to do the voice of Herzl for your upcoming film? If you do, I would be glad to do it.... As you can see, I have had an accident, and this is the first time in months I've been out.... By the way, I'm Christoph Waltz."

I was stunned. Christoph Waltz was an exceptionally talented actor best known for his work with director Quentin Tarantino. In 2009, Waltz received an Oscar and a Golden Globe for his portrayal of ss-Standartenführer Hans Landa in Tarantino's *Inglourious Basterds*.

"I'm curious," I asked him, "Why do you want to be the voice of Herzl?"

"Look, I am not Jewish, but I have two reasons. First, my grandfather was an actor in a Viennese theater where some of Herzl's plays were performed. My grandfather told my father what a tough time even Vienna's Jews gave poor Herzl. Second, I used to be married to a Jewish woman. We are now amicably divorced. Two of our children are studying in Israel."

"At the Hebrew University?" I asked.

"No, one of them is at a yeshiva called the Mir. Have you heard of it? The head rabbi is called Rabbi Finkel."

"Of course I've heard of it! The Mir is one of the largest yeshivas in the world."

"Yes. So, since some of my children might live in Israel one day, I want to make sure they know what an important role Herzl played in the Jewish people's return to the land of Israel."

"Christoph, I can't think of a better reason for you to provide Herzl's voice for our film. And I have a feeling that a force larger than you and me sent you on this mission. We hadn't found someone to do Herzl's voice until now, because we needed to wait for you to recover from your injury. As my grandmother used to say, '*Alles in leben iz*' (Everything in life is meant to be)."

Two years later, Christoph volunteered his time to provide the voice of Menachem Begin in *The Prime Ministers*. Along with Sandra Bullock, Michael Douglas, and Leonard Nimoy, who provided the voice of Levi Eshkol, he helped us bring Israel's prime ministers to life. As I told the film's primary donors, my long-time friends, Syd and Joanne Belzberg, and philanthropist and Holocaust survivor, Lou Kestenbaum, "No Hollywood studio could boast a better cast."

While I am proud of all of Moriah's films, I am especially attached to a documentary Rick and I produced and wrote in 2004, *Unlikely Heroes*. The film tells the true stories of seven ordinary Jews who accomplished the extraordinary feat of saving the lives of others while they themselves were trapped in the nightmare of the Holocaust. It was Moriah's privilege to honor these heroes by recreating their stories in film, and sharing them with moviegoers around the world.

Pinchas Rosenbaum was a member of a distinguished Hungarian rabbinic family. When most of Hungary's seven hundred and fifty thousand Jews clung to the belief that they would be spared Hitler's rampage across Europe, twenty-year-old Rosenbaum and his Zionist youth movement friends formed a resistance organization, Hatzala, to alert Jews of impending deportations to the death camps. After learning that his entire family had been murdered, Rosenbaum posed as a high-ranking Nazi officer to infiltrate meetings at the infamous Arrow Cross headquarters. He arranged false identity papers, and escorted children to safe houses in neutral countries.

Once, parents of children Rosenbaum was trying to help begged him not to take away their children. Fearing his identity would be discovered, he spoke to them quietly in Yiddish, "My dear brothers and sisters, I am also a Jew. I have come to save your children. I am taking them to the Glass House [the refuge for Jews in Budapest] where they will be saved." The parents followed his orders, enabling

Rosenbaum to save their children's lives. By the war's end, Rosenbaum had helped save hundreds of children.

Willie Perl was a twenty-two-year-old Jewish Viennese lawyer in 1938 when Adolf Eichmann interrogated him at gunpoint. Perl belonged to the Zionist Revisionist Organization, which advocated illegal Jewish immigration to Palestine. Touting his connections with the revisionists, Perl told Eichmann, "The Führer wants the Jews out and we can do the job for him." When Eichmann rejected the idea, Perl went to Eichmann's superiors in Berlin, who approved his plan.

Perl made arrangements for nearly four hundred children to board a ship for Palestine. As the ship prepared to set sail, Perl stood on the gangplank between Eichmann and other top Nazi officials and addressed the children:

> You are leaving, but you are coming.... You are leaving the country in which most of you were born, but in which you were always a minority, sometimes treated better sometimes worse, but always as a minority. You are going home to a country in which we will shape our future, to the country, which God promised us in which we were great and heroic...the trip will not be easy but the reward will be great...as you reentered these railroad carts, you leave behind a country and a people who do not want you, on the way to your brothers and sisters who are longing for you. A happy homecoming, happy *aliya*.

When one child began singing "*Hatikvah*," the other children and assembled parents joined in in what was surely the only instance in the history of the Third Reich in which Adolf Eichmann and other Nazi officials stood at attention while the Jewish national anthem was sung. Willie Perl and his team of rescuers secured additional ships, and over several years, helped eighteen thousand Jews make their way to Palestine.

Recha Sternbuch was a Swiss Jew who devoted years to aiding Jewish refugees from neighboring countries. Sternbuch brought them into her home, helped them acquire visas, and developed a network of people to transport and hide them. She was arrested in 1939, and sent to jail for a brief period, because she refused to divulge the names of those who helped her, stating, "Your demand that I should denounce human beings who haven't harmed anyone, this I cannot do."

Sternbuch's devotion to saving Jews knew no bounds. When Swiss police arrested three Jews who had escaped occupied France, Sternbuch violated the Sabbath to drive to police headquarters to rescue them, then rushed back to synagogue, arriving late for her only son's bar mitzvah. When she received a coded message revealing that ten thousand Jews a day were being murdered at Auschwitz, she relayed the information to the Allied Forces and Jewish organizations abroad. She succeeded in getting fourteen hundred Jews released from Theresienstadt by bribing former President of Switzerland, Dr. Jean-Marie Musy, to speak with his friend, ss Chief Heinrich Himmler. After the war, Strenbuch visited survivors in DP camps, sought out Jewish children who had been placed in convents and Christian homes during the war, and opened schools and camps.

Pinchas Rosenbaum, Willie Perl, Recha Sternbuch and the other characters in *Unlikely Heroes* were, like the Maccabees in the second century BCE, or the Palmach fighters during the British Mandate for Palestine, the Jewish heroes of their generation. With courage, daring, and pride, they gave meaning to the words of the Prophet Samuel: "*Netzach Yisroel lo yeshaker*" (the Eternity of Israel will never be forsaken).

Chapter Nine

Expanding the Vision

By the late 1980s, the Simon Wiesenthal Center and Moriah Films had established international reputations. Our social action campaigns were effective and widely covered by the press, and our films were being screened in theaters and shown on television stations around the world. The Center had an active board, a national staff of thirty, and a membership approaching one hundred thousand.

But our only public facility remained a modest four thousand-square-foot Holocaust museum located on the Yeshiva University of Los Angeles campus. Its inadequate size limited our ability to teach the vital lessons of the Holocaust and to have a significant impact on the diverse population of Los Angeles, which was comprised of more than one hundred and forty ethnic groups that spoke more than two hundred and twenty languages. I recommended to the board, and they unanimously concurred, that we acquire additional land, when it became available, to build a larger Simon Wiesenthal Center museum.

Miraculously, an opportunity soon came knocking on our door. One winter day in 1988, the owner of a large plant nursery located next door to our yeshiva informed me that he was putting his property up for sale, and asked if we might be interested in purchasing it. We seized the moment and bought the property. Over the next five years, inspired by multi-million dollar gifts from the Belzberg, Peltz, Milken, Snider, Winnick, and Casden families, dozens of major gifts from loyal supporters, and thousands of smaller gifts from people throughout the country, we would build a major, new Los Angeles museum.

A new, larger facility provided the opportunity to broaden the scope of our message. We decided not to limit the Museum's focus to events that took place between 1933 and 1945, but rather to link those events to post-Holocaust history, which was rife with examples of atrocities that resulted from racism and hatred. We wanted both to teach the story of the Holocaust and to apply its lessons to the present and the future in a Museum of Tolerance.

Our internal discussion about the Museum's mission spilled over into the public arena. Holocaust survivors debated whether building a Museum of Tolerance, rather than a Jewish Holocaust museum, was a good idea. Many, including Simon, vehemently argued that the Museum should include the stories of non-Jewish minorities persecuted by the Nazis, and the stories of post-World War II atrocities. He made the point that had Hitler defeated England and America, minorities, including African-Americans and Latinos, would certainly have been persecuted, and insisted that Jews needed friends and allies to conquer hatred. Opponents feared that by including other examples of man's inhumanity to man, we would misrepresent what was unique about the Holocaust: that it was an industrialized program specifically designed to exterminate the Jewish people.

In the end, we adopted Simon's approach, but with the stipulation that the Museum of Tolerance be divided into two sections with different messages and visitor experiences. The first would present the Holocaust—from the birth of Nazism in the 1920s through the destruction of European Jewry and the defeat of the Third Reich in May 1945—for the average visitor, who knew little Holocaust history, through a controlled visitor experience built around a film and computerized visual effects. The atmosphere would be dark, and the experience personal, as each visitor would be given a passport of a

Jewish child that would accompany him or her from one epic event to the next, until the end of the exhibit, where the child's ultimate fate would be revealed. The second section would be a social laboratory designed to challenge and inspire people of all backgrounds to confront the racism, prejudice, and miscarriage of justice that has plagued our world since Auschwitz. The Social Laboratory would focus both on American and international issues, from gender inequalities and prejudice against homosexuals, to anti-Semitism, racism, terrorism and genocide, including recent events in Biafra, Bosnia, Rwanda and Darfur. The atmosphere would be open and accessible, to encourage visitors to engage with a variety of exhibits and issues.

A remarkable team of staff and trustees diligently worked to transform the Museum concept into a reality. Rabbi Abraham Cooper developed content, Rabbi Meyer May raised funds, and Susan Burden served as Staff Liaison to the Board's Museum and Building Committees. Janice Prager, who would later be in charge of our national fundraising events and major gifts, would join the team, which would be indispensable and involved in every major undertaking by the Center.

Trustees Sam and Frances Belzberg, William and Barbara Belzberg, Roland Arnall and Esther Cohen devoted countless hours to developing and managing the project. Alan Casden, Chairman of the Building Committee, oversaw construction and Frances Belzberg chaired the Content Committee. Dr. Efraim Zuroff, Dr. Alex Grobman and Dr. Gerald Margolis, directors of the former Museum, provided important input. James Gardner of London and Karl Katz from the Metropolitan Museum of Art, who had designed many museums and exhibits around the world, helped design the facility. Rick Trank, our Academy Award-winning executive producer of Moriah Films, oversaw the production of the Museum's film exhibits. Development consultants, Sidney Green and Leslie Belzberg, helped us launch a national fundraising campaign. By January 1993, the nearly one hundred thousand-square-foot, fifty four million dollar Museum of Tolerance neared completion.

As the February opening approached, I was both excited and nervous. Our recent Annual National Tribute Dinner celebrating the forthcoming opening had been thrilling, especially when I was named a Chevalier of the Ordre national du mérite by French President François Mitterrand. But I was anxious, because the opening of the Museum of Tolerance represented a major milestone in the life of the Simon Wiesenthal Center.

The opinion that mattered most to me was that of the man who had given us his most precious possession, his good name. Simon had requested a private tour of the Museum prior to its opening, and I proudly served as guide. As I accompanied him through the Museum on the Friday morning before our "Fulfill the Vision" weekend and Monday's official opening, I closely watched his reactions. Simon walked slowly through the Museum, his eyes fixated on the exhibits rather than the building itself, despite his background in architecture. He never once glanced down at the newly laid carpeting or the four-story rotunda. Instead, he paced among the exhibits, as if each one brought back another episode from his long years in Hitler's concentration camps. When we reached a reenactment of the Wannsee Conference, tears welled up in Simon's eyes. Perhaps it reminded him of how, as a teenager, he had tried in vain to chase down a train that was taking away his mother, eventually delivering her to the gas chambers. At that moment, I knew that Simon was proud of what we had accomplished; as he wiped his eyes with a handkerchief, I was confident that he believed his work over so many years had been worthwhile, and that American Jews understood and accepted the responsibility of remembering the Holocaust.

That Sunday night at the Beverly Hilton Hotel, it was my turn to express feelings of pride to 800 Simon Wiesenthal Center trustees, supporters and friends, gathered to celebrate the Museum opening:

In August of 1977, when the idea first came to me to do something about creating an institution to perpetuate the memory of the most vivid example of man's inhumanity to man, I was struck by the fact that, with the exception of an oral history project in Flatbush, no major institution on the Holocaust existed outside Israel.... As if the great academies of Western thought had, by their acquiescence and silence, concurred that such a phenomena as the Holocaust was best preserved by the victims themselves…. That it wasn't relevant enough for the Yard at Harvard, or for the Archdioceses of our nation's co-religionists, or the curriculums of America's schools. Simply put, the *Shoah* was homeless in America. It had no address here in the great hub of Western Civilization.

That made no sense to me. As the Angel who wrestled with Jacob reminded him in the Book of Genesis: "You ask me for my name…well, listen well…I have no particular name…" Because, you see, evil is nameless, colorless, it is of all faiths; it brooks no geographic boundaries, it cannot be confined to a specific time; its appearance is not like the morning mist that automatically evaporates with the rising of the sun…. To defeat it, you must go out and take her on; you must attempt to excise the malignancy before it is too late, to educate the uninformed, to anticipate the unexpected and to always be there when evil appears…

The Museum of Tolerance became a great success, thanks, in large part, to the dynamic stewardship of Liebe Geft and her exceptional staff. Under Liebe's direction, over the next two decades, the Museum of Tolerance would become recognized as an international leader in tolerance education. Nearly six million visitors—one and a half million of them high school students, and ninety-five percent of them non-Jews—would pass through its doors. Over time, more than two hundred thousand professionals would participate in its Tools for Tolerance™ program, the largest sensitivity training program in the US.

Given the Museum's success, we decided to expand its reach by seeking grants from the federal government, the State of California, the City and State of New York, and major foundations such as Wells Fargo, greatly aided by trustees Norm Brownstein, Stu Isen, Steve Ghysels, and spearheaded by Rabbi Meyer May and Cliff Berg. We opened satellite facilities in other locations. With the help of trustees Nelson Peltz, Ira Lipman, Peter May, Alan Adler, Marc Utay and Michael Fuchs, we transformed the Wiesenthal Center's New York office on 42nd Street in the heart of Manhattan into a seventeen thousand-square-foot Tolerance Center, a professional development training facility for teachers, law enforcement officials, and government employees. In 2014, with the assistance of Jona Rechnitz, the New York Center received generous grants from the State of New York Department of Corrections and the City Council of New York.

At the same time, the Canadian Friends of the Simon Wiesenthal Center greatly expanded its activities under the lay leadership of longtime friends Gerry Schwartz and his wife Heather Reisman, as well as Lawrence Bloomberg, Philip Reichman, Honey Sherman and many others. Led by Avi Benlolo, the Friends organization opened the Tom and Anna Koffler Tolerance Training Centre in Toronto, and created the Tour for Humanity in order to take our message on the road to communities throughout Canada.

In 2000, at the urging of Wiesenthal Center trustee, Judah Hertz, the Center bought a new building caddy-cornder to the Museum of Tolerance in Los Angeles to serve as our international headquarters, to house staff offices and archives and to expand our Tools for Tolerance programs.

Over the years, we developed many successful and creative exhibits at the Museum of Tolerance. One exhibit came to us from Billy Crystal. Billy and his wife Janice approached me in 2001, after they had been researching their family tree. Billy was fascinated by the way his family had moved up in American society. He explained how his great-grandparents had come to New York from Austria and Russia, how his great-grandfather had opened a music store, and how his grandfather, Milton Gabler, had turned that store into a meeting place for jazz musicians, and created Commodore Records, which produced albums for Billie Holiday, Louis Armstrong and Ella Fitzgerald.

Billy and Janice proposed an exhibit to tell the American immigrant tale by showcasing individual stories from families of diverse backgrounds who came to America with nothing and built productive lives. Such an exhibit, they pointed out, would celebrate the possibility America offers to overcome adversity and achieve success, and would encourage museum visitors, especially young people, to seek out their own family histories and heroes. I thought it was a wonderful idea.

Billy and Janice devoted many months to developing the exhibit. They brought in audio-visual experts, including Doris Woodward, Don Molitar, Julie Green Williams and other professionals from Electrosonic and Walt Disney Imagineering, who worked closely with our own Susan Burden and Liebe Geft. Billy recorded the narration for the exhibit.

When Malkie and I were in New York in January 2003, Billy invited us to the studio where he was recording the narration, and spiced up the invitation with the offer of a kosher lunch. While we were eating our corned beef sandwiches, a man abruptly approached me from behind, placed his hands over my eyes, and began to sing, "*Oy hut er gedavent*" (Oh did he pray).

I was certain the sonorous voice belonged to my long-time acquaintance, Joseph Malovany, cantor of New York's Fifth Avenue Synagogue.

"Cantor Malovany, you can't fool me!" I said with a smile.

But when I spun around and the mystery singer removed his hands, I found Billy's close friend, Robin Williams, standing before me.

Thoroughly amused, I quipped, "Robin, when you've had enough of being a comedian, there's a future for you as a cantor!"

In February 2003, we opened the "Finding Our Families, Finding Ourselves" exhibit. In addition to telling Billy's family story, we shared the remarkable stories of African-American author Maya Angelou, Mexican-American rock musician Carlos Santana and Italian-American baseball player and manager Joe Torre. Through images, video clips and re-created home environments (including Billy's childhood apartment, complete with warped wood floor and furniture held in place by rope), we explored these accomplished individuals' distinctive journeys, and highlighted the lives and dreams of the family members who inspired them.

The exhibit was a popular success. School groups flocked to it. Oprah Winfrey highlighted it on her television show. Billy explored his family history further in a Broadway play, *700 Sundays*, which he named for the limited number of days he spent with his father before he died.

At our 2003 National Tribute Dinner, we awarded Billy and Janice the Wiesenthal Center's highest honor, its Humanitarian Award. The one thousand-guest star-studded event, was meticulously organized by our multi-talented National Director of Development, Janice Prager, and held in the ballroom of the Beverly Hilton Hotel. Maya Angelou, Joe Torre and Carlos Santana graced us with their presence. I used the occasion to joke about the fundraising Billy and I had undertaken for the exhibit, and the countless meetings we attended:

When we first started out two years ago, we needed a few million dollars. Billy agreed to accompany me to Florida to kick off our fundraising effort. In Florida, we met Don Soffer, who gave the first very generous gift to start the project.

So in the hotel, Don says to me, "If Billy will come down for cocktails tonight, I think I'll have a good prospect for you." Billy agreed, and we went down to meet Don. I take one look at Don's prospect and realized he's had a little too much to drink. Billy tells him all about the *Finding Our Families* exhibit, and this man starts talking to us about finding our golf clubs! Miraculously, he agreed to contribute one hundred thousand dollars, but he started to make out the check to Tiger Woods!

But, ladies and gentlemen, fundraising was nothing for Billy, compared to those meetings. Billy sat through them all, saying to himself, "*Oy vey*, do the Jews love meetings! Give them a meeting and their day is made.... If you meet a Jew who looks invigorated, it's not because he just came back from the spa, it's because tonight there's a meeting! Just the thrill that he might get a chance to second a motion or, if he is lucky, resolve this or resolve that, repeat this for the forty-sixth time or argue about that for the forty-ninth time.... A non-Jew might wonder, 'What's so special about a Jewish meeting?' Let me tell you, a Jewish meeting is where everyone talks at the same time, even the fellow who is taking the minutes, and then everybody is angry at everybody else for not listening.... There is only one exception: when the food is brought in. Then you can hear a pin drop, and all eyes are on the waiter as everyone tries to figure out who is in a better position to lunge at it."

The good news, Billy and Janice, is that after tonight, there will be no more meetings. But because of you, millions of people will embark on journeys to discover who they are and where they came from.

Over time, we collected many important historical documents and artifacts to display in the Museum of Tolerance. The most significant is "the Hitler letter," the only letter in the world signed by Adolf Hitler, in which he expresses his opinion of what should be done with the Jews. The four-page, typed letter, dated September 1919, was housed in an ss archive in Nuremberg that a us army unit came upon in April 1945. A member of the unit, William F. Ziegler, collected a handful of documents from the archive as souvenirs, which he stored in a closet of his home when he returned to the us. In the mid-1980s, he noticed Hitler's letter among the documents, and sold it to a rare documents dealer, Profiles in History, which is owned by Ben Shapell, son of Wiesenthal Center trustee, David Shapell. When my devoted assistant, Dana Mones, informed me that Ben wanted to come over and show me the letter, I knew it was something that belonged at the Simon Wiesenthal Center.

Charles Hamilton, Jr., one of the world's foremost autograph dealers and handwriting experts, who in 1983 had correctly determined that a diary attributed to Hitler was a forgery, examined the letter in 1988 and again in 1990. Hamilton authenticated the signature, stating that the document was, "a seminal letter of enormous importance, not only to Germany, but to the world. For in it, Hitler outlines in detail, the reasons for his anti-Semitic views. It is Hitler's blueprint for the catastrophe that was to overwhelm the world twenty years later."

The Hitler letter is one of the most important documents of World War II. In it, Adolf Hitler makes his first political statement regarding the Jewish question:

Anti-Semitism stemming from purely emotional reasons will always find its expression in the form of pogroms, but anti-Semitism based on reason must lead to the systematic legal combating and removal of the rights of the Jew…its final aim, however, must be the uncompromising removal of the Jews altogether. Both are possible, only under a government of national strength, never under a government of national impotence.

These hair-raising words prove that Hitler conceived of the idea of the elimination of Germany's Jews as early as September 1919, years before he wrote *Mein Kampf,* and without the input of his future partners, Heinrich Himmler, Reinhard Heydrich or Adolf Eichmann. Even though the letter does not refer to the annihilation of the Jews, it proves that the removal of the Jews from Germany was fundamental to Hitler's thinking from the onset.

Hitler wrote the letter when he served in the German Armed Forces during World War I. In early 1919, he was assigned to the propaganda section of the Bavarian Army under the command of Captain Karl Mayr in Munich. On September 12 of that year, Captain Mayr ordered him to monitor the meeting of the small German Workers' Party. Although sent as an observer, Hitler could not resist speaking up. His remarks made such an impression on the forty people present that the group's founder, Anton Drexler, invited Hitler to join. Soon after, Hitler took over the party, which would grow into the Nazi Party. On September 16, 1919, Captain Mayr, who now regarded Hitler as the resident expert on the Jews, asked him to answer an inquiry from Adolf Gemlich, an army undercover agent, about the appropriate attitude toward the Jews. The now-famous letter is Hitler's reply.

The letter is exceptionally rare, because the Nazis destroyed most documents in the waning days of the war, and because historians believe that Hitler orally transmitted most orders to his deputies regarding the extermination of the Jews. For these reasons, no documents with Hitler's signature were discovered or introduced into evidence during the Nuremberg Trials.

The New York Times and other international media outlets covered the story of our acquiring the letter in 2011. We made the letter the centerpiece of an interactive exhibit in the Holocaust section of the Museum of Tolerance, which includes a timeline and hundreds of photographs of key events in the history of the Third Reich. There, it reminds visitors that what began as a private letter eventually became state policy that led to the murder of millions, and warns them that demagogues must be taken seriously, for they mean what they say, and under the right circumstances, will carry out what they promise.

Long-time benefactors, Michael and Lori Milken, made an important contribution to our collection by donating pen-pal letters sent by Anne Frank and her sister Margot to two American girls in 1940, just before the German invasion of the Netherlands sealed the Frank family's fate. In September 2013, we included the letters in "Anne," a one-of-a-kind, multi-media exhibit on the life of Anne Frank made possible by generous grants from Larry and Carol Mizel, David and Fela Shapell, and Wells Fargo Bank, and developed in cooperation with the Anne Frank House in Amsterdam and the Anne Frank Fonds in Basel. Visitors enter the exhibit through a sweeping streetscape of Frankfurt, the Frank's hometown, and are lured by the sights and sounds of Amsterdam, the city to which they fled in 1933. As Anne mentions in her astutely observed diary, a tower bell chimes and the leaves of a chestnut tree change color. Visitors enter the secret annex and Anne's room, in which major scenes from her diary are brought to life through an intense, surround presentation. Academy Award nominee Hailee Steinfeld provides the voice of Anne Frank, which accompanies visitors through the exhibit:

> Countless friends and acquaintances have gone to a terrible fate. Evening after evening, the green and gray army lorries trundle past. The Germans ring at every front door to inquire if there are any Jews living in the house. If there are, then the whole family has to go at once. I often see rows of good, innocent people accompanied by crying children, walking on and on in the charge of a couple of these chaps, bullied and knocked about until they almost drop....
>
> I must have something besides a husband and children, something that I can devote myself to. I want to go on living

even after my death. And that's why I'm so grateful to God for having given me this gift, which I can use to develop myself and write, to express all that's inside me…. But, and that's a big question, will I ever be able to write something great? Will I ever become a journalist or a writer…?

We have been pointedly reminded that we are in hiding, that we are Jews in chains, without any rights, but with a thousand duties…. Who has made us Jews different from all other people? Who has allowed us to suffer so terribly up till now? It is God that has made us as we are, but it will be God, too, who will raise us up again. If we bear all this suffering and if there are still Jews left when it is over, then Jews, instead of being doomed will be held up as an example. Who knows, it might even be our religion from which the world and all the peoples learn good, and for that reason and that reason only do we have to suffer now. Be brave! God has never deserted our people….

The night before the exhibit opened to the public in the Museum's Jaime and Marilyn Sohacheski Gallery, Jeffrey and Marilyn Katzenberg and Ron and Kelly Meyer hosted a special preview. Many Hollywood figures attended the event, including Tom Cruise, Roma Downey, Mark Burnett, Barbra Streisand and James Brolin. Barbra was so moved that she later told the press, "If the Museum of Tolerance's enthralling new Anne Frank exhibit were experienced by every person, it would leave us incapable of tolerating oppression. To be imbued with Anne's beautiful spirit and courage for this riveting sixty minutes is to make both your heart and your world a better place." Ron Meyer added that the Frank family's desperate attempt to escape its fate particularly resonated for him, because his parents were fortunate to have been able to leave Germany for the US in 1938, just before the borders were sealed.

The exhibit provides the perfect context for displaying the pen-pal letters. Indeed, the interlinking of the Anne Frank story with the Museum of Tolerance's mission is fateful, for it was Simon Wiesenthal, who, in 1963, tracked down Karl Silberbauer, the Gestapo officer who arrested Anne Frank and her family. With Silberbauer's arrest and confession, the authenticity of Anne Frank's diary could no longer be denied.

The Museum of Tolerance collection also houses Simon Wiesenthal's Vienna office, exactly as he left it when he died. We preserved Simon's desk and chair, his original oil paintings depicting life in the concentration camps, and other furnishings, documents and decorations. Thanks to a major gift from Alan Casden, a long-time benefactor, trustee and personal friend of Simon's, and his wife Susan, we transformed the artifacts into one of the most popular multi-media exhibits at the Museum of Tolerance. The exhibit includes a recorded presentation about Simon's life, from the tragedies of his youth to his accomplishments as a Nazi hunter. Simon's voice tells visitors that his work was not about the past, but the future, for it served "as a warning for the murderers of tomorrow, that they will never be able to rest. They must know that a moral duty is not defined by time, and that a murderer, even after forty years, remains a murderer." He insists that his work was not about vengeance, but justice: "What is revenge? Can you take revenge against a man who was responsible for the death of seven hundred thousand people? What can be the revenge… ?"

Over the years, the Museum of Tolerance has attracted visitors from a wide variety of backgrounds. Most are deeply affected by the experiences the Museum provides. Many send us emails or letters afterwards to express their gratitude.

One young mother wrote:

> I visited your museum in the summer of 1997…I had just found out I was pregnant with my first child…. We were given a card…mine was a little girl named Liliana Fano…her story was so tragic and she perished…. I left wishing there was a way to keep her memory alive…. On February 26, 1998, six months later, I gave birth to a little girl and the answer became clear. I named her Liliana so that in some small way, the name and story of Liliana Fanos can live on. The reason I shared it with

you is I want you to know that your museum is powerful and its message carries on with visitors long after they have walked out the door. —Elissa

Another memorable letter came from an eighth-grade teacher who had visited the Museum with students from a middle school in California. The day after the visit, one of the students, fourteen-year-old Richy, was fatally shot by gang members:

> Richy was one of the eight-graders that we brought with us to the Museum last Friday—a mere day before his death. I'm so incredibly proud and thankful that he was able to go on the trip with us.... Please know that we hold the MOT [Museum of Tolerance] in our highest regards, now more than ever. As we continue to help our students grieve this loss and grapple with the concept of violence in our world, we will draw upon so much of what we learned at the Museum. Thank you, Thank you, Thank you. —Nicole

Colonel Richard Seibel, who had served as commanding officer of the US Army's Eleventh Armored Division during World War II, once visited the Museum. Colonel Seibel had earlier donated an artifact to us that had become one of our most prized possessions: the Mauthausen Flag, an American flag secretly sown by inmates of the infamous Mauthausen Concentration Camp out of tattered clothing, days before their liberation on May 5, 1945. After Seibel's division liberated Mauthausen, its soldiers flew the flag at the camp's entrance to mark the defeat of Hitler's Third Reich, then presented it to Colonel Seibel. When he discovered that Simon was one of the survivors his division had liberated, Colonel Seibel donated the flag to the Simon Wiesenthal Center.

During his visit to the Museum of Tolerance, Colonel Seibel penned a poignant note:

> Every act of hatred based solely on race, heritage, religion, poverty, wealth, disability is like a miniature Mauthausen. Do

not allow these daily concentration camps to exist. It is not in some grand war that you will bring peace on earth, but in your daily lives with singular acts of kindness.

Some museum visitors have been world political leaders, including three Presidents of the United States, each of whom struck an important chord. Ronald Reagan first addressed a Simon Wiesenthal Center National Tribute Dinner in 1988, where he invoked Israel:

> Out of the ashes of the Holocaust came a great thing called the State of Israel...America and Israel share an understanding forged in the blood and horror of the Second World War. It is not enough to invoke our common traditions...we must also defend our traditions, our morality, and our decency... the West knows all too well what happens when the barbarians believe they can act unchecked.
>
> All we need do is look at Simon Wiesenthal's life...we must follow his example and never waver in our pursuit of justice...we must remain strong and we must be willing to use force when we're under threat.... For the fact is, a strong Israel depends upon a strong America. An America that loses faith in the idea of a strong defense is an America that will lose faith in a nation at arms like Israel.

In 1989, when he returned to California after serving two terms in the Oval Office, President Reagan unexpectedly dropped by the Museum and shocked a group of high school students by giving them an impromptu speech on the importance of public service.

When President George H.W. Bush spoke at our National Tribute Dinner in 1991, he described the significance of the Mauthuasen flag:

> I must say what was running through my mind when the Holocaust survivors brought in the Mauthausen Flag. What a story those men and women creating out of scraps this symbol of the values that gave them hope.... I just wish every American could

hear their story. I wish every American could see this flag and feel the same emotion I felt when these survivors brought it to the stage. The two pledges of Simon Wiesenthal's life inspire us all: "Never forget" and "never again"…yes, like many here, Barbara and I have been to Auschwitz. We've seen the images of human evil. And literally when I left, I left part of me. But I took something away in its place—the determination not just to remember, but to act. I say this to you as a World War II veteran—and now as President of the United States—the haunting images compel us to guard against tyranny and inhumanity. Remembering makes us strong. Remembering makes us act.

President George W. Bush spoke about leadership:

All of you are supporting a great work. For more than a generation now, the Simon Wiesenthal Center has fought against anti-Semitism and all forms of bigotry. Not just here but around the world…anti-Semitism once destroyed the moral foundations of one of the most educated nations on earth. It is a fact that barbarism can appear even in the most outwardly civilized society. Tolerance can never be assumed; it must be taught…a leader must do more than hold his conviction. He must give it voice and he must give it force…. This place bears the name of a man who has never tired of righting wrongs and seeking justice…. Your work is always urgent and always unfinished.

Israel's leaders have been visitors to the Museum of Tolerance as well. Prime Ministers Menachem Begin and Yitzhak Shamir spoke at the Museum. Yitzhak Rabin and Ariel Sharon visited when they served as Ministers of Defense. Shimon Peres came when he was Foreign Minister.

In March 2014, Prime Minister Benjamin Netanyahu came to the Museum of Tolerance during a three-day visit to California following a meeting with President Barack Obama. Larry Mizel, Merv Adelson, Syd and Joanne Belzberg, Elliott Broidy, Janet Crown, Stuart Isen, Jimmy Lustig, Ron Meyer, Cheston Mizel, Brett Ratner, James

Packer, Burt Sugarman, Mary Hart, David and Fela Shapell, Jay Snider, Sol and Ruth Teichman and other Simon Wiesenthal Center trustees and supporters greeted the prime minister in the Museum's Mizel Boardroom. Then, knowing that the thorny America-Iran nuclear negotiations were on the Prime Minister's mind, I directed him to a conference room to see something he had never seen before, the Hitler Letter. Although we provided him with an English translation, Prime Minister Netanyahu focused on the original German text, on Hitler's signature and the chilling words, "its final aim, however, must be the uncompromising removal of the Jews altogether. Both are possible, only under a government of national strength, never under a government of national impotence." The letter must have made an impression, because Prime Minister Netanyahu referred to it in his remarks to Los Angeles Jewish community leaders in the Museum's Peltz Theater:

> The [Hitler] Letter I was shown a few minutes ago, a letter of intent to liquidate the Jewish people stated clearly.... It wasn't believed, it was discounted as ranting for internal consumption. It turned out to be very different. We have paid a terrible price that the powers of the world did not heed that warning nor did they act on it...
>
> I think it is outrageous that seventy years after the Holocaust, this [the Iranian call for the annihilation of the Jewish state] could be accepted with virtual silence. When somebody says that they are going to annihilate you, you take them seriously and prepare, and warn, and make an issue of it. The mere statement, this brazen approach, that one can call for the liquidation of the Jewish state and people don't get excited about it, means that goal entrenches and re-entrenches in the minds of the fanatics and they think they can get away with it. We need to expose their deception.
>
> While they say that [they will destroy Israel] in Tehran, and while they say that while putting on smiling faces, internally where it counts, they continue to talk about the liquidation of the Jewish state and they continue to act for the liquidation of the Jewish state...

If there is something I can say here at the Museum of Tolerance, it is that we cannot be tolerant to the intolerant. These people are out to destroy a section of humanity called the Jewish people. We will not let them, we will expose, and we shall fight them, and we shall beat them.

Other important political and religious leaders have visited the Museum of Tolerance. In August 1996, during a five-day tour of California, the leader of Tibetan Buddhism, the Dalai Lama, paid us a visit. Draped in gold and maroon robes, he meandered through the Museum, taking in each exhibit through large, half-rimmed glasses. Following the tour, we convened in the Peltz Theater to present the Dalai Lama with our 1996 Peace Award. Actors Pierce Brosnan, Richard Gere and Steven Seagal, Senator Tom Hayden and Assemblyman Richard Katz were in the audience, along with hundreds of other guests. In his acceptance speech, the Dalai Lama spoke about family, education and world events. He then described his admiration for the Jewish people: "The Jewish people never gave up their hope, their determination...they kept their traditions very alive.... So since then, we are always trying to steal your secret," he joked, revealing his inimitable, infectious smile.

The most surprising visit of a foreign leader was that of King Hussein in March 1995. One month earlier, during the Simon Wiesenthal Center's second mission to Jordan, I had extended a standing invitation to King Hussein and his family to visit the Museum. But I had little hope that the King would accept my offer; after all, a visit by the leader of the Hashemite Kingdom to a museum devoted, in large part, to the Holocaust, would surely cause a stir in the Arab world.

But then the Office of the Jordanian Ambassador to the United States called with the news: "Their Majesties, King Hussein and Queen Noor will soon be visiting Washington, DC. While in the United States, they have requested a visit to the Museum of Tolerance." Within days, the trip's details were confirmed. The King and Queen would be coming to Los Angeles with their children, the Prime Minister of Jordan, and senior government officials. I, along with members of the Los Angeles Jewish community, and many others, were astonished.

On March 24, 1995, a procession of black limousines streamed toward the Museum as a Marine Corps band offered a brassy salute. California Governor Pete Wilson, his wife Gayle and I welcomed the royal family and the rest of the entourage, and led them to the Museum entrance. Surrounded by bodyguards muttering into their palms and reporters snapping photographs, I accompanied King Hussein and Queen Noor on a brief tour of the Museum. The King, noticeably moved, spent an hour-and-a-half in the Holocaust Exhibit, holding back tears as he watched a video about Nazi cruelty against children. He attentively viewed a documentary on the American Civil Rights Movement, and a film clip of the 1992 Los Angeles riots following the infamous Rodney King event.

Aware of our limited time, Queen Noor said, "This is really something.... We'll have to come back." At the end of the tour, King Hussein wrote in the Museum guest book, "Words cannot express my feelings," then signed his name in Arabic and English. He had become the first Muslim leader to visit an American Jewish museum.

Following the tour, I led the King and Queen and their three children to the Museum's Peltz Theater, where we held a ceremony to grant King Hussein the Museum of Tolerance's first Peace Award. One year earlier, the King had displayed monumental courage and trust when he signed the Israel-Jordan Peace Treaty with Israel's Prime Minister, Yitzhak Rabin. Senator Dianne Feinstein made brief remarks, then the King spoke. "We look forward with confidence to a day when the words 'Arab-Israeli' no longer evoke images of strife," Hussein said, when "future generations will one day enjoy a life free from fear, a life free from want, a life in peace." He spoke of "a new era where the enemies of yesterday become the good neighbors of today and the friends of tomorrow...where disputes cede to dialogue and conflict is replaced by cooperation." He described the Museum of Tolerance as "a haunting reminder to all mankind of the many inexplicable acts of cruelty...of the tragedy and shame that result from blindness, illogical hatred and intolerance."

I presented King Hussein with a silver shofar inscribed with the words: "He who pursues peace will find his prayers answered." He accepted the prize to a standing ovation. I thanked his Royal Highness for coming to the Museum of Tolerance, and reinforced its message:

A few moments ago, your Majesties, you saw, first-hand, the results of unmitigated hatred when you visited the Museum, particularly the Holocaust section that highlights the evil brought upon mankind by the Third Reich. But the story of mankind need not be written in crematoria or in death camps. It need not be written in the carnage left by a terrorist attack. It can be written in the fertile fields that feed the hungry, in the wonders of modern medicine that cure the sick. It can be written in the classrooms of our schools and universities that help defeat ignorance or our synagogues and mosques that nourish the soul and in the halls of our legislatures that pro-tect the rights of free men and women.

As we sat together enjoying a luncheon that followed the ceremony, King Hussein innocently turned to me and said, "I would like to become a member of your Museum." Assuming he was speaking figuratively, I did not go into details of our membership policies. But His Majesty pressed on, "Is there a membership card I could fill out and keep with me?"

Realizing now that he was serious, I instructed a staff member to run over to the Museum's entrance lobby and fetch some member-ship materials. When he returned, I presented the King of Jordan, a descendant of the Islamic prophet Mohammed, with a membership card to the Simon Wiesenthal Center's Museum of Tolerance. He removed a fine ballpoint pen from his jacket pocket, signed the back of the card, and tucked it into his wallet.

That Museum visit cemented my personal relationship with King Hussein. Exactly one year later, in March 1996, I visited King Hussein while he was recuperating from surgery at the Bel Air Hotel in Los Angeles. I invited Mary Hart, who had organized the Museum's award ceremony, to join me.

Despite his post-operative condition, head bandages and all, the King was eager to share with me something he had brought from home. He asked me to wait a moment while he retrieved an old suitcase, which, he explained, had belonged to his grandfather, King Abdullah. From this modest but royal heirloom, he withdrew a letter written by one of his sons, that he read aloud. The letter's significance soon became clear: it was a heartfelt, personal tribute to Israeli Prime Minister Yitzhak Rabin, who, four months earlier, had been assassinated by Jewish Israeli extremist, Yigal Amir.

In 1997, King Hussein surprised me once again. I was driving down Pico Boulevard on my way to a dental appointment when my cell phone rang. It was General Ali Shukri, King Hussein's senior advisor: "Rabbi," he said, "If it's not an inconvenient time, I would like to put His Majesty on the phone."

I tried to conceal my surprise with a simple, "Of course," as I quickly pulled my car off to the side of the road.

"Rabbi," King Hussein began. "It is so kind of you to take my call. I have something important that I need your help with. Let me be frank. Unfortunately, my relationship with Prime Minister Netanyahu has deteriorated, and I think that it's probably best if the two of us could have a private discussion. I'm turning to you with a suggestion. I would like to ask you to contact the Prime Minister directly, and tell him that I will be in my home in London. I know that he is coming to the United States to speak to the Jewish community. My suggestion is that on his way back to Israel, he stop in London and stay in my home, where the two of us can sit down face to face, restore our relationship and do what we can to restore peace in our region. Is there any way that you could speak to the Prime Minister, convey my message and get back to General Shukri with a response?"

I knew that King Hussein's relationship with Prime Minister Netanyahu had become tense in the last month, following a botched attempt by the Mossad to assassinate Khaled Mashaal, political chief of the terrorist Palestinian organization, Hamas, in the Jordanian capital. But I was shocked that King Hussein would turn to me rather than go through normal diplomatic channels to help repair the rift. "Your Majesty, it so happens that after the Prime Minister speaks to the Council of Jewish Federations, he is coming to Los Angeles to the Simon Wiesenthal Center, where we have a program scheduled at the Museum of Tolerance. I think I will be able to deliver your message to him directly."

King Hussein was pleased. He offered one suggestion: "Perhaps you could arrange a telephone conversation so that the Prime Minister and I can speak while he is visiting with you."

"That is an excellent idea, Your Majesty," I responded. "I will pass on the suggestion."

Still in my car on the side of Pico Boulevard, I phoned my Israeli contacts, who passed the information on to the Prime Minister. Prime Minister Netanyahu agreed to speak with King Hussein.

As the visit approached, the Prime Minister's team arranged for a secure phone line to be set up in the Museum of Tolerance's Mizel Boardroom. On a Monday morning, the Prime Minister's motorcade pulled up to the Museum. Arnold Schwarzenegger, who was chairing the official welcoming program, met Prime Minister Netanyahu at the Museum entrance. Without eliciting the slightest suspicion from Arnold, who knew nothing of the plan, the Prime Minister excused himself, saying he needed to use the washroom. He and his security detail headed straight for the fourth floor board room. Thirty seconds later, the board room phone rang. It was, of course, King Hussein. Prime Minister Netanyahu and King Hussein spoke for nearly ten minutes. The Prime Minister accepted the King's invitation to meet with him the next day at his London residence. There, the two worked out their differences and repaired the fragile Israeli-Jordanian relationship, a symbol of the possibility of peace between Israel and its Arab neighbors.

Chapter Ten

Moguls and Stars
Are People, Too

I n 2011, I spent an unforgettable day touring Jerusalem with comedian Jerry Seinfeld and my good friend, DreamWorks Animation CEO Jeffrey Katzenberg, who along with this wife Marilyn, has chaired the Wiesenthal Center's annual dinners for twenty years and who heads its International Leadership Council that has raised many millions of dollars for the Simon Wiesenthal Center. Together, the three of us visited Shimon Peres, the President of Israel, at his official Jerusalem residence. In his thick accent, President Peres called on us to elicit greater support for Israel:

> Gentlemen, Israel needs you. We are now before the festival of Chanukah, and I want to tell you: Don't think that miracles are only in the Bible or occurred in the past. The greatest miracle of all is here before your eyes.... We are a small country. One-third of our people were murdered in the Holocaust. We survived. We started with nothing. We have no oil. But look at what we have

done in just over six decades in the sciences, in technology.... Imagine what we could do if we had everyone's support?

Informed that Jeffrey and Jerry were in the country to promote a movie, President Peres asked Jerry, "What is the movie called?" Jerry replied, "The Bee Movie." President Peres joked, "Look, Jerry. I'm sure a man of your talent doesn't make B movies. You only make A movies."

Jerry retorted deadpan, "Mr. President, do you mind if I ask you a question? Do you ever get out of the office?"

That Friday evening, I led Jeffrey and Jerry through Dung Gate into the Old City's Jewish Quarter. As we filtered into the stone-paved plaza in front of the Western Wall, a Chassid in full regalia picked Jerry out of the crowd: "Welcome home to Yerushalayim, Mr. Seinfeld!"

Jerry turned to me in surprise, "Rabbi, I thought those guys don't watch TV. How did he know who I am?"

"Jerry," I replied, "Chassidim have their own communications network."

Jeffrey and Jerry then spontaneously joined a circle of jubilant Chassidim dancing before the ancient wall. When Jeffrey broke away to drum on a nearby table, Jerry followed. The Chassidim came next, encircling the two Jews from Hollywood—one a movie mogul, the other a star—creating a scene that could not have occurred anywhere else in the world.

Soon after, in March 2012, Shimon Peres was scheduled to make his first official trip to Los Angeles as Israel's President. He was eager to meet with key Hollywood personalities to update them on critical issues facing Israel. I suggested to the President's staff, and they concurred, that Jeffrey Katzenberg was the right person to host the meeting at his DreamWorks Animation Studios.

First, President Peres spoke briefly to hundreds of Dream-Works Animation employees, drawing parallels between California and Israel:

> When California was founded, many thought it too wild and too windy to inhabit. You started as a mistake, and we started

as a doubt. But look what you did from a mistake and what we did from a doubt.

Then he met with the group that Jeffrey had organized, including Hollywood executives Ron Meyer, Haim Saban, Michael Lynton, Les Moonves, Steven Spielberg, Tom Rothman, Rick Ross and Peter Rice; actors Barbra Streisand and Billy Crystal; Israel's Ambassador to the US, Michael Oren and Israel's Consul General, David Siegel. He spoke forcefully about the Iranian nuclear threat. "A nuclear Iran would be a disaster for the entire Middle East...every Arab country would seek to follow Iran's example.... Israel would never tolerate a nuclear Iran...the destiny of Israel cannot be held hostage by the mullahs of Iran..."

He also made a strong case for a two-state solution to the Israeli-Palestinian problem, which, he insisted, was the only way to assure a secure Israel. He concluded by reminding the group gathered that one of Judaism's most important contributions to the world is the state of being unsatisfied: "Jews are never satisfied...Jews, without a land, without resources, have come so far, because when you're not satisfied, you keep dreaming."

Years earlier, in the fall of 1997, I had had another unforgettable experience with Hollywood personalities in Israel. Malkie and I were planning to be in Jerusalem during the holiday of Sukkos with our friends and Wiesenthal Center trustees, producer Burt Sugarman and his wife, Entertainment Tonight host Mary Hart. Burt had just watched the evening news, which included an item about three Hamas suicide bombers who had blown themselves up on Jerusalem's popular Ben Yehuda Street pedestrian mall. I reassured him, saying, "Burt, it's like cancelling a trip to New York because of a homicide."

The following week, Burt and Mary's trip proceeded as scheduled. I met them in the elegant lobby of the King David Hotel to discuss their itinerary. I promised Burt I would take him to a *tish*, a gathering of Chassidic men around their mentor and teacher, the Rebbe. Taking note of Burt's excitement over the possibility of receiving a personal blessing from a Chassidic rebbe, Mary insisted on coming along. I explained that in the Chassidic world, women simply do not participate in events like these, but Mary would have none of it. "I'm coming," she said matter-of-factly.

The next day I visited the Boyaner Rebbe's *gabbai* and explained the situation, "I, of course, understand that the honor of participating in a *tish* is reserved for men, and that women's holiness is derived from other sources. But I think this woman would grow spiritually simply from peering in on this most holy occasion."

The *gabbai* offered a viable suggestion. "The *tish* will take place in a large *sukkah* we build each year outside the Tiferes Yisroel Yeshiva. Next door, there is a building that might offer a view. If this woman opens an upstairs window and squats down at just the right angle, she might just get a glimpse of the Rebbe."

Mary was game. That evening, cloaked in a long-sleeved dress, her blond hair tucked within a patterned silk scarf, Mary boarded a taxi with my daughter-in-law, Annie, and headed for the yeshiva in Jerusalem's *Ge'ula* neighborhood. Just as the *gabbai* had described, she found a corner in a chilly, third-floor walk-up next door to the yeshiva, and through bamboo mats that formed the *sukkah's* temporary roof, watched the evening's spectacle.

The Boyaner Rebbe, Nachum Dov Brayer, delivered a speech in Yiddish from the head of an enormous table draped in an unadorned white cloth. A throng of hundreds of followers dressed in knee-length, black silk coats and *shtreimels* (fur hats) surrounded him—some seated in coveted positions around the table, others swaying on metal bleachers that extended from the central table to the *sukkah's* outer limits. They hung on the Rebbe's every word, then joined him in singing traditional Ukrainian Chassidic melodies.

Following the tish, Burt, Mary, Malkie and I reconvened. Mary could hardly contain her excitement of seeing her husband raise his cup of wine and wish *"L'chaim"* to the Rebbe. When Burt described how he had received a piece of the *shirayim*, a portion of fish from the Rebbe's meal, signifying a personal blessing, Mary exclaimed, "This was more exciting than interviewing a Hollywood superstar!"

When I was a kid, there was nothing I loved more than a Sunday double-header at Yankee Stadium. From way up in the bleachers, I followed every play. Between innings, I imagined I was sitting in the dugout shmoozing with the Yankee greats. So when Zach Samuels called to ask me if I wanted to be a dugout guest of Tommy Lasorda, I needed no convincing.

On a breezy spring evening the following week, I arrived at Dodger Stadium and excitedly announced to a ticket collector that I was a guest of Tommy Lasorda. A security guard appeared moments later and escorted me to Tommy's office. Tommy looked very much as he did on television: squat and stocky, with eyes that matched the royal blue Dodgers cap perched above his downy white sideburns. He shook my hand and made small talk.

"So, Rabbi, where are you from?"

"Originally, New York City."

"Uh huh. So…the Yanks or the Mets?"

"Well, as a kid, I was a diehard Yankees fan. Those were the days…Joe DiMaggio…Yogi Berra…"

"Have you ever been out on the field?"

"The closest I've come is watching pitchers warm up in the bullpen."

"Well then, you're in for a treat."

Unsure why I was getting special treatment, I dutifully followed him out to the field, where the players were warming up. The pitcher's fastballs whirred past. Outfielders, who appeared to be positioned miles apart from one another, effortlessly lobbed and snagged high flies. My eyes swept across the manicured field and up to the tiered bleachers packed with fifty thousand noisy fans.

Tommy interrupted my hypnotic gaze to introduce me to the game's umpire. We shook hands, and stood at attention as the Star Spangled Banner echoed through the stadium. Then Tommy turned to me and said, "Well, now would be a good time to say it."

"Say what?" I asked, perplexed.

"You mean Zach didn't tell you?"

"Zach didn't tell me what?"

"Well, look, I had my priest here. Then I tried a minister," Tommy explained. "But neither one could help me break our losing streak. So now I'm looking for someone else, someone whose calls God is taking.... I asked Zach to get me a rabbi, and here you are. So now, whatever blessing there is in your religion, say it for the Los Angeles Dodgers."

I thought on my feet and decided that a modified form of the *Mi Sheberach* prayer, which is recited in synagogue for people who are ill, might just cover it: "May the One who blessed our ancestors, Abraham, Isaac and Jacob, bless and heal the Los Angeles Dodgers. May the Holy One restore them and strengthen them. And let us say Amen."

"Amen," Tommy grunted, as he made his way to the dugout, adding, "You can sit with my wife right over there." Tommy pointed to a prime spot in the first row near the Dodgers dugout. I joined his wife, Jo, who was expressing her team spirit in a royal blue and white outfit.

The close-up view of the game was breathtaking. Balls whizzed over home plate at lightning speed. Batters swung as if their lives depended on it. Infielders leapt and dove with swiftness and grace.

But when I turned my look inward, I realized my allegiance to the home team was compromised. I had a chronic soft spot for the underdog, and tonight, the underdogs were the Chicago Cubs.

When, in the top of the third inning, Cubs superstar Andre "The Hawk" Dawson hit a three-run home run to take the lead, I had to suppress my desire to cheer so Jo wouldn't take offense.

Maybe my prayer had been half-hearted, too. As the ninth inning drew to a close, the Cubs were ahead six to three. I apologized to Tommy for failing to bring him a win: "Sorry, Tommy," I said, "I guess God wasn't taking any calls from a rabbi either."

Thankfully, most of the prominent figures I have come to know have not relied on me as a conduit for their prayers. Instead, I have had the pleasure of becoming acquainted with many well-known people, especially Hollywood celebrities, due to their involvement with the

Simon Wiesenthal Center, Moriah Films and the Museum of Tolerance. Many of them have been great supporters of our work, and have helped our organization grow. From time to time, some have turned to me for advice.

Arnold Schwarzenegger has been a loyal supporter of the Wiesenthal Center and the Museum of Tolerance for twenty-five years, beginning long before he became Governor of California. He has been involved in many advocacy issues, such as our effort to prevent the distribution of a controversial video game, KZ Manager, in which players took on the role of commandants of Nazi death camps, and earned points for gassing prisoners and selling gold fillings. In 1991, Arnold flew to Austria and successfully lobbied officials of the Austrian Ministry of Education to ban the game.

When accusations were made that Arnold's father, Gustav Schwarzenegger, had been a member of the Nazi party, Arnold asked Simon Wiesenthal and the Wiesenthal Center to investigate. Our research showed that Gustav Schwarzenegger had joined Austria's Nazi Party before the Anschluss in 1938, and had served in the German Army in World War II, but had no connection to the SS or to Nazi war crimes. I always maintained that one generation cannot be held responsible for another, and that Arnold had done great work to further the cause of Holocaust awareness, sometimes at our behest, especially in Austria.

Arnold was not the only member of his family to support Jewish causes. In August 2000, he and his wife, Maria Shriver, held a reception in their Brentwood, California home in honor of Joseph Lieberman, the Jewish US Senator from Connecticut who had recently been selected as the Democratic nominee for US Vice President. While Malkie and I were shmoozing with guests in Arnold and Maria's gorgeous backyard, we noticed a man capped in a shiny white yarmulka waiting on line at a meat-carving station. Intrigued that perhaps Arnold and Maria had ordered kosher food out of respect for Senator Lieberman, I approached the man to see if he knew, for a fact, that the food was kosher. Once in conversation range, I realized he was Maria's father, politician and activist Sargent Shriver, who himself had been a Democratic Party nominee for US Vice President in 1972.

"Mr. Shriver, when I saw a man waiting in line wearing a yarmulka, I thought the corned beef might be kosher," I said.

Shriver replied, "Rabbi, I don't know about the food. I'm just wearing this out of respect to Joe Lieberman, and to celebrate this great day when an Orthodox Jew was nominated to the office of Vice President of the United States."

When I first met Angelina Jolie in 2007, I did not know that she had a personal connection to the Museum of Tolerance. We had invited her to speak at a Museum screening of *A Mighty Heart*, a film in which she plays the wife of Daniel Pearl, the American journalist brutally murdered in Pakistan in 2002. Overcome with emotion, she told the audience how difficult it was to speak with Daniel Pearl's parents seated before her, and how her tears were connected to a memory she had of coming to the Museum of Tolerance with her family as a teenager:

> It was here that I began thinking about the horrible crimes committed on our planet, and about the need of every person to do whatever he or she can to speak out…. My volunteer work today as a UN Ambassador of Goodwill, speaking out against atrocities, is directly related to exhibits at the Museum of Tolerance that left a lasting impression on me when I first came here as a teenager.

One of the most interesting Hollywood encounters I've had was with one of the greatest actors of all time, Marlon Brando. When Rabbi Cooper called me during the week of Passover in April 1996 to convey the message that Marlon wanted to speak with me, I had a feeling he was not seeking my opinion on kosher-for-Passover foods. Instead, I figured his call had something to do with a disastrous interview he had given on *Larry King Live* the previous Friday night.

Marlon's remarks that evening had been outrageous. He had stated that Hollywood was run and owned by Jews; that Jews should have a greater sensitivity to human suffering; that Jews had exploited other minorities by stereotyping them in Hollywood. I was unwilling to forgive his tirade, but agreed, at least, to hear him out.

After the holiday, Rabbi Cooper and I met Marlon at the home of his friend and attorney, David Ross. At several periods in his life, Marlon had put on quite a bit of weight, and this was one of those times.

He began with an admission, "What I said on *Larry King* was offensive."

I concurred: "It was blatantly anti-Semitic. And you're now being quoted by anti-Semites around the world."

"But," he continued, steering the conversation in an unexpected direction, "*Vi ken ich zein a Antisemit? Hust du gehert of mein lerer, Stella Adler?*" Marlon Brando, the American cultural icon and Hollywood bad boy was speaking to me in the old language of Ashkenazi Jews, Yiddish. He had asked, "How can I be an anti-Semite? Have you heard of my teacher, Stella Adler?"

Stella Adler, the Jewish-American actress and acting teacher, was part of the famous Adler acting clan, which had its start in New York City's Yiddish Theater District. Marlon had studied with her after dropping out of high school. More than a teacher, Marlon explained, she had been a surrogate mother to him, teaching him, among other things, Yiddish.

Marlon described how Stella had helped earn him a role in the 1946 Broadway play, *A Flag Is Born*, about the creation of a Jewish state in the ancient land of Israel: "Stella arranged for me to have a major part in *A Flag is Born*. I played David, a Holocaust survivor."

Then Marlon went a step further: "Stella didn't just teach me Yiddish, and how to act, she converted me to Zionism. She was a great supporter of Ze'ev Jabotinsky and Menachem Begin. Soon after I was part of her circle, I began speaking on New York City street corners on behalf of the Irgun, calling for a Jewish homeland in Palestine."

Marlon topped that off with a story that left me incredulous: "When I worked for the Irgun, I went on an arms smuggling mission to Palestine. I was arrested in Italy, placed in jail for a week, and grilled to reveal the names of the people who had hired me. But I refused to give them up…. How many Jews would do that? Do you think a Jew-hater could do that?"

By the end of our two-hour meeting, I was convinced that Marlon Brando was no anti-Semite, and that his terrible remarks did not reflect who he really was. Marlon was flabbergasted by the accusation that he was an anti-Semite, repeating again in Yiddish at the end of our conversation, "*Vi ken ich zein a Antisemit?*" (How can I be an anti-Semite?) and concluding with words of gratitude to the many Jews, including Adler, who had helped shape his phenomenal career, "Rabbi, without Jews I would not be who I am," he said.

As for what to do about his public relations problem, I offered Marlon the following parable:

> A man comes to a rabbi and asks him for advice on how to make amends for having said something terrible about his friend. The rabbi tells him, "It is very simple. Go to the butcher and get a bunch of feathers. With the feathers, make a path from the butcher shop to my house. When you arrive, you will be forgiven." The man does exactly as the rabbi has instructed him, only when he knocks on the rabbi's door, the wind blows all the feathers away. He asks, "So, Rabbi, am I forgiven?" The rabbi answers, "You will be forgiven, but only when you collect the feathers."

"That's your situation, Marlon. The only way to redeem yourself is to go public. You have to use the same airwaves that carried your interview with Larry King to carry an apology."

I offered to hold a press conference for Marlon at the Simon Wiesenthal Center the following week. He agreed. While Marlon did not attend the event, which I attributed to his embarrassment over his appearance, his lawyer, David, read an eloquent apology.

A short while after the press conference, we received a ten thousand-dollar check in the mail from Marlon Brando. We refused the donation, and suggested Marlon redirect it to the local Jewish Federation's UJA campaign, which he did.

Years later, another prominent actor called me for my advice. On Christmas Eve, 2007, Steven Spira, President of Worldwide Business Affairs of Warner Brothers Pictures, and an active member of the Los Angeles Jewish community, called on behalf of actor and producer Will Smith. I was surprised that Will was seeking the advice of a rabbi, especially on Christmas Eve, but said I'd be happy to help.

A few minutes later, Will was on the phone from Vail, Colorado. He had just finished shooting the post-apocalyptic science-fiction movie, *I Am Legend,* and had gotten into some hot water in a press interview. "Rabbi," he said, "I need your advice. A reporter from a Scottish newspaper asked me about human mutants and degeneration, which are themes in the film, and about good and evil. I told him that I don't believe that people are born evil. Then he asked me, 'What about Hitler?' I said 'Even Hitler didn't wake up going: Let me do the most evil thing I can do today. I think he woke up in the morning, and using a twisted, backwards logic, set out to do what he thought was good.' The next thing I know, the paper's published an article saying, 'Will Smith thinks Adolf Hitler didn't understand the extent of pain and suffering he was causing…' The media picked up the story, and it's everywhere…. Rabbi, what can I do?"

I understood Will's dilemma very well. It seemed to me that he was simply trying to say, as Judaism does, that human beings are inherently good. But, as often happens with the media, Will's words were misconstrued. I advised him, "Will, if you don't rebut this, it will be very damaging to you. We live in the world of the internet and the internet does not take Christmas vacations. I would advise you to call your publicist and tell him to put out a statement of your views, even on Christmas Eve."

"But he's on Christmas vacation," said Will.

"I'm sure you have your publicist's cell phone number. He needs to put out a statement, even on Christmas Eve."

Will thanked me for my advice. The next day, as I skimmed the day's headlines, I saw that he had issued a statement: "I am incensed and infuriated to have to respond to such a ludicrous interpretation. Adolf Hitler was a vile, heinous, vicious killer responsible for one of the greatest acts of evil ever committed on this planet…."

The statement, which appeared in print and on the web on Christmas Day, refuted any absurd accusation that Will Smith was soft on Nazism.

In the years following the incident, Will became a close friend of the Wiesenthal Center and through the Will and Jada Smith Family Foundation, partnered with the Museum of Tolerance on a number of inner-city youth programs to combat prejudice and anti-Semitism.

The press was the subject of an improbable encounter I had in April 1989 with Israel's Prime Minister Yitzhak Shamir and the Heavyweight Boxing Champion of the World Mike Tyson and his wild-haired promoter, Don King. Prime Minister Shamir had stopped in New York before a planned visit with President George Bush in Washington, DC. By coincidence, he was staying at the Park Lane Hotel on Central Park, just one block from a reception we were holding in Simon's honor.

Nelson Peltz was chairing the Wiesenthal Center event, and many celebrities were scheduled to attend, including Tyson and King. When King learned that Prime Minister Shamir was staying nearby, he asked me if there was a possibility the champ could drop by and meet him. I put in a call to one of the Prime Minister's aides, Harry Horowitz, who informed me that Prime Minister Shamir had just returned to his hotel suite, and was willing to meet with Tyson if he could come to the hotel in the next ten minutes.

Tyson, King, Nelson, Rabbi May and I walked up Central Park South to the Park Lane. When we reached the Prime Minister's suite, an aide invited Tyson in to meet him while Harry pulled me aside for a little chat. He relayed how the Prime Minister hadn't known who Tyson was, and had asked Harry what he did for a living. When Harry demonstrated with a quick right-left-right, Prime Minister Shamir had responded incredulously in Yiddish, *"Der vos er git klepp?"* (He hits people?)

The next day, I traveled to Washington, DC to attend a White House reception for Prime Minister Shamir. When I reached the front of the receiving line at the entrance to the State Dining Room, President Bush introduced me to Prime Minister Shamir.

"Yes, Mr. President," Prime Minister Shamir interjected, "I know the rabbi. I will be attending his son Avi's wedding in a few days." The Prime Minister motioned me to come back to speak with him when he was finished with his official duties.

I followed his instructions, and returned a few minutes later. "Rabbi Hier," the Prime Minister said, in obvious frustration, "I cannot begin to figure out the American media. My whole purpose in coming to the United States was to get one positive article in the newspaper about Israel's strategic needs, but I did not succeed.... Then this morning, I woke up, and what did I see in the newspaper? A picture of me, together with a man, "*Vos er git klepp*," that hits people for a living! An article about Israel? No, there is no interest. But an article about the Prime Minister and a boxer? For this they come running!"

That day, April 5, 1989, an unforgettable image had appeared in dozens of newspapers around the world: hulking Mike Tyson and flamboyant Don King shaking hands with little Yitzhak Shamir. The caption read, "Some World Heavyweights."

Sometimes my interactions with Hollywood celebrities have involved controversy. Such was the case with one of the greatest entertainers of our time, the "King of Pop" Michael Jackson. In 1995, Michael released a single, "They Don't Care About Us," which included the offensive lyrics:

> You can never kill me
> Jew me, sue me
> Everybody do me Kick me, kike me
> Don't you black or white me

I was shocked by Michael's anti-Semitic language, especially because I assumed he had learned a few lessons about hate speech when he visited the Museum of Tolerance in 1993.

Along with other organizations, the Wiesenthal Center called on Michael to retract, "They Don't Care About Us." After I spoke with him on the phone, Michael sent a letter of apology addressed to Rabbi Cooper and me in which he wrote:

> There has been a lot of controversy about my song, "They Don't Care About Us." My intention was for this song to say "no" to racism, anti-Semitism and stereotyping. Unfortunately, my choice of words may have unintentionally hurt the very people I wanted to stand in solidarity with. I just want you all to know how strongly I am committed to tolerance, peace and love, and I apologize to anyone who might have been hurt.

A controversial film was the reason for my encounter with actor-director Mel Gibson. In 2004, Gibson directed *The Passion of the Christ*, an epic biblical drama that portrayed Jews in classically anti-Semitic ways, and undermined the gains made by the landmark Second Vatican Council of 1962-65 regarding the role of Jews in the crucifixion of Jesus. The film portrayed Jews who remained faithful to Judaism as bloody tyrants or buffoons, and those who converted to Christianity as saints.

In a *Readers' Digest* interview, Gibson tried to defend himself:

> I have friends and parents of friends who have numbers on their arms. The guy who taught me Spanish was a Holocaust survivor. He worked in a concentration camp in France. Yes of course. Atrocities happened. War is horrible. The Second World War killed tens of millions of people. Some of them were Jews in concentration camps. Many people lost their lives. In the Ukraine several millions starved to death between 1932 and 1933. During the last century, twenty million people died in the Soviet Union.

When a reporter for *The New York Times* asked me to comment on the interview, I said, "I think he was lobbed an easy question. He could've used the occasion to take us on a different road. Instead he marginalized the Holocaust, he diluted its significance..."

And I wrote directly to Mel Gibson:

> While it is true that tens of millions of people were killed in
> unspeakable catastrophes, most of those were as a direct conse-
> quence of the war. But it was the Jews alone who were singled out
> and targeted for total annihilation by a deliberate policy that the
> Nazis called "The Final Solution to the Jewish Question," where,
> for the first time, it became a government's central policy to plan
> the murder of an entire people—men, women and children....
> Indeed Hitler's government succeeded in murdering nearly six
> million Jews.... That would be equivalent today to murdering
> forty-seven million Russians or sixty million Americans or twenty
> million British. We are not engaging in competitive martyrdom,
> but in historical truth. To describe Jewish suffering during the
> Holocaust as "some of them were Jews in concentration camps"
> is an afterthought that feeds right into the hands of Holocaust
> deniers and revisionists.

In March 1993, I had the special opportunity to spend time with
director-producer Steven Spielberg. Steven had graciously invited
Malkie and me to join him in Krakow, where he was shooting his
epic historical drama, *Schindler's List*. We were delighted to join him
on the set of this most important film. Together with Steven's mother
and stepfather, Leah and Bernie Adler, and Liebe and Dr. Ivor Geft,
we flew to Krakow in Steven's private plane via Paris.

The *Schindler's List* set was extraordinary. Steven had recon-
structed the Plaszow concentration camp in an abandoned quarry
near the site of the real camp in order to avoid the modern high-rise
buildings that had cropped up since the war. Hundreds of extras—a
small number of the thousands employed in making the film—were
dressed in tattered uniforms, their heads shaven. Child actors portrayed Jewish children being torn away from wailing mothers. The
images were disturbingly realistic.

We were not the only ones overwhelmed by the scenes being
enacted before us. Ralph Fiennes, the English actor who portrayed

Amon Goeth, the sadistic commandant of the Paszow camp, told us that one day on the set, an elderly Polish woman had mistaken him for a real German officer, and had let loose an anti-Semitic comment, saying, "The Germans were charming people. They didn't kill anybody that didn't deserve it."

I was still unsettled when we flew back to Paris a few days later. When we hit turbulence, Steven's wife, actress Kate Capshaw, noticed my white knuckles and joked, "Rabbi, have a little faith, will you?"

A few months later, back in Los Angeles, Steven invited me to an early screening of the film. It was utterly gripping. I told Steven it was a remarkable achievement. But as a rabbi, I felt compelled to point out two problematic details: "The first issue," I hesitantly told him, "is in the film's opening scene. The voice reciting the kiddush uses Sephardic Hebrew pronunciation. The Jews that lived in Krakow in the 1940s were Ashkenazi. Their pronunciation was very different…. The second issue has to do with the wedding scene. You have a woman officiating at the ceremony, but there were no women rabbis in Poland in the 1940s."

With the film set to open in just a few months, Steven was concerned that there was not enough time to find someone to re-record the kiddush. I contended that the film would lose some of its authenticity if the kiddush were not re-recorded, and assured him that I could find someone to do it right away. He was skeptical, but gave me the go-ahead.

I suggested Emil Katz, a Polish Holocaust survivor, who was hired and did a wonderful job. Emil would later joke that his kiddush was heard by more people than any other kiddush in the three thousand five hundred-year-long history of the Jewish people.

As for the wedding scene, I made a suggestion: "There is a story of the great Chassidic Rebbe Levi Yitzchok of Berditchev…Reb Levi Yitzchok sees a man opening a shop on Yom Kippur, a day when work is strictly forbidden. The Rebbe looks to the heavens and declares, 'Oy, Lord, have pity on this man. Can You imagine how needy he must be if he must open his store on the holiest day of the year?' Maybe you could have the woman rabbi look up to the sky and say something like, 'God, look how impossible our circumstances are in this terrible place. Please have pity on us and look kindly upon this marriage.'"

Steven liked the idea and incorporated it into the film.

In December, before the film opened around the country, we held a special screening of *Schindler's List* at the Museum of Tolerance for Steven's family and close friends. Like all future audiences, we found ourselves mesmerized and finally speechless, when the film concluded with the tender image of Oskar Schindler's rescued Jews filing past his Jerusalem grave.

One morning on a return flight from New York to Los Angeles, a flight attendant informed me that a passenger had upgraded me from economy to first class. Thoroughly delighted, I asked to thank my patron in person. The attendant accompanied me to the first-class section, where the donor, having had a bit too much to drink, mumbled something about being a shoe manufacturer with great respect for rabbis, and something else about his nephew being a rabbi of the largest synagogue in New York. I thanked him for the upgrade, and sat next to him, thinking we would continue our conversation. But as soon as the plane took off, he was out cold.

A moment later, there was a tap on my right shoulder. "Rabbi Hier? Is that you?"

Seated behind me was the famous actress and fitness guru, Jane Fonda. Jane and I had known each other from the days of the Soviet Jewry movement, when she had worked vigorously on the campaign to free Soviet refusenik Ida Nudel. "Why don't you come sit next to me so we can catch up?" Jane suggested, "I think your friend there is out for the duration."

Jane told me that she had just appeared on *The Today Show* to discuss her new book about coping with middle age. Next, our conversation moved to matters of faith. Jane confided in me that while she and her husband, Tom Hayden, were brought up in non-religious homes, and were not "religiously inclined," she was seeking some kind of faith-based ritual, especially for her children, who she felt were "missing something." She divulged, "I've heard a lot about the Jewish Sabbath, but I've never experienced it."

"Well," I offered, "My wife and I would love to have you over for a Shabbos meal. When are you free in the next few weeks?"

Jane checked her calendar and asked, "Do you think you could manage next Friday night?"

"Of course," I replied, consciously setting aside the complicating factor that our kitchen was in the midst of a renovation.

"But one request," Jane proceeded. "No other Hollywood guests. I spend every day of the week with people in the industry. I want my family to experience a real Jewish Sabbath without any Hollywood interference."

"It will be our pleasure," I assured her.

The following Friday night, Jane arrived on our doorstep in a snappy pantsuit, with her two teenage children, Troy and Lulu. As I had agreed, there were no other Hollywood celebrities, though I had invited six students from the Yeshiva University of Los Angeles, who couldn't believe their luck when Jane Fonda sauntered into the living room.

We began by singing *Shalom Aleichem* (Peace Be Upon You), the Kabbalistic liturgical poem to welcome Shabbos. Next we sang *Eshes Chayil*, a tribute to the woman of the house. I made the traditional kiddush, blessing the wine and the braided bread, the *challah*.

Jane helped serve the roast chicken, potatoes and vegetables, which Malkie somehow managed to prepare despite the half-demolished state of our kitchen. She hummed along and encouraged her children to do the same when we sang the final melodies to give thanks for the meal.

At nearly 11:00 pm, Jane was the last to leave. "We don't have anything like this, you know," she told me. "I hope you realize what a jewel your Sabbath is."

I stayed in touch with Jane through the years. In 1987, I invited her to serve as mistress of ceremonies at a banquet at the Los Angeles Bonaventure Hotel at which the Simon Wiesenthal Center presented Soviet dissident Natan Sharansky with a Humanitarian Award. Jane's introduction made many people in the audience aware, for the first time, of her involvement in the Soviet Jewry movement:

It's a great thing that Mr. Sharansky is here tonight to accept his award in person. For me, his presence itself is an award to all of us. It is concrete, living proof of the effectiveness of the commitment, the steadfastness, the persistence and the articulateness of his wife, Avital, and I want to thank her and send her our love. And it's proof of Natan's own moral integrity and courage, and it rewards the efforts of tens of thousands of people all around the world who over the years have made up the movement for Soviet Jewry that former prisoner of conscience, Anatoly Shcharansky, now Natan Sharansky of Jerusalem, Israel, is here, is proof that we must never ever give up.

Jane mentioned how she had traveled to Moscow to meet with Jewish refuseniks, including Ida Nudel:

So it is particularly moving to me to see him here and I know that Ida is still writing her letters. I know that she's still keeping the spirit, and I hope that all of us will remember her, and will write for her, and fight for her, and for all of the Soviet prisoners of conscience. And that when we feel discouraged, let us reflect on the lesson of Natan Sharansky's presence here tonight.

Given Jane's commitment to the Jews of the Soviet Union and our lovely Shabbos meal together, I was shocked when in September 2009, her name appeared among the signatories of a protest letter directed at the Toronto International Film Festival regarding its decision to spotlight Tel Aviv and the work of Israeli filmmakers at its upcoming thirty-fourth annual festival. The letter read in part:

As members of the Canadian and international film, culture, and media arts communities, we are deeply disturbed by [the Toronto International Film Festival's] decision to host a celebratory spotlight on Tel Aviv. We protest that TIFF, whether intentionally or not, has become complicit in the Israeli propaganda machine. We do not protest the individual Israeli filmmakers included in City to City [one of the programs at the festival], nor do we in any way suggest that Israeli films should be unwelcome at TIFF. However, especially in the wake of this year's brutal assault on Gaza, we object to the use of such an important international festival in staging a propaganda campaign on behalf of what South African Archbishop Desmond Tutu, former US President Jimmy Carter and UN General Assembly President Miguel d'Escoto Brockmann have all characterized as an apartheid regime.

Jane's name was one of the most prominent among the more than fifty signatories, which included actor Danny Glover, musician David Byrne, film-maker Ken Loach and authors Naomi Klein and Howard Zinn.

I happened to be in Toronto preparing for the Canadian premiere of Moriah Films' newest documentary, *Against the Tide*, when the film festival controversy erupted. I immediately issued a rebuke:

As a documentary filmmaker and as a member of the Academy, I can tell you that this protest is nothing less than a call for the complete destruction of the Jewish state. By calling into question the legitimacy of Tel Aviv, they are in fact supporting a one-state solution, which means no Israel. I applaud the organizers of the festival for celebrating the one hundredth anniversary of Tel Aviv. If every city in the Middle East would be as culturally diverse and as open to freedom of expression as Tel Aviv, then peace would long have come to the Middle East. The signatories to this protest may have been filmmakers, authors, directors and actors, but it is clear that the script they are reading from might as well have been written by Hamas.

My piece was picked up by the international media. Within hours, my secretary phoned to say that Jane Fonda was on the line: "Rabbi, I am outraged by your remarks, particularly your comments that this was an attack on the heart and soul of Israel. You misstated my position."

"Jane, I am equally shocked that you would attach your name to a protest that calls into question the legitimacy of the city of Tel Aviv."

"How long have we known each other, Rabbi? For some thirty years? You know I would never question the legitimacy of Israel... Rabbi, when will you be back in LA?"

"I'm flying home tonight."

"Can we continue our conversation in person?"

Shortly after I returned home that evening Jane arrived. Despite her recent hip replacement surgery, she looked as young and fit as ever. She took a few sips of tea then reiterated what she had said in our phone conversation: "Rabbi Hier, I would never call for the destruction of Israel."

I responded by reading her parts of the protest letter she had signed, and added, "You know that even Hamas doesn't challenge the legitimacy of Tel Aviv. They confine themselves to Jerusalem, to talking about the 1967 borders. How could you sign a statement that calls Tel Aviv occupied territory?"

Suddenly, Jane asked Malkie to bring her some tissues, and through tears admitted, "Rabbi, to be truthful, I didn't write that protest letter and I didn't even read it. I signed it because my good friend, Naomi Klein, whom I respect, asked me to. I regret not having read it, because it could have been more balanced."

"Jane," I said, "This is a one-sided narrative. If you never saw the letter, you should not be a part of this, and you should say so publicly."

"At this point, what do you suggest I do?"

"If I were you, I would issue a direct statement to the media stating the facts that you just shared with me."

Before leaving, she asked if I would send her information on the recent Hamas rocket fire into Israel. The next day, she sent me an email.

"Many deepest thanks. Our meeting was helpful and I appreciate your hospitality. I will send you the statement I'm working on over the weekend. It won't make everyone happy, but hopefully it will clarify my position. Onward, Jane."

The following day, Jane's statement appeared in the *Huffington Post*. In it, she said, "I signed the letter without reading it carefully enough, without asking myself if some of the wording wouldn't exacerbate the situation rather than bring about constructive dialogue." The statement was picked up by the international media, many of whom ran it with the headline, "Jane Fonda Withdraws Her Protest."

Another Shabbos guest of ours was actor Tom Cruise. Tom has been a long-time supporter of the Wiesenthal Center. In 2011, we honored him with the Simon Wiesenthal Center Humanitarian Award. At the tribute dinner at the glamorous Beverly Wilshire Hotel, he spoke movingly about the Holocaust:

> When I visited the Museum of Tolerance, I remembered the story of eleven-year-old Lillian Bernstein, who on April 6, 1944, together with forty-three other children, were arrested in Izieu, in the French province of Ain, and sent to the Auschwitz-Birkenau death camp. Before leaving, she left behind a letter to God in which she wrote, "God, how good You are, how kind, and if one had to count the number of good and kind deeds You have done for us [we] would never finish.... God, it is thanks to You I had a beautiful life before, but I was spoiled but had lovely things that others do not have. God, may I ask You one thing only. Make my parents come back. My poor parents, protect them even more [than] You protect me so that I may see them again as soon as possible. Make them come back again...I have such faith in You that I thank You in advance."
>
> Our challenge, ladies and gentlemen, is to make sure that we do all in our power to see to it that there will be no more Auschwitz-Birkenaus, no more Rwandas, no more Darfurs on our planet. That our children (like Lillian Bernstein)...may be free to live in a world where men and women are judged by their accomplishments and deeds rather than by their race or religion.

At the end of the evening, I invited Tom and his wife, actress and model Katie Holmes, to join Malkie and me for a Shabbos dinner.

A few weeks later, Tom, Katie, Tom's sister and mother arrived at our home in jeans and casual shirts, relieved that there were no other Hollywood celebrities around the table, and no paparazzi stationed outside. Our only other guests were our children, grandchildren and Mohamed Alabbar, our friend from the United Arab Emirates, whose Dubai mega-skyscraper was the spectacle from which Tom had recently performed hair-raising stunts for the action film *Mission: Impossible 4*.

After the opening melodies and kiddush, I gave a short introduction to the meaning of Shabbos, based on the teachings of Rabbi Joseph B. Soloveitchik:

> For Rabbi Soloveitchik, the biblical mandate, "Six days you shall work, and on the seventh day you shall rest" hinges on the difference between the six days and the seventh day of the week. The six days, he says, are about "how": How does the world function? The seventh day is about "why": Why was the world created, why were humans?
>
> People live in both worlds—the world of "how" and the world of "why." Success in each is measured differently. Success in the "how" world is achieved by conquering: the more you conquer, the more successful you are. But in the "why" world, success is measured by your willingness to allow yourself to be defeated, to retreat, to accept surrender in the face of the overwhelming power of the Creator of the world.
>
> Rabbi Soloveitchick's point is that every human being lives a life that oscillates between the "how" and the "why." You cannot live exclusively in one world. If you live entirely in the utilitarian "how" world, your life will lack meaning. If you live your whole life in the "why" world, your life will be unproductive. Powerful civilizations have collapsed because they did not achieve the right balance. Jews have survived because they have always engaged themselves both in the "how" and the "why," and they have always had Shabbos to bring the two into proper balance.

Malkie served a lovely meal, and we talked about our families. Tom and Katie indulged our grandchildren's every question about their latest Hollywood projects. They asked about our family, and wanted to see the photo albums from our children's weddings. We sang the traditional Shabbos songs and Tom, Katie and Mohamed clapped and followed along with English transliterations. Katie told Malkie how much she enjoyed the food, especially the potato kugel. Malkie gave her a doggy bag, and promised to send her the recipe.

While our guests came from vastly different backgrounds and faiths, the spirit of Shabbos enveloped us all. As we said our good-byes, I was reminded of the story of the man who travels to distant lands in search of a lost treasure only to discover that the treasure he seeks is within easy reach, within his own family, in his own home.

A few days later, I received a thank you card from Tom and Katie that made it clear that they, too, felt the special atmosphere of our Shabbos together: "It was a beautiful evening," the card read. "We can't thank you enough. It was an honor to share the Sabbath with you and your wonderful family."

Chapter Eleven

The Heart and Soul of It

W hen I returned to Los Angeles from a brief trip to Washington, DC in February 1993, two weeks after the opening of the Museum of Tolerance, I learned that a special visitor had dropped by the Museum unannounced during my absence. The older gentleman was given a tour of the exhibits by my colleague, Rabbi Meyer May, and upon leaving, left a message with my secretary. It read: "Call me as soon as possible. —Teddy"

"Teddy" was the one-and-only Teddy Kollek, the charming, energetic Mayor of Jerusalem. Since taking office in 1965, he had transformed the neglected backwater that was Jerusalem into a modern metropolis. He had created the city's landmark cultural institutions: the Israel Museum, the Jerusalem Theater, the Biblical Zoo and the Cinematheque. With the help of an impressive, international network of donors, Teddy had built and improved hundreds of city parks, schools, sports facilities and libraries.

Teddy endeavored to create a peaceful Jerusalem. He worked to foster co-existence between divisive populations: religious and non-religious Jews, Jews and Arabs, Muslims, Christians and Jews.

After Jerusalem's 1967 reunification, he reached out to the Arab community to elicit its involvement in municipal affairs, and ensured Muslim access to Al-Aksa Mosque and the Temple Mount. But he was also adamant that Jerusalem remain unified under Israeli sovereignty. Teddy had once aptly stated Jerusalem's eternal significance to the Jewish people: "Jerusalem is the one essential element in Jewish history. A body can live without an arm or a leg, but not without a heart. This is the heart and soul of it," he said.

When I called Teddy at the Beverly Wilshire Hotel, he praised the Museum of Tolerance. "Rabbi Hier, what you've created is magnificent. I'm sure this Museum will be a great success."

What he next ventured came as a surprise: "Rabbi, I want to talk to you about creating a Museum of Tolerance in Jerusalem. Of course, we already have Yad Vashem, so the Holocaust portion of the Museum won't be necessary. But what we need desperately is a museum that focuses attention on the values of tolerance and mutual respect."

I was honored by Teddy's request, but raised doubts, "Mr. Mayor, thank you for the compliment. But we just raised fifty four million dollars to build our Museum here. How could I possibly undertake construction of another museum in Jerusalem?"

"I understand," Teddy acknowledged. But demonstrating the determination that had earned him the title, "Jerusalem's greatest builder since Herod the Great," Teddy pressed on: "Look, all I'm telling you is that Jerusalem needs this kind of project. What I'm asking is for you to come to Jerusalem to discuss the idea."

A few months later, I was in the backseat of an old European car with the irrepressible, eighty-two-year-old, Hungarian-born Mayor of Jerusalem, as he instructed his driver on the best routes to take to crisscross the city. Teddy was on a mission to show me the city's available building plots—from the French Hill neighborhood near Hebrew University's Mount Scopus campus to sites near the Israel Museum and in the German Colony.

Again, I tried to dampen Teddy's enthusiasm. I reminded him that we were just getting our LA Museum off the ground, and that our Board of Trustees would never approve another building project. "Rabbi," he interrupted, "We are not building. What we are doing is seeing if we can find and put away a piece of land for you. Nothing in Jerusalem gets built overnight. The important thing is to know that when you are ready, you have a plot to build on."

After an extensive tour, Teddy admitted that none of the plots we had seen was quite right. Nonetheless, he instructed me, "Rabbi Hier, come back to Jerusalem next year, and I will have for you the prime piece of real estate that your Museum deserves."

Before I could make the follow-up trip to Jerusalem, however, Teddy's political influence waned. After serving a record six terms of office as Mayor of Jerusalem, he lost a seventh bid to Israeli cabinet minister Ehud Olmert. During his last weeks in office, Teddy invited me back to the Mayor's Office to introduce me to Jerusalem's soon-to-be mayor, whom he asked to make the search for a building site for a Museum of Tolerance a top priority.

As the search for a proper building site continued over the next ten years, the idea that Teddy had put in my mind developed into a passion.

I thought about all that Israel represented and had achieved. I recalled growing up on New York's Lower East Side in the aftermath of the Holocaust, when the world perceived Jews as perennial victims with little hope for reversing their tragic fate, and how a group of idealistic Zionists had created a new reality by establishing a modern country in the ancient land of Israel. In a remarkably short period of time, that country had surpassed all expectations by becoming a home to millions, and a thriving democracy in a region of the world without a democratic tradition.

I thought about the way in which Israel gave the Jews a permanent address in the world. We learn in the Torah that the Almighty Himself, recognizes the importance of carving out an identity and creating a physical presence in the world when He instructs His faithful servant, Moses, to build Him a sanctuary. Israel is our people's sanctuary.

I contemplated how the establishment of Israel had raised the status of Jews everywhere. My own meetings with presidents, prime ministers and kings could not have taken place if a Jewish nation-state, identified by a flag, represented by an anthem and protected by an army, did not exist. Without it, we would have remained, at best, like the Dalai Lama and his Tibetan Buddhists: sometimes invited into halls of power through back doors only, so as not to upset the Chinese.

A distinct memory from a trip I had taken to Israel with a group of Vancouver NCSY teenagers in 1971 floated through my mind. We had met the man destined to inform the world that a Jewish state had come into being, David Ben-Gurion, in Sde Boker, the kibbutz in the Negev desert where he had retired. The tiny founding father rose from a simple wooden chair, addressed us, and predicted, "We could not have established Israel without the help of Jews in the diaspora. But I believe a time will very soon come when Jews in the diaspora will need the help of Israel."

Ben-Gurion was right. Israel had not only provided Jews around the world with a home, it had restored Jewish national identity and pride. Israel was a gift to Jews everywhere.

I decided I too should contribute to that irrevocable Israel-diaspora relationship that Ben-Gurion so eloquently defined. What I had to offer was an educational, interactive, experiential Museum of Tolerance that could strengthen the principles of mutual respect and human dignity that are the very pillars of our faith. It would be the Simon Wiesenthal Center's gift to Israel.

Fortunately, I was not alone in my passion for the project. Leading members of the Board of the Simon Wiesenthal Center and senior staff concurred that building a museum in Jerusalem was a worthy endeavor.

In 2003, Mayor Ehud Olmert made us the extraordinary offer of a three-acre site in the heart of the city, blocks from Jerusalem's major hotels, that catapulted the project forward. Eight months later, we held an exciting groundbreaking ceremony attended by many dignitaries, including Knesset Member and Chairman of the Labor Party Shimon Peres, Finance Minister Benjamin Netanyahu, US Ambassador to Israel Daniel Kurtzer, and California Governor Arnold Schwarzenegger, who was on his first official trip abroad.

At the gala dinner that night at the King David Hotel, I joked that Governor Schwarzenegger had stolen some his best lines from the Torah. "For example," I said, "In the Book of Genesis, we read the story where Abraham is called upon to sacrifice his son, Isaac, on Mount Moriah. The story includes a well-known verse in which Abraham tells Eliezer and Yishmael, who accompany him up to the mountain, 'You stay here with the flock, while Isaac and I go up to the summit.' Then Abraham says to them '*V'nashuva Alechem!*' I'll be back! Or in the Book of Exodus, when Pharaoh is fed up with Moses, he says to him, "Moses, I don't want to see your face again." And what happens? The next time they see each other, Moses splits the sea and Pharaoh and his chariots come charging at him. They stare each other down, and what do you think Moses says to Pharaoh? 'Hasta la vista, baby!'"

Governor Schwarzenegger responded, "Rabbi, with all due respect, I think you have it all wrong. I didn't steal my lines from the Torah, from the Book of Genesis or the Book of Exodus. I stole them from you. When we first got to know each other, I came to you and I asked how I could help the Simon Wiesenthal Center, and you said by giving a nice donation and becoming a major supporter. So I gave you one hundred thousand dollars and what did you say to me? Arnold, thank you very much, but I'll be back!"

Arnold then set a more serious tone when he spoke of the Museum of Tolerance as an example of Israel moving beyond daily strife and terrorism toward a better future: "We look past the suicide bombers, the terrorists, past the blood," he said. "We look ahead to the time people can live side by side." He spoke for all of us when he cited the "darkness that pervades the Middle East," and predicted that, "this building will be a candle to guide us."

The design and planning process got underway. Architect Frank Gehry developed a conceptual design that we displayed in Jerusalem's City Hall in accordance with municipal regulations. We posted project notices in the Hebrew and Arabic press. No complaints were registered.

But the gift of a magnificent parcel of land in the heart of Jerusalem by the government of Israel, with the full backing of its future Prime Minister, Benjamin Netanyahu; its future President, Shimon Peres; and subsequent Jerusalem mayors, was not enough to steer the project clear of Middle East politics. When site excavation began, and bones dating back four centuries were discovered, Shiek Raad Saleh, a Hamas loyalist and leader of the Northern Branch of the Islamic Movement in Israel, seized the opportunity to petition Israel's Supreme Court to halt construction. He argued that the site was part of the old Mamilla Cemetery, and did not belong to Israel.

But our lawyers were able to refute that. They presented evidence to the Supreme Court that Muslim clergy had at least twice in the past authorized construction on the grounds of the former cemetery: in 1929, the Grand Mufti of Jerusalem, the Muslim cleric in charge of Jerusalem's Muslim holy places, built the Palace Hotel (which would later become the Waldorf-Astoria), and in 1946 approved plans to develop a Muslim university campus. They also demonstrated that Muslim authorities had petitioned the British prior to Israel's establishment for permission to build a bank and commercial center over portions of the cemetery. They argued that in endorsing these projects, Muslim authorities had invoked the concept of *mundras*, which holds that cemeteries not in use for thirty-seven years can be considered abandoned and de-sanctified.

Since the Israeli government and the Jerusalem municipality had given us the land, and the precedent for construction was so clear, we assumed the case would be resolved in a few months. Instead, it took the court nearly three years to reach its verdict. Finally, in 2008, Israel's Supreme Court rendered a unanimous decision in favor of the Museum of Tolerance Jerusalem, stating:

> For almost fifty years, the compound has not been a part of the cemetery, both in the normative sense and in the practical sense, and it was used for various public purposes.... During all those years, no one raised any claim, on even one occasion, that the planning procedures violated the sanctity of the site, or that they were contrary to law as a result of the historical and religious uniqueness of the site...

Israel is a small strip of land, of great antiquity, with a history that extends over thousands of years.... For decades this area was not regarded as a cemetery by the general public or by the Muslim community. No one denied this position. In our case, the area of the Museum compound was separated from the Moslem Mamilla cemetery as long ago as the 1960s, and it was classified as an open public area...and it was made available for various kinds of planning activity. A multi-story car park was built on it, a road was paved on it, and plans were made to construct multi-story buildings on it.

In its ruling, the Supreme Court also stressed the Museum's importance:

The Museum of Tolerance Jerusalem embodies an ideal of establishing a spiritual center that will spread a message of human tolerance between peoples, between sectors of the population and between man and his fellow-man. The establishment of the Museum is likely to make an important national contribution to the whole country, in which no center has yet been built with the purpose of addressing the issue of tolerance in all its aspects, and to bring about the assimilation of this idea among the general public.... The location of the Museum in the center of Jerusalem has special significance, since it is a city that has a special ethical significance for three religions and an ancient history, which is unique to human civilization.

With this unequivocal validation, we faced a further delay when in the fall of 2008, world financial markets crashed, dramatically weakening the not-for-profit sector. The Chairman of the Wiesenthal Center's Board of Trustees, Larry Mizel, prudently recommended that we downsize the project, and seek a less costly, more streamlined design than Gehry's two hundred and fifty million-dollar, multi-building scheme. The board approved.

We engaged the Israeli firm Chyutin Architects, who developed an elegant conceptual design of one hundred and sixty thousand square feet that significantly reduced the cost of the project to one hundred million dollars. We later rounded out the design team: Michal Sedlacek of Aedes Los Angeles would serve as project architect for the Museum's exterior and public interior spaces; Mehrdad Yazdani from Yazdani Studios of Cannon Design would be principal designer for the exhibition spaces; Joe Cortina of Cortina Productions would be creative director of the Museum exhibits, and Chris Conte of Electrosonic would be senior design consultant for the Museum's audio-visual and technology features.

In June 2011, the City of Jerusalem approved our building plans. The city's new mayor, Nir Barkat, was an advocate for the project both at home and abroad. He called the Museum, "a twenty-first century idea essential for the future of Israel's capital."

The leadership of the Simon Wiesenthal Center remained steadfast and undaunted over the course of many years, as we worked to overcome the formidable challenges we faced in beginning construction of the Museum of Tolerance Jerusalem. We recognized that building in Jerusalem, like all worthy efforts in Israel, requires patience and dedication, sometimes beyond initial expectations. The leadership remained committed to the belief that the potential the Museum represented for conveying critical messages to millions of people, both Jews and non-Jews, far outweighed any temporary delays.

The project would not have gotten off the ground without the unstinting support of a group of visionaries deeply devoted both to Israel and the mission of the Simon Wiesenthal Center.

Roland and Dawn Arnall were extraordinary supporters. First, in 2005, they helped raise millions of dollars by bringing a small group of trustees aboard their plane to see the Jerusalem site for themselves. Roland made his pitch mid-air, and when the plane encountered turbulence, told his guests, "This, my friends, is definitely the time to declare your support and make a difference." He announced his own multi-million dollar gift to the project, and urged other trustees to follow suit. When Roland unexpectedly passed away in March of 2008, Dawn stepped in and furthered his exceptional leadership. In

2014, she made a legacy gift to name the Museum of Tolerance Jerusalem building in Roland's memory.

Gordon and Leslie Diamond, who are among our closest friends and whom we first met in Vancouver in 1962, followed the example of their beloved parents, Jack and Sadie Diamond, when they made the first legacy gift to the project. In 2014, they gave an additional extraordinary gift, placing them among the Center's largest donors. We will have the pleasure of naming the Museum's one thousand-seat amphitheater in their honor.

Ed Snider, owner of the Philadelphia Flyers hockey team, who began his association with the Wiesenthal Center as a small, direct-mail donor, and eventually became one of its greatest supporters, became a major benefactor of the Museum of Tolerance Jerusalem; the Museum's Theater of the Performing Arts will be named for him.

Early supporters of the Wiesenthal Center, Gary and Karen Winnick, became major benefactors to the Museum of Tolerance Jerusalem, and prodded their friends to do the same. The Winnicks agreed to be honored at a major fundraising event that helped raise millions of dollars for the project, and to which President Bill Clinton sent a special message: "There is no better place on earth to continue the Museum of Tolerance mission than Jerusalem.... If this mission of hope is embraced there, it can be proclaimed everywhere."

Barbara Greenspun, together with her children, Susan, Brian, Danny, Jane and their spouses, demonstrated her unfailing commitment to the Wiesenthal Center by providing major support toward the project's Children's Museum, which will be named in honor of the Greenspun Family. Barbara and her late husband, the legendary publisher of the *Las Vegas Sun*, Hank Greenspun, were members of the Center's original Board of Trustees, and Brian and Danny became trustees after their father passed away. The Greenspun family's support exemplifies their love for Israel, which Hank heroically demonstrated when he served as an arms smuggler for the Hagganah in 1948.

That same love of Israel moved self-made businessman and trustees Rowland and Sylvia Schaefer to become major benefactors to the Museum of Tolerance Jerusalem. The Museum's Education Center will be named for the Schaefer Family. Rowland believed strongly in the Museum's message that greater Jewish unity and mutual respect could build a stronger, safer Israel. We are indebted to Rowland and his wife Sylvia for their vision, which extended well beyond the local Miami community, and to their daughters, Bonnie and Marla, for continuing their father's devotion to the Center.

The project was recently bolstered by multi-million dollar gifts from long-time devoted trustees and friends: Jack and Gita Nagel; Rabbi Jacob and Leah Friedman; David Shapell, of blessed memory, and his wife Fela; Burt Sugarman and Mary Hart; Lee Samson and his wife Anne, of blessed memory; Jimmy and Debbie Lustig and Herb and Karen Baum.

The central figure behind construction of the Museum of Tolerance Jerusalem is unquestionably Larry Mizel. Larry and his wife Carol, long-time activists in charitable and community causes both locally and nationally, are among the Wiesenthal Center's largest donors. In September 2003, Larry succeeded Sam Belzberg as Chairman of the Board of Trustees; he previously served as Chairman of the Building Committee, succeeding Merv Adelson, who devoted much time in the early years to negotiating with the Israeli authorities. Larry believes whole-heartedly in the Museum concept and its importance to Israel's future. As Chairman and Chief Executive Officer of Denver-based MDC Holdings, a major home-building company, he also understands property and construction issues better than anyone.

Larry formed an outstanding construction management team with the indefatigable Yoni Riss of Coleridge Capital and the Center's multi-talented and adept Chief Financial Officer/Chief Administrative Officer, Susan Burden. The threesome began regularly traveling to Jerusalem to meet with Mayor Nir Barkat, and to work with the relevant municipal agencies. Larry was exactly the right man at the right time to move the project forward. He reassured me many times, "Rabbi, don't worry, I am going to get this done whatever it takes." Without Larry's leadership and commitment, there would not be a Museum of Tolerance Jerusalem project.

Michael Milken, one of the world's most prominent Jewish philanthropists, has been a great friend and supporter of the Wiesenthal

Center. When the Center was in its infancy, Michael introduced me to some of the country's most important businesspeople. Many became Wiesenthal Center supporters, including Nelson Peltz, who has served as Co-Chairman of the Board of Trustees for thirty years. When the Museum of Tolerance opened in Los Angeles, Michael and his wife Lori were among the major benefactors.

I had shown Michael the site when he visited Jerusalem and had kept him appraised of our progress over the years. In early September 2014, Trustee Cheston Mizel and I met with Richard Sandler, the executive vice president and a trustee of the Milken Family Foundation, and a national leader in the Federation movement, and followed this up with an extensive meeting with Michael. On September 24, 2014, Michael called with exciting news that he and Lori had decided to join Larry and Carol Mizel in making a legacy gift to the Museum of Tolerance Jerusalem. When the Museum is completed in 2017, its campus will proudly be named the Lori and Michael Milken and Carol and Larry Mizel Families Campus.

Since its creation in 1948, the State of Israel has been virtually the only country in the world that has had to explain and justify its right to exist. Israel's detractors and enemies insist on defaming and delegitimizing the country by accusing it of intolerance and lack of human dignity.

The Museum of Tolerance Jerusalem will not be a museum about the past; it will not be a Holocaust museum and will not compete with Yad Vashem. Instead, it will be a museum with a twenty-first-century idea first proposed by Mayor Teddy Kollek back in 1993.

The Museum of Tolerance Jerusalem will deal with today's and tomorrow's crucial issues. It will promote universal respect, Jewish unity and co-existence, themes that are absolutely vital to Israel's future and are ground-zero issues in Jerusalem.

Today, issues of tolerance and human dignity dominate discussions in bilateral and multi-national forums. These topics top the agendas of every major world leader addressing the challenges of an increasingly complex and rapidly changing world, making the museum the logical platform for visiting world leaders. Unlike any other museum, the Museum of Tolerance Jerusalem will be a museum about Judaism's core values. It will ask the fundamental question, "How did Jews survive thousands of years of exile, expulsion and persecution, yet continue to make vital contributions to humanity?" It will answer the question by demonstrating how we have always retained our core values: education, family, community, respect toward people of all backgrounds, the sanctity of human life, the necessity to fight for social justice and to confront and stand up to evil.

The Museum's interactive, multi-media exhibit, *The People's Journey*, will immerse visitors in epic moments in Jewish history. Visitors will speak with Maimonides, stand beside Alfred Dreyfus, experience a Chassidic *tish*, listen to Theodor Herzl, witness the establishment of Israel, visit Soviet refuseniks and watch Israeli paratroopers capture the Western Wall. They will encounter the stories of men and women, religious and secular, rabbis and laymen, dreamers and doers, who have sustained the Jewish people in all its diversity over the millennia.

In the Social Laboratory, visitors will be challenged to apply these core values to contemporary issues vital to Israeli society, such as the relationship between Israeli Jews and non-Jews, and conflicts between Jewish religious and secular worldviews, and to international issues of terrorism, political extremism, resurgent anti-Semitism, human rights abuses and economic inequities. The Social Laboratory will engage Jews, Christians and Muslims, adults and children, in the challenge of inter-ethnic and inter-religious coexistence.

Each time I visit the construction site of the Museum of Tolerance Jerusalem, I am reminded of a walk I took as a child with my grandfather one rainy day on Canal Street on the Lower East Side. We had gone together to buy an *esrog* for the holiday of Sukkos. My grandfather carefully selected and purchased an unblemished citron, then opened its cardboard box to inhale its fragrance as we walked home under a large black umbrella. I asked him, "Zaide, it's raining. Why don't you wait until we get home to open the box?"

"Moishe," he responded, "I am an old man. I will never have the privilege of going to Israel. The best I can do is to smell this *esrog* grown in Israel and imagine I'm there."

The Museum of Tolerance Jerusalem represents the culmination of my personal journey from Lower East Side *yeshiva bocher*, to American rabbi, and Jewish organizational leader. It seeks to transmit the Jewish values on which I was raised, which I have worked to impart, and which I hold dear, and is infused with the American values that have shaped my identity.

For two thousand years, Jews like my grandparents were subjected to pogroms and inquisitions in almost every country in which they lived. No one seemed to care; few came to their rescue. The idea of a Jewish state with Jerusalem as its capital was unimaginable. Today, we are all the representatives of those generations who did not live to see the miracle of modern Israel reborn. Therefore, ours is both the privilege and responsibility of fulfilling that dream for future generations. As Reuven Rivlin, President of the State of Israel said: "At a time when…the paralyzing forces of apathy…and the forces of violent extremism, threaten to rip the citizens of Israel asunder, we must invest all resources…in an effort to build bridges to bring people closer together…. I pay tribute to all those participating in the task of setting up this museum, for their dedication to the vitality important goal of promoting tolerance in this land of ours."

Epilogue

On May 20, 2004, I was deeply honored to receive an Honorary Doctorate of Humane Letters from Yeshiva University. President Richard Joel, whom I had known since we led a Yeshiva University Torah Leadership Seminar to Europe and Israel together more than forty years earlier, presented me with the degree at the university's seventy-third Annual Commencement Exercises. Before a crowd of thousands of students and their proud families at New York City's Madison Square Garden, President Joel said:

> From the yeshivot of the Lower East Side to the stage of the
> Academy Awards, Marvin Hier's journey has given the Jewish
> people strong defense, advocacy of justice and the goodness of
> a gifted rabbi with a pixie-ish smile, incomparable humor and
> an unending concern for the dignity of the Jewish people. You
> have guided communities as rabbi and, while not a Yeshiva
> University alumnus until today, you have always been a part of

the YU family. More than a quarter century after you founded the Simon Wiesenthal Center, it is impossible to conceive of a world without Rabbi Marvin Hier tirelessly fighting for the welfare of the Jewish people and teaching generation upon generation the lessons of the Holocaust, and exposing evil wherever it exists. You are truly a hero of the Jewish people.

My only regret was that my parents and grandparents, who were no longer alive, could not be there. I'm sure my grandmother, Freidel, would have reminded me, *"Alles in leben iz barshert"* (Everything in life is meant to be).

As I look back over the trajectory of my life from New York's Lower East Side to Vancouver, Los Angeles and Jerusalem, from *yeshiva bocher* to rabbi, political activist, film producer and museum founder, I realize that I have always held firm to that deceptively simple idea. I have always believed that no matter how many people try to extinguish the light of the Jewish people, they will never succeed, because the irrevocable covenant God made with Abraham will always produce unexpected helpers and new circumstances to rekindle it. I have always believed in miracles, whether the ancient type, staves that turn into snakes, seas that split, manna that falls from trees, or the greater miracles of our own time, the creation of Israel, the incredible victories of the Israeli army and the renaissance of yeshivas and Jewish day schools throughout the world.

I have always believed in my grandmother's words, too, when it comes to my greatest joy in life, my family.

I could not be prouder of my two sons: Ari, who served in the Israel Defense Forces and directs the Wiesenthal Center's Campus Outreach Programs to combat anti-Semitism and Israel de-legitimization on college campuses, and Avi who has raised tens of millions of dollars for the Wiesenthal Center as Director of its Leadership Missions, and who, together with his wife Annie, spends much time in Israel, spearheaded a campaign to renovate Jerusalem *mikvahs*.

My grandchildren have followed their parents' example:

Yehudeet and her husband, Jacob Counne, who live in Chicago, together with friends, raised twenty four thousand dollars from around the world in a few days to assist Israeli women whose husbands were called up as reservists during the 2014 Gaza War.

Miriam and her husband, Yehuda Dubin, took upon themselves the mitzvah of comforting hospitalized soldiers and their families in Jerusalem during the Gaza flotilla raid in 2010.

Rachel and Yael volunteer to help cancer patients and their families. Yael's husband, AJ Stern, coordinated the 2014–15 Israel Festival, the largest Jewish gathering on the West Coast.

Isaac, who works at Bloomberg LP, was a recipient of a scholarship through Yeshiva University's Jay and Jeanie Schottenstein Honors Program, studied at Israel's Yeshivat Kerem B'Yavneh and was active in B'nei Akiva.

Hanna was the only student in a class of three hundred at the University of San Diego who challenged a professor for using a map of the Middle East that did not include Israel. (The professor apologized and ordered a new map.)

Devorah was an active member of AIPAC at the Yeshiva University of Los Angeles High School, and is a pro-Israel activist at Yeshiva University's Stern College for Women.

Joseph is the president of YULA's Israel Advocacy Club for his short multi-media film linking the Holocaust to contemporary anti-Semitic attacks. In the film, he wrote, "What would you do if you woke up to this? …I take a stand for what I believe in…not because I want to, because I have to."

Like Jacob, who Rabbi Joseph B. Soloveitchik noted is the only patriarch the Talmud refers to as an elder, because he leapt over the generations to bring the *Mesorah* directly to his grandchildren, I have had the good fortune to be able to communicate my beliefs and values to two generations that have come after me. I am grateful to the Almighty to have been given the privilege to watch my children and grandchildren follow in the footsteps of our ancestors, making their own marks down the paths of Jewish commitment and activism.

May they continue on their way.

Reception for Yeshiva University hosted by Jack Diamond for Dr. Samuel Belkin of YU in Vancouver

Private audience with Pope John Paul II; standing, left to right: Roland Arnall, Dawn Arnall, Shimon Samuels, Rabbi Abraham Cooper and Ira Lipman

With Ed Snider (left) and Rabbi Meyer May (center) in Rome

With Dawn Arnall in Rome

Wiesenthal Center board meeting at Rome's Villa Miani; seated, left to right: Martin Rosen, Gary Winnick, Marc Utay, George Feldenkreis, me, Don Soffer, Larry Mizel and Jack Nagel; standing: Rabbi Steven Burg, Malkie Hier, Janice Prager, Herb Baum, Rabbi Abraham Cooper, Ed Snider, Rabbi Meyer May, Dawn Arnall, Stu Isen, Rosalie Zalis, Gordon Diamond, Judah Hertz, Jimmy Lustig, Leslie Diamond, Jaime Sohacheski, Lee Samson and Alan Casden

Private audience with Pope Francis

With Pope Francis

Recording the narration for *Genocide* with Elizabeth Taylor and Arnold Schwartzman

Genocide premiere at the Kennedy Center; left to right: Simon Wiesenthal, Abe Pollin, Sam Belzberg, Elizabeth Taylor, Frank Sinatra and me

293

Frank Sinatra and I joking that the Kennedy Center premiere was Elizabeth Taylor's "earliest arrival ever"

With Simon Wiesenthal and Frank Sinatra at the Los Angeles premiere of *Genocide*

At the Los Angeles premiere of *Genocide*; left to right: Carol Mizel, Simon Wiesenthal, Elizabeth Taylor, Sam Belzberg, Larry Mizel and me

June, 1982

FS

Dear Rabbi Hier,

Many thanks for sending us Simon's new book "Max and Helen"....we will enjoy reading it, and we appreciate your thinking of us!

Please send our very best to Simon -- and the same to you...we are well, and getting ready to go on the road again to Atlantic City! But we wanted to thank you for being so thoughtful.

Warmest regards,

Frank Sinatra
Frank Sinatra

Letter from Frank Sinatra

Telling the story of "a rabbi, a movie star and a missing dress" at a Wiesenthal Center National Tribute Dinner honoring Elizabeth Taylor at Beverly Hills' Beverly Hilton Hotel

Arnold Schwartzman and I with Richard Benjamin and Paula Prentiss after they presented us with an Academy Award for *Genocide*

Robert DeNiro presenting me with an Academy Award for *The Long Way Home*

With Kirk and Michael Douglas at a Wiesenthal Center National Tribute Dinner in
Michael's honor at the Beverly Hilton Hotel

297

With Nicole Kidman

With Michael Douglas and my grandaughter, Yehudeet

With Dustin Hoffman, when he recorded the narration for *Against the Tide*

With Rick Trank and Sandra Bullock, when she recorded the voice of Golda Meir for *The Prime Ministers*

With Rick Trank and Sir Ben Kingsley, when he recorded the narration for *It Is No Dream*

At the premiere of *It is No Dream* at the Basel Municipal Casino; front row, left to right: Rabbi Meyer May, me, Rita and Jack Sinder and Rabbi Abraham Cooper; second row: Avi Hier, Sol Teichman, Annie Hier, Yvonne Kerrigan, Leslie Diamond, Jose Liberman and Kathy and Rick Trank; third row: Ruth Teichman, Lauri Glotman and Esther Liberman; fourth row: Malkie Hier, Brad Krevoy and Roz Cooper; fifth row: Rosalie Zalis, Susie Krevoy, Elizabeth Leigh, Barbara Leigh and Syd Belzberg; back row: Dr. Ed Zalis, Brian and Tammi Kerzner, Janice Prager and Joanne Belzberg

Rabbi Abraham Cooper and I showing Simon Wiesenthal the Museum of Tolerance construction site in Los Angeles

Alan Casden at the opening of the Museum of Tolerance in Los Angeles

301

With Billy and Janice Crystal at a Wiesenthal Center National Tribute Dinner in their honor at the Beverly Hilton Hotel

Malkie with Robin Williams

With Caroline Kennedy (center) and Liebe Geft (right) at the Museum of Tolerance

Michael Milken speaking at the opening of the Museum of Tolerance's "Anne" exhibit

With the Dalai Lama at the Museum of Tolerance; Janice Prager is to my left

Speaking at a Wiesenthal Center National Tribute Dinner honoring President Ronald Reagan; front row, left to right: Arnold Schwarzenegger, Frances Belzberg, President Reagan, Sam Belzberg, Bill Belzberg, First Lady Nancy Reagan and Barbara Belzberg; back row: Malkie Hier, Charlton Heston, Lydia Heston, Robert Stack, David Flynn and Jane Seymour

Giving President Ronald Reagan a tour of the Museum of Tolerance

Presenting a Cup of Elijah to President George H. W. Bush at a Wiesenthal Center
National Tribute Dinner in his honor in Los Angeles

Presidential nominee George W. Bush and Laura Bush visiting the Museum of Tolerance in Los Angeles

Rick Trank and me accepting the Oscar for "The Long Way Home"

Prime Minister Netanyahu at the Museum of Tolerance, March 2014, greeting trustees Ron Meyer, Burt Sugarman, Mary Hart, James Packer and Brett Ratner

Showing Israeli Prime Minister Benjamin Netanyahu the Hitler Letter with Larry Mizel at the Museum of Tolerance

With Tommy and Jo Lasorda at Dodger Stadium

With Joe DiMaggio

Jane Fonda serving as mistress of ceremonies at a Wiesenthal Center National Tribute Dinner in honor of Natan Sharansky at Los Angeles' Bonaventure Hotel; Natan Sharansky and Simon Wiesenthal are seated to her right

On the set of *Schindler's List* with Steven Spielberg and his mother, Leah Adler, in Krakow

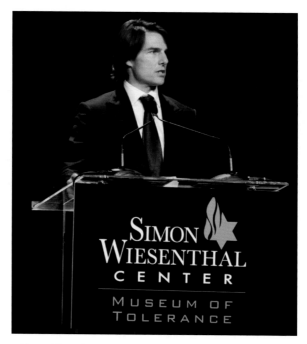

Tom Cruise speaking at a Wiesenthal Center National Tribute Dinner in his honor at the Beverly Wilshire Hotel

Will Smith bringing teens to the Museum of Tolerance in Los Angeles

With Mary Hart and Burt Sugarman

With Jerry Seinfeld and Jeffrey Katzenberg at the MOTJ site in Jerusalem

President Shimon Peres discussing the Museum of Tolerance Jerusalem with
Yoni Riss, me, Larry Mizel and Susan Burden

Israeli President Shimon Peres meeting with leaders of Hollywood's entertainment industry; left to right: Ron Meyer,
Haim Saban, Michael Lynton, Les Moonves, Barbra Streisand, Steven Spielberg, President Peres, Tom Rothman, Jeffrey
Katzenberg, Rick Ross, Billy Crystal, me, David Siegel, Michael Oren and Peter Rice

Attending a Canadian Friends of the Simon Wiesenthal Center's Spirit of Hope Dinner; standing, left to right:
Rabbi Meyer May, Rabbi Abraham Cooper, me, Gerry Schwartz, Heather Reisman, Avi Benlolo, Alan Dershowitz
and David Gergen; seated: Bob Woodward and Robert Gibbs

Opening ceremony of the first Museum of Tolerance International Film Festival honoring Clint Eastwood; left to right: Taylor Hicks, me, Clint Eastwood, Mike Melvoin, Governor Arnold Schwarzenegger and George Lopez

With Lester Crown at the Simon Wiesenthal Center dinner in Chicago

At a Wiesenthal Center National Tribute Dinner; left to right: Marilyn Katzenberg, Brett Ratner, Nicole Avant, Ted Sarandos, Ron Meyer, Haim Saban, Jeffrey Katzenberg, Larry Mizel and me

At a Wiesenthal Center National Tribute Dinner; left to right: Jeffrey and Marilyn Katzenberg, Christoph Waltz, Lori and Michael Milken, me and Rabbi Meyer May

Museum of Tolerance Jerusalem Mission to Dubai, March 2014, hosted by Mohamed Alabbar

With Ron Meyer (left) and Jeffrey Katzenberg (right)

Attending Prime Minister Netanyahu's speech to the United States Congress on Iran; Rabbi Meyer May, Larry Mizel, Rabbi Abraham Cooper and Norm Brownstein

With Jerusalem Mayor Nir Barkat, Larry Mizel and Rabbi Meyer May at the Museum of Tolerance Jerusalem construction site

With Israeli Prime Minister Benjamin Netanyahu, holding a rendering of the Museum of Tolerance Jerusalem

With Israeli President Reuven Rivlin

317

Me, Bob Book, Yehuda Avner, Rabbi May, Michael Weinberger, Jona Rechnitz

At the Museum of Tolerance Jerusalem construction site

Yitz Woolf.

With Malkie and Yeshiva University President Richard Joel at the University's
Commencement Exercises at New York's Madison Square Garden

With Malkie

The Hier family; in strollers, left to right: Katie Stern and Elana and Ariel Counne; standing: Isaac Hier, Ari Hier, Hanna Hier, Devorah Hier, Yehuda and Miriam Dubin, A J, Serina and Yael Stern, me, Malkie Hier, Ann and Avi Hier, Yehudeet and Jacob Counne, Joseph Hier and Rachel Hier

Jonathan Lax.

320

Appendix I

Testimony Presented before
the Foreign Relations Committee of
the US House of Representatives,
Ninety-Ninth Congress
Concerning Allegations Against Kurt Waldheim
Washington, DC, April 22, 1986

Mr. Chairman:

The Simon Wiesenthal Center has reviewed all available documentation on the Kurt Waldheim case and has during the last four weeks,
undertaken its own independent investigation into some areas here-
tofore not fully scrutinized.

At the outset, let me state for the record that the Simon Wiesenthal Center has reached the conclusion that Kurt Waldheim deliberately concealed his past. Contrary to his contention that after being
wounded on the Russian front his military career ended in 1941, it
would be more correct to say that his military career, in effect, started
then; since it is only after 1942 that records indicate that Kurt Waldheim distinguished himself in the service of Hitler's army.

The Center believes that Waldheim concealed his past not only because he did not want people to know where he was during that period, but also because he did not want people to know for whom he was working. Waldheim worked on the command staff of two Wehrmacht generals: General Von Shtahl and General Von Loehr, both of whom are amongst a handful of regular army generals who were convicted and executed as war criminals. It would have been impractical for Waldheim to have listed that kind of a resume early on in his post-World War II career. The names Von Shtahl and Von Loehr would have raised more than a few eyebrows in world capitals. For a budding world-class diplomat, it was much better that such a past be erased from memory and later described as merely irrelevant data that would "tend to bore people." The Wiesenthal Center, however, believes that rather than bore people, it would have alerted them.

Mr. Chairman, in 1944, Kurt Waldheim, on his last vacation from the front, completed his doctoral thesis on Konstantin Frantz. After much searching, the Center obtained a copy of Waldheim's dissertation. In both of his autobiographical books, Waldheim says he wrote the dissertation on the Federalist principles of Konstantin Frantz. A much more accurate description would be that his dissertation was on the Reichsidees of Konstantin Frantz.

Konstantin Frantz was a notorious nineteenth-century anti-Semite who believed one way or another that the Jewish question would have to be solved, either, as he put it, by chopping the head off of every Jew and replacing it with a head that does not refer back to the Talmud, or by driving the lot out to Palestine. Although Waldheim is careful not to cite any of the anti-Semitic references of Konstantin Frantz, his dissertation extolls and endorses Frantz's "Greater Reich" concept, which sees Austria and other European countries absorbed by Germany, and the creation of a Greater Germany. There is no criticism of Frantz in Waldheim's doctoral thesis, only appreciative and laudatory statements along with the recognition that Frantz was, in effect, before his time and that the true realization of Frantz's ideas would be realized later.... Later being the Third Reich. The most illuminating way of explaining the thinking of Waldheim is his selection of a closing quote to his dissertation from another notorious

German anti-Semite, Friedrich Gentz: "*Europa ist durch Deutschland gefallen, durch Deutschland muss es wider auferstehen*" (Europe through Germany fell, through Germany it must rise again).

It is interesting that in Waldheim's autobiography, he comments that in 1941 there was much anti-Nazi sentiment in the army and that he had managed to read all of the available anti-Nazi literature. Waldheim writes, and I quote, "I found men who shared my views and our long discussions gave us a chance to air our feelings." This, referring to a time when many in Germany and Austria believed that they would win the war. Yet when he was working on his dissertation (1943–1944), most well informed Germans and Austrians knew that Germany was going to lose the war. Waldheim did not even pick an innocuous topic, but rather presented to the Law Faculty of the University of Vienna a criticism-free celebration of a leading proponent of Greater Germany. Konstantin Frantz's ideas hardly befit the image of an anti-Nazi thinker, which Waldheim so carefully cultivates about himself in his autobiographies.

Strange, too, Mr. Chairman, is the fact that in a comprehensive two-volume work on dissertations submitted to the University of Vienna in all disciplines between the years 1937–1949 by Dr. Lisl Alker, published in 1954, neither Kurt Waldheim's name nor subject of dissertation is listed in this authoritative University of Vienna source. This, despite the fact that thirty-seven doctoral dissertations in the Faculty of Law in 1944 are listed, some even on the National Socialist concepts. We do not know why Mr. Waldheim's dissertation was, for example, only placed in the University library in 1985 and in the University archives only in the late 60s or early 70s. Apparently, it was held somewhere else (perhaps in the Dean's Office of the Faculty of Law), but it was not listed in the first or subsequent editions of Dr. Alker's reference work. One thing is clear: the Wiesenthal Center has confirmed, from a University of Vienna archivist, that Mr. Waldheim's dissertation was not lost during Allied bombings of Austria late in the war. Could it be that the topic and thrust of this dissertation was something that a recent recipient of a doctor of law degree from the University of Vienna would not want exposed to a post-war environment, universally repulsed by Nazi ideology?

Mr. Chairman, the Simon Wiesenthal Center does not know if the assertions linking Kurt Waldheim to war crimes are true. But the whole world knows that he has violated a sacred trust in lying about his past. And if he is interested in truly setting the record straight, for once and for all, he himself should publicly and immediately demand that the government of Yugoslavia release all documents relevant to the charges listed against him by the Yugoslavian War Crimes Commission in 1947.

Appendix II

Letter to Pope John Paul II
Regarding the Canonization of Pope Pius XII

September 10, 1998

His Holiness Pope John Paul II Vatican City
00120 Vatican City State

Your Holiness:

I am writing to you about a very disturbing matter. There have been persistent reports that Your Holiness plans to canonize three of your papal predecessors including Pius XII. When this possibility was first raised in June 1992, I shared my grave concerns with Cardinal Cassidy, but unfortunately I must say those concerns have been all but ignored.

Under your papacy, great strides have been made by the Church in reaching out to the Jewish people—the Vatican's recognition of the State of Israel, the Church's historic document on the *Shoah*, your visit to the Rome Synagogue and to the concentration camps. Jews around the world have admired your courage and saluted those gestures.

But I am afraid the sainthood of Pius XII will significantly detract from those accomplishments.

While it is normally not the practice of non-Catholics to comment on the worthiness of the Church's candidates, Pope Pius XII must surely qualify as an exception to that rule. During his pontificate, the most horrific war known to mankind was fought, a war in which fifty million people lost their lives. During that war, the Nazis unleashed their diabolical plot to murder all the world's Jews. Indeed, they succeeded in exterminating six million—one-third of the entire Jewish population. From the outset of the conflict to its conclusion, Pope Pius XII sat on the throne of St. Peter in stony silence, as the trains carrying millions of unsuspecting victims crisscrossed Europe en route to the gas chambers.

The overwhelming body of scholarly evidence from Jewish and non-Jewish sources, including the released Vatican documents on the Second World War, shows that Pius XII was perhaps the best informed leader on what was really happening in Europe at the time. Yet, not once did the supreme Pontiff muster the courage to condemn the Nazis publicly.

Not once did the Pope lift his voice in unequivocal terms to protest the deportations and murder of the Jews, as the Archbishop of Ponlouse or the Bishop of Montauban did in France, or as Bishop Giuseppe Placido Nicolini did in Italy, or Father Bernard Lichtenberg did in Germany, or as Bishop Apor of Gyor did in Hungary, all placing themselves at much greater risk than Pope Pius XII.

In fact, when Hitler attacked the Soviet Union in June 1941, Pius XII was jubilant, knelt in prayer and said a novena for the total victory of the Führer's armies, a sentiment he was still invoking as late as 1943, even though that was tantamount to endorsing Hitler's entire extermination policy (given the fact, well-known in 1943 at the Vatican, that the Nazis followed up all their military campaigns by deporting and murdering all the Jews).

Some defenders of Pius XII often cite the following paragraph from his 1942 Christmas speech: *"This is a vow that mankind owes to the innumerable exiles whom the hurricane of war has torn from their homeland and scattered abroad. This is a vow that mankind owes to the hundreds of thousands of people who, through no fault of their own, and sometimes only on grounds of nationality or origin, are destined for death or slow deterioration..."*

This speech, which the Church knows was received with great disappointment by President Roosevelt, Prime Minister Churchill and by the Poles, was found to be so ambiguous that *The New York Times*, in its December 25, 1942 edition used the headline, "Pope Assails Peril of Godless State" in describing it. An examination of the captured German documents after the war reveals that it was never even noticed by the Nazis, much less interpreted as a Papal defense of the Jews.

Let us compare that ambiguity with the same Pius XII's decisive denunciation of the euthanasia program against the infirm and mentally handicapped, which he refers to in his pastoral letter of June 1943:

> We see the bodily deformed, the insane and those suffering from hereditary disease at times deprived of their lives, as though they were a useless burden to society. This procedure is hailed by some as a new discovery of human progress, and is something that is altogether justified by the common good.
>
> Yet what sane man does not recognize that this not only violates the natural and divine law written in the heart of every man, but flies in the face of every sensibility of civilized humanity? The blood of these victims, all the dearer to our redeemer, because deserving of greater pity, "cries to God from the earth."

The distinction is quite obvious. By forcefully condemning euthanasia, the Pope could anticipate finding a responsive chord among the German people, but to publicly defend the Jews would be an act of courage that was beyond the capacity of Pope Pius XII.

Not only did the [P]ope's silence extend to the Jews, but it even applied to Catholic Poland, as President Raczkiewicz wrote to Pius from London on January 2, 1943: *"In this tragic moment my people are struggling not only for their existence.... They do not want revenge, but justice, they are not asking for material and diplomatic help...but they beg for a voice that points to the evil clearly and strongly and condemns those who are at the service of this evil."*

But his voice was never heard.

The sad truth is that only at the end of 1943 and early 1944, when most of the Jews had already been murdered, and when it was abundantly clear to the entire world that Nazi Germany had lost the War, only then did Pius XII entertain the notion of saving Jews. (It was for his belated efforts in 1944 that Chief Rabbi Herzog, among others, would later thank him.)

It is my firm belief that had Monsignor Angelo Giuseppe Roncalli (the future John XXIII) been pope at the time or had Your Holiness been pope then, the Vatican most certainly would have publicly and vigorously protested Adolf Hitler's policies!

Even senior Church officials such as Cardinal Tisserant knew the truth about Pius XII when he wrote: *"I am afraid that history may be obliged in time to come to blame the Holy See for a policy accommodating to its own advantage and little more...and that is extremely sad...above all when one has lived under Pius XL."*

The successor to Cardinal Faulhaber, in Germany, Cardinal Julius Doepfner, in a sermon commemorating Pope Pius XII said: *"The retrospective judgment of history provides every ground for the view that Pius XII should have protested with greater firmness."*

The heroic priest, Father Salvatore Rufmo Niccacci, who was among those who risked their lives to provide safe haven for 300 Jews in Assisi, wondered of Pius XII: *"Isn't his role as the spiritual leader of the Church more important than his role as politician or head of state?"*

I must say, Your Holiness, the Church's insistence of moving ahead with Pius XII's Beatification and Canonization, even in the lifetime of tens of thousands of Holocaust survivors who endured unspeakable suffering and witnessed his silence firsthand, is especially troubling. For the survivors of the Holocaust, Your Holiness, granting sainthood to Pius XII desecrates the memory of our ancestors and millions of martyrs by allowing the world to think that a saint was enthroned nearby in Rome while they were being taken to the crematoria without even an echo of a protest.

Undoubtedly, there were saints in those terrible years. But the historical record shows that Pope Pius XII was not one of them.

Respectfully,

Rabbi Marvin Hier
Dean of the Simon Wiesenthal Center

Appendix III

Address Delivered
at the Organization for Security and Cooperation in
Europe Conference on Anti-Semitism
and Other Forms of Intolerance
Cordoba, Spain, June 8, 2005

Last month, the world commemorated the sixtieth anniversary of the defeat of Nazism. Shortly after the Holocaust, its major perpetrators were brought to Nuremberg to stand trial. Those in the dock were not only generals and admirals who had conducted Hitler's war of annihilation, but bankers and economists who had plundered Europe's economy, amongst them newspaper editors and publishers whose words tore into the flesh of innocent people like bullets.

Every day, during the twelve-year history of the Third Reich, Josef Goebbels, Hitler's Minister of Propaganda, and Julius Streicher, Publisher of the infamous *Der Stuermer* newspaper, each with his own audiences, served up daily potions of hate that helped sell Hitler's need for a "Final Solution to the Jewish Question." Goebbels committed suicide and avoided the court's judgment. But to Julius Streicher, Justice Lawrence handed down the death sentence, charging him with incitement to commit murder and extermination. The judgment at Nuremberg made it clear that words have consequences and those who author incitements to hate-based violence and crime bear responsibility.

What should be the responsibility of the media in today's battle against anti-Semitism, when almost every day, particularly in the Middle East and at times in Europe, there appear anti-Semitic articles under the guise of freedom of the press?

Clearly, the safest guarantee of a free society is to have a vibrant, aggressive and free press that serves as check and balance against abuse by the government or by the more powerful groups in society. But on the other side of the spectrum, there is also a need to speak out when the media validates lies and becomes the perpetrator and advocate for distortions, when it seeks to manufacture the truth rather than to search for it, and when it has an agenda and then looks for the facts to fit that agenda.

It is precisely the blurring of those lines that led France's Versailles Court of Appeals last week to rule against three reporters and directors of that nation's most respected newspaper, *Le Monde*, saying they committed "a racist defamation" by publishing an article which said of the State of Israel, "One has trouble imagining that a nation of refugees, descendants of people who have suffered the longest period of persecution in the history of humanity...would be capable of transforming themselves into a dominating people...and with the exception of an admirable minority into a scornful people finding satisfaction in humiliating others." The court ordered the newspaper to publish a condemnation of the article because it constituted incitement.

We live in a different world. In today's world, you don't have to attend a rally to become a bigot, or be present at the orchestrated, giant rallies that the Nazis organized at Nuremberg to be imbued with hate. Today, when a newspaper article or television broadcast appears in a foreign country and is instantly transmitted via satellite, cable and the internet into the homes of millions of people throughout the world, you can become a bigot and anti-Semite in your own living room, watching the Iranian produced television series, *Zahra*

Blue Eyes, depicting Israelis kidnapping Palestinian children and transplanting their organs in Jewish children...or the Syrian mini-series, *Al Shattat* (The Diaspora) about the alleged secret Jewish government that controls the world...or reading the words of Portuguese Nobel Laureate Jose Saramago:

> The Jews endlessly scratch their own wound and keep it bleeding to keep it incurable, as if it were a banner.... Israel in short is a racist state by virtue of Judaism's monstrous doctrines, not just against the Palestinians but against the entire world which it seeks to manipulate and abuse...or the Lithuanian newspaper, *Respublika*, which published a series, "Who Rules the World?" and answered, "The Jews."

It is simply unconscionable that sixty years after the Holocaust, in spite of numerous films and books on the subject, anti-Semitism is again in vogue in Europe and around the world. In such a world, the media has a special role to play in exposing the lies and defending truth. It can help by debunking the myth of *The Protocols of the Elders of Zion*, interviewing Holocaust survivors involved in promoting tolerance, highlighting schools that commemorate Yom Hashoah, putting the spotlight on political leaders who aren't doing enough to stop the hate, focusing attention on institutions in Europe and around the world that are promoting tolerance, covering the tensions in the Middle East fairly and objectively without hurling anti-Semitic slurs comparing Israel's Prime Minister Sharon to Hitler, or the Israeli army to the Nazis.

What is at stake is nothing less than the future of civilization, and the future of our children and grandchildren. History has taught us that we have paid a grave price for indifference. There can be no bystanders in this battle. As Edmund Burke reminded us, "The only thing necessary for evil to triumph is for good men to do nothing."

Index

A

Abbas, Mahmoud, 113, 130
Abdullah, King, 144, 153-154, 245
Abdullah II, King, 152-153, 172
Abrams, Ron, 171
Abramson, Dov, 59-60
Adelson, Merv, 240, 280
Adler, Alan, 229
Adler, Bernie, 261
Adler, Leah, 261, 309
Adler, Leo, 74
Adler, Stella, 255-256
Alabbar, Mohamed, 155-156, 196,
    269-270, 315
Alkin, Michele, x, 108, 124
Altar, Yisrael, 47-48
Angelou, Maya, 231-232
Anne, Princess, 38, 40
Arafat, Yasser, 188
Arnall, Dawn, 170, 193, 278, 291
Arnall, Ronald, 57, 60, 66-67, 163,
    227, 290
Avant, Nicole, 314
Avner, Yehuda, 217, 318

B

Bak, Pinchos (Pinky), 26-31
Bakshi-Doron, Eliyahu, 186
Balitzer, Alfred, 145
Barad, Rhonda, 74

Barak, Ehud, 10, 186
Barkat, Nir, 278, 280, 316
Bass, Saul, 200-201
Bathily, Lassana, 174
Baum, Herb, 72, 171, 280, 291
Baum, Karen, 171, 280
Beer, Ginka, 179
Begin, Menachem, 33-34, 221, 240, 255
Belkin, Samuel, 33, 55, 289
Belzberg, Barbara, 137, 227, 304
Belzberg, Chantal, 31
Belzberg, Frances, 28, 52, 137, 227, 304
Belzberg, Hyman, 49
Belzberg, Joanne, 37, 170, 221, 240, 300
Belzberg, Leslie, 227
Belzberg, Marc, 28, 31
Belzberg, Samuel (Sam), 48-50, 52,
    57, 60, 62, 73, 77, 280, 293,
    295, 304
Belzberg, Syd, 37, 170, 193, 221, 240,
    300
Belzberg, William (Bill), 52-53, 210, 304
Ben-Gurion, David, 274
Benedict XVI, Pope, 189-192, 195, 197
Benjamin, Richard, 207, 296
Benlolo, Avi, xi, 74, 100, 170, 230, 312
Berg, Cliff, 229
Berger, Razie and Sendy, ix
Berger, Stanley, 180
Bergson, Peter, 216

Bernstein, Lillian, 268
Bertram, Heribert, 103
Bienenfeld, Shimshon, 19
Bin Laden, Osama, 115
Bin Rashid Al Maktoum,
     Mohammed, 155, 173
Bint Al Hussein, Haya, 155, 173
Blair, Tony, 175
Bloomberg, Lawrence, 230
Blum, Annette, 170
Blum, Richard, 76
Bokova, Irina, 118-122, 125, 173
Borgen, Sheppie, 19
Bradley, Tom, 73, 164
Brando, Marlon, 254-256
Brier, Seymour, 2
Brodlieb, Ken, 171
Brodlieb, Timothy, 171
Broidy, Elliot, 240
Brolin, James, 236
Brown, Jerry, 73, 164
Brownstein, Norm, 229, 316
Buchwald, Herb, 171
Bullock, Sandra, 215, 217, 221, 299
Bulz, Emmanuel, 138
Burden, Susan, ix, 227, 231, 280, 312
Burg, Steve, 291
Burke, Patrick, xi
Bush, George H.W., 239, 258, 305
Bush, George W., 240, 306
Bush, Laura, 306
Byrne, David, 266

C

Capshaw, Kate, 262
Carlebach, Shlomo, 33
Carson, Johnny, 207
Carter, Jimmy, 106-109, 266
Casden, Alan, 193, 227, 237, 291, 301
Casden, Susan, 237
Chamberlain, Neville, 115, 194
Chrenenko, Konstantin, 135-136
Churchill, Winston, 116, 128, 194, 201,
     218-219, 327

Clary, Robert, 94-95
Clinton, Bill, 77, 165, 279, 283
Clinton, Hillary Rodham, 165
Cohen, Esther, 57, 72, 227
Cohen, Kelly, 34, 42, 161
Cohn, Arthur, 214
Cooper, Abraham, ix, 27-28, 56,
     89, 100, 109, 119-120, 122,
     129, 137, 144, 153, 155, 166,
     170, 171, 174, 227, 254-255,
     260, 290, 291, 300, 301,
     312, 316
Cooper, Roz, 300
Counne, Ariel, 320
Counne, Elana, 320
Counne, Jacob, 287, 320
Counne, Yehudeet, 287, 298, 320
Crown, Lester, 74, 313
Cruise, Tom, 236, 268-270, 310
Crystal, Billy, 213-214, 230, 249,
     302, 312
Crystal, Janice, 233, 302

D

Dalai Lama, 242, 274, 304
Dalfen, Alan, 148
D'Amato, Alfonse, 86
Daoud, Abu, 63
Dayan, Moshe, 33-34
DeNiro, Robert, 213-214, 297
Dershowitz, Alan, 112, 312
Diamond, Gordon, 32-33, 167, 171,
     193, 279, 291
Diamond, Jack, 25, 45, 49, 289
Diamond, Leslie, 167, 171, 193, 279,
     291, 300
Diamond, Sadie, 279
Diefenbaker, John, 47
DiMaggio, Joe, 1, 8, 251, 308
Dolgen, Jonathan, 193
Douglas, Kirk, 218, 297
Douglas, Michael, 215, 218, 221,
     297, 298
Drexler, Anton, 234

Dubin, Miriam, 287, 320
Dubin, Yehuda, 287, 320

E

Eastwood, Clint, 313
Eaton, Rick, xi
Eban, Abba, 33-34
Eisenberg, Arnold, 8
Elizabeth II, Queen, 38-40
Esses, Ilya, 141-142
Ewing, Jack, 103-104

F

Fattaha al-Sisi, Abdel, 129-130
Faurisson, Robert, 98
Feinstein, Dianne, 76, 243
Feinstein, Moshe, 2, 15
Feldenkreis, George, 170, 193, 291
Feldstein, Meyer, 24
Fiennes, Ralph, 261
Flantzgraben, Yankele, 7, 9, 19, 159
Flynn, David, 304
Fonda, Jane, 206, 263-268, 309
Fouks, Arthur, 21
Fox, Audrey, xi
Francis, Johnnie, 71
Francis, Pope, 192-198, 292
Frank, Anne, 138, 235-237
Friedman, Howard, 193
Friedman, Jacob and Leah, 280
Fuchs, Michael, 229
Fugman, Max, 32

G

Galbut, Russel, 72
Gardner, James, 227
Gecas, Anton (Anthony), 92-93
Geft, Ivor, 261
Geft, Liebe, x, 229, 231, 303
Gehry, Frank, 275, 277
Gergen, David, 312
Ghysels, Steve, 193-194, 229
Gibbs, Robert, 312
Gibson, Mel, 260-261

Gilbert, Martin, 201, 219
Gindi, Jack and Rachel, 59
Ginzberg, Hersh, 159
Glass, Heshy, 59
Glotman, Lauri, 300
Glover, Danny, 266
Goldberg, Yakov, 19
Goldenberg, Bernard, 18, 22-24
Goldenberg, Mark, 62
Goldman, Murray, 32
Gorbachev, Mikhail, 136, 143
Goren, Shlomo, 34
Graff, Jacob and Pnina, 58
Gray, Irio, 41
Green, Sidney, 227
Greenspun, Barbara, 279
Greenspun, Hank, 279
Greenspun, Brian, 279
Greenspun, Daniel, 279
Greenspun, Jane, 279
Greenspun, Susan, 279
Greenwald, Dovid, 19
Grobman, Alex, 227
Gyongyosi, Marton, 105-106

H

Hager, David and Judy, 58
Hamilton, Charles Jr., 233
Hardman, Leslie, 138
Harper, Stephen, 172
Harris, Mark Jonathan, 214
Hart, Mary, 241, 244, 249, 280, 307, 311
Hartman, Robert, 74
Hassan, Prince, 150
Hayden, Tom, 242, 263
Hayman, Fred, 210
Hertz, Judah, 193, 230, 291
Herzl, Theodor, 197, 217-221, 282
Heston, Charlton, 304
Heston, Lydia, 304
Hexter, Herbert, 59
Hicks, Taylor, 313
Hier, Annie, 171, 250, 286, 300, 320

Hier, Ari, 25, 30, 46-48, 57, 61, 74, 166, 208, 286, 320
Hier, Avi, 25, 46-48, 57, 61, 74-75, 156, 170, 171, 259, 286, 300, 320
Hier, Esther, xi
Hier, Hanna, 287, 320
Hier, Devorah, 287, 320
Hier (née Mermelstein), Marlene (Malkie), xi, 17-19, 21-32, 38-41, 46-50, 57, 60-62, 71-74, 140-141, 158, 170, 171, 172, 206-209, 213-215, 231, 249-253, 261-270, 291, 300, 302, 304, 319, 320
Hier, Rachel, 18, 287, 320
Hier (née Frost), Raisel, 3-4, 208
Hier, Yankel (Jack), 2, 3
Hier, Isaac, 320
Hier, Joseph, 320
Hitchcock, Alfred, 200
Hitler, Adolf, 3-6, 12, 61, 70-71, 78-82, 89-90, 102-104, 115-116, 131-132, 136-147, 181-194, 206, 221, 226, 228, 233-234, 238-241, 257, 261, 307, 321, 326-328, 331-333
Hochbaum, Fishel, 15, 19
Hochbaum, Jerry, 19
Hoenig, Harvey, 19
Hoffman, Dustin, 215-216, 299
Hollande, Francois, 100-101, 126, 170
Holmes, Katie, 268-270
Horowitz, Azer, 32
Horowitz, Harry, 258
Huberfeld, Laura, 170
Huberfeld, Murray, 170, 190, 193, 217
Huberfeld, Pinchus, 190
Huberfeld, Rae, 190
Huberman, Sandy, 74
Hussein, King, 143-145, 148-155, 169, 173, 242-246

I

Isen, Stuart (Stu), 193, 229, 240, 291
Isner, Shavie and Elchanon, ix

J

Jackson, Michael, 259-260
Joel, Richard, 285, 319
John XXIII, Pope, 184-185, 328
John Paul II, Pope, 177-179, 185-199, 290, 325
Jolie, Angelina, 254
Juppé, Alain, 118

K

Kahn, Leon, 33, 41
Kahn, Evelyn, 33
Kaminetzki, Max, 15, 19
Kanin, Fay, 199-200, 207-208
Katz, Emil, 262
Katz, Ezra, 72
Katz, Karl, 227
Katzenberg, Jeffrey, 212, 215, 217, 236, 247-249, 311-312, 314-315
Katzenberg, Marilyn, 236, 247, 314
Kempthorne, Walter, 86
Kennedy, Caroline, 303
Kennedy, Ted, 164
Kerry, John, 121, 125, 196
Kerzner, Brian, 300
Kerzner, Tammi, 300
Kestenbaum, Lou, 221
Kidman, Nicole, 215, 298
Ki-Moon, Ban, 174
King, Coretta Scott, 37
King, Don, 258-259
King, Larry, 220, 254-256
King, Martin Luther Jr., 37
Kingsley, Ben, 215-218, 300
Klein, Jessica and Jason, xii
Klein, Myra and David, ix
Klein, Naomi, 266-277
Klein, Naomi and Scott, ix
Klein, Shayna and Daniel, xii
Klemp, Stefan, 102-103
Kluger, Jerzy, 179
Knobel, Shobsie, 19
Kolberg, Al, 32
Koffler, Tom, 230

Koffler, Anna, 230
Kollek, Teddy, 271-273, 281
Kotler, Aharon, 13-15, 157
Koussevitsky, Moshe, 35-36
Kravitz, Mendel, 13, 19, 158, 159
Krevoy, Brad, 300
Krevoy, Susie, 300
Kurnzer, Yehuda, 159
Kurtzer, Daniel, 274

L

LaFarge, John, 182-183
Lamm, Maurice, 55
Lamm, Norman, 33, 55-56, 62
Landesman, Dovid, 59
Lasorda, Tommy, 251, 308
Lasorda, Jo, 308
Laulicht, Linda, 171
Laulicht, Murray, 171
Lazarowitz, Lorraine, Irving, Ronald,
    Marla, and Jimmy, ix
Leibowitz, Bernard, 43, 162
Lederer, Hans, 89
Lehrer, Willie, 2
Leigh, Barbara, 300
Leigh, Elizabeth, 300
Lemmon, Jack, 214
Lerman, Jack, 71
Levin, Stephen, 72
Levine, Hanna, xi, 17, 158, 159
Levine, Harry, xi, 17, 158, 159
Levy, Bernard-Henri, 126
Levy, Linda, 171
Liberman, Esther, 181, 196, 300
Liberman, Jose, 181, 196, 300
Lichtenstein, Aaron, 33-35
Lieberman, Joseph (Joe), 253-254
Lipman, Estee and Menachem, ix
Lipman, Ira, 179, 188, 213, 229, 290
Litman, Sol, 74
Loach, Ken, 266
Lopez, George, 313
Lowy, Leo, 41
Lowy, Peter, 193

Lukash, Leslie, 87
Lustig, Jimmy, 193, 240, 280, 291
Lynton, Michael, 249, 312

M

Malkin, Judd, 74
Malovany, Joseph, 231
Margolis, Gerald, 227
Mashaal, Khaled, 245
Matthau, Walter, 214
May, Meyer, ix, 57, 59, 100, 144,
    153-155, 166, 170, 171, 174,
    214, 227-229, 258, 271, 291,
    300, 312, 314, 316, 318
May, Peter, 229
Mayr, Karl, 234
M'bala M'bala, Dieudonné, 98-100
Meir Lau, Yisrael, 186
Meiselman, Moshe, 56, 59
Melvoin, Mike, 313
Mendelsohn, Martin, xi, 82
Mengele, Josef, 81-91
Merah, Muhammed, 100
Merkel, Angela, 171
Mermelstein, Adele, xi, 17
Mermelstein, Elisa and Chaim, ix
Meyer, Ron, 212, 215, 236, 240, 249,
    307, 312, 314, 315
Milken, Lori, 235, 281, 314
Milken, Michael, 235, 280-281, 303, 314
Miner, Sheldon, 2
Mitterrand, François, 96, 101,
    135-136, 228
Mizel, Carol, 235, 280-281, 295
Mizel, Cheston, 137, 171, 194,
    240, 281
Mizel, Larry, 137, 171, 193, 196, 235,
    240, 277, 280-281, 291, 295,
    307, 312, 314, 316
Molitar, Don, 231
Mones, Dana, xi, 233
Moonves, Les, 249, 312
Murdoch, Rupert, 215
Muskin, Elazar, 60

N

Nagel, David, 60
Nagel, Jack, 59-60, 193, 196, 280, 291
Nagel, Gitta, 59, 196, 280
Nemmouche, Mehdi, 100
Netanyahu, Benjamin, 124, 130, 197,
    240-241, 245-246, 274-276,
    307, 316, 317
Nichols, Margaret, 170
Nimoy, Leonard, 215, 221
Nissel, Raphael, 100, 170, 171
Noor, Queen, 150, 242-243
Novak, Bobby, 74, 214
Nudel, Ida, 263-265

O

Obama, Barack, 112-115, 124, 130,
    175, 240
Olmert, Ehud, 273-274
Oren, Michael, 249, 312
Orenstein, Bill, 32
Orzen, David, 179
Orzen, Rosa, 179

P

Packer, James, 194, 241, 307
Pearl, Daniel, 254
Peerce, Jan, 33
Peltz, Claudia, 152, 215
Peltz, Nelson, 152, 155, 168, 173, 215,
    226, 229, 258, 281
Peres, Shimon, 105, 167, 168, 197, 240,
    247-248, 274-276, 312
Perl, Willie, 85, 222-223
Philip, Prince, 38-40
Pius XI, Pope, 182-184
Pius XII, Pope, 180-184, 188, 191, 197,
    325-329
Platt, Larry, 62
Pohl, Willi, 63
Pollak, Michael, 171
Pollak, Shereen, 171
Pollin, Abe, 293
Potok, Chaim, 33

Powell, Bruce, 59
Prager, Janice, x, 119, 170, 171, 214, 227,
    232, 291, 300, 304
Preis, Moishe, 41
Prentiss, Paula, 207, 296
Press, Alan, 19
Pure-Slovin, Alison, xi, 74

Q

Qichen, Qian, 146-147, 168

R

Rabin, Yitzhak, 129, 166, 218, 240-245
Rabinowitz, Jacob, 55-56
Rania, Queen, 154
Ratner, Brett, 193, 240, 307, 314
Reagan, Nancy, 304
Reagan, Ronald, 77, 84-85, 137, 145,
    239, 304, 305
Rechnitz, Jona, 230, 318
Reisman, Heather, 230, 312
Resnick, Jack, 212
Resnick, Pearl, 212
Rice, Peter, 249, 312
Richter, Felice, x, 108
Rivlin, Reuven, 317
Robinson, Steve, 194
Rosen, Martin (Marty), 69-70, 193, 291
Rosenbaum, Pinchas, 221-223
Rosenblut, Jorge, 170
Ross, David, 255
Ross, Rick, 249, 312
Rothman, Tom, 249, 312
Rothschild, Jacob, 170
Rubin, Harold, 37
Rudin, Mickey, 71
Rufus, Jack, 54-55
Russell, Bertrand, 72, 116
Ryzman, Betty and Zvi, 58

S

Saban, Haim, 249, 312, 314
Safsel, Yakov, 11
Saleh, Raad, 276

Samson, Anne, 170, 215, 280
Samson, Lee, 29, 170, 193, 215,
      280, 291
Samuels, Shimon, xi, 94, 100, 119-120,
      191, 290
Samuels, Zach, 251
Santana, Carlos, 231-232
Sarandos, Ted, 314
Sauer, Nachum, 59
Sawoniuk, Anthony, 93
Sayyid Tantawy, Muhammad, 129
Schaefer, Rowland, 279
Schaefer, Sylvia, 279
Schallinger, Samuel, 78
Scheel, Walter, 63
Schell, Maximilian, 220
Schindler, Oskar, 263
Schmidt, Helmut, 89-91
Schneier, Arthur, 90
Schuster, Velvel, 42-43, 162
Schwartz, Danny, 71
Schwartz, Gerry, 230, 312
Schwartzman, Arnold, 200, 204,
      293, 296
Schwarzenegger, Arnold, 246, 253,
      274-275, 304, 313
Seagal, Steven, 242
Sedlacek, Michal, 278
Sedlmeier, Hans, 86
Segal, Joseph (Joe), 33
Segal, Rosalie (Rose), 33
Seibel, Richard, 238
Seinfeld, Jerry, 247-248, 311
Seymour, Jane, 304
Shafron, Dave, 41
Shafron, Morley, 32
Shamir, Yitzhak, 240, 258-259
Shapell, Ben, 233
Shapell, David (Dave), 149, 233, 235,
      241, 280
Shapell, Fela, 149, 235, 241, 280
Shapiro, Avra, x, 103, 123
Sharansky, Avital, 265
Sharansky, Natan, 135-136, 264-265, 309

Sharon, Ariel, 240, 333
Sharpe, Karen, 220
Sharpe, Stanley, 220
Sheinberg, Sidney (Sid), 193
Sherman, Honey, 230
Shriver, Maria, 253
Shukri, Ali, 144, 150, 245
Siegel, David, 119, 161, 249, 312
Silberbauer, Karl, 236
Sinatra, Barbara, 71-72
Sinatra, Frank, 71-72, 76, 205-206, 293,
      294, 295
Smith, Will, 257-258, 310
Snider, Ed, 193, 279, 291
Snider, Jay, 193, 241
Sinder, Jack, 219, 300
Sinder, Rita, 219, 300
Soffer, Don, 72, 193, 232, 291
Sohacheski, Jaime, 196, 236, 291
Sohacheski, Marilyn, 236
Sokol, Sheldon, 55
Solomon, Wilfred, 37
Soloveichik, Ahron, 33-35
Soloveitchik, Joseph, 28, 35, 42, 56,
      194, 269, 287
Specter, Arlen, 86
Spielberg, Steven, 249, 261-263,
      309, 312
Spira, Steven, 257
Sponder, Leonard, 8
Stack, Robert, 304
Steinfeld, Hailee, 235
Stern, Abraham, 30
Stern, A.J., 287, 320
Stern, Joe, 171
Stern, Katie, 320
Stern, Serina, 320
Stern, Suri, 171
Stern, Yael, 287, 320
Sternbuch, Recha, 222-223
Streep, Meryl, 206
Streisand, Barbra, 236, 249, 312
Sugarman, Burt, 193, 241, 249, 280,
      307, 311

T

Tannenbaum, Cheri, 52
Tannenbaum, Harvey, 52, 62
Taylor, Elizabeth, 202-215, 293, 294, 295, 296
Teichman, Ruth, 241, 300
Teichman, Sol, 97, 241, 300
Tendler, Shalom, 59
Tendler, Yitzchok, 7, 12-15, 19, 159
Tischler, Izzy, 41
Torre, Joe, 231-232
Trank, Kathy, 300
Trank, Richard (Rick), x, 170, 212-216, 227, 299, 300, 306
Triantopoulos, Lydia, 96
Truman, Harry, 2
Tyson, Mike, 258-259

U

Utay, Marc, 193, 229, 291

V

Villaraigosa, Antonio, 171
Von Stauffenberg, Franz-Ludwig, 90

W

Walker, Alice, 114-118
Waltz, Christoph, 215, 220, 314
Warner, John, 202
Warshavchik, Dovid, 12-19, 158
Wasserman (née Dunner), Laura, 31-32
Wein, Berel, 47
Weinberger, David, 41
Weinberger, Michael, 318
Weinreb, Heshie, 19
Weitzman, Mark, xi, 174
Weizman, Ezer, 186

Welles, Orson, 202, 212-215
Widelitz, Stacy, 170
Wiesenthal, Cyla, 64, 75
Wiesenthal, Paulinka, 75
Wiesenthal, Simon, 64-73, 77-79, 89, 101, 108, 154, 163, 164, 165, 178, 206-207, 215-216, 218-219, 236-237, 239-240, 253, 293, 294, 295, 301, 309
Williams, Julie Green, 231
Williams, Robin, 213, 231, 302
Williamson, Richard, 191
Wilson, Gayle, 243
Wilson, Pete, 243
Winfrey, Oprah, 231
Winnick, Gary, 137, 193, 279, 291
Winnick, Karen, 137, 279
Wistrich, Robert, 119-120
Woodward, Bob, 312
Woodward, Doris, 231
Wosk, Abrasha, 43-46, 161
Wosk, Morris, 33
Wosk, Dena, 33

Y

Yazdani, Mehrdad, 278
Yitzchok, Levi, 262

Z

Zalis, Ed, 215, 300
Zalis, Rosalie, 193, 215, 291, 300
Zell, Sam, 74
Zell, Rivka, 74
Ziegler, William F., 233
Zinn, Howard, 266
Zsolt, Agnes, 88
Zuroff, Efraim, xi, 92, 171, 227

The fonts used in this book are from the Garamond family.